REMAINS™

STEVE NILES
KIERON DWYER

D1437739

IDW PUBLISHING
SAN DIEGO, CA

Story:
STEVE NILES

Art:
KIERON DWYER

Coloring:
HARPER JATEN

Lettering & Design:
ROBBIE ROBBINS
& CINDY CHAPMAN

Original Series Editors:
KRIS OPRISKO
& JEFF MARIOTTE

Editor:
ALEX GARNER

WWW.IDWPUBLISHING.COM

ISBN: 1-932382-38-0
07 06 05 04   1 2 3 4 5

Ted Adams, Publisher
Chris Ryall, Editor-in-Chief
Robbie Robbins, Design Director
Kris Oprisko, Vice President
Alex Garner, Art Director
Cindy Chapman, Operations Manager
Tom B. Long, Designer
Beau Smith, Sales & Marketing
Chance Boren, Editorial Assistant
Jeremy Corps, Editorial Assistant
Yumiko Miyano, Business Development
Rick Privman, Business Development

POINT/COUNTERPOINT: FAST ZOMBIES V. SLOW ZOMBIES
INTRODUCTION BY SCOTT IAN AND PATTON OSWALT

Scott: The case for **FAST ZOMBIES**:

Among the many definitions of the word "fast" in the "definitions book," I found that many of them apply to why fast zombies are better than slow zombies (besides their killer quads).

Let's take a look, shall we?

"Fast"

1. Acting, moving, or capable of acting or moving quickly, swift: *Holy shit, those zombies are fas... aaaaaggggghhhhhhhhhhhhhhhhhhh*

Photo: Andy Buchanan

From personal experience, I can tell you with the utmost certainty that when someone is trying to eat you, it is much worse if that someone can run faster than you can. Yes, a slow, shambling, stumbly zombie is just as relentless but at least if you fuck up (as you would be wont to do if a zombie was trying to eat you), you get a second chance. Against a fast zombie? No second chances, chappy.

2. Accomplished in relatively little time: *The zombie horde paid a fast visit, leaving nary a scrap for the vermin that inevitably follow.*

Fast zombies, much more so than the over-hyped piranha or the so-called "perfect eating machine," the shark, are the most efficient eaters in the known and unknown worlds. A shark leaves enough waste for a pilot fish to live off its scraps. Fast zombies, like the indigenous peoples of this country (Indians), use all the pieces, therefore doing their part to end the ever-pesky vermin problem that plagues society even now!

Slow zombies have been sharing their kills with rats and flies and hyenas and dogs and even the occasional confused bum forever. Ewwww.

3. Quick to understand or learn; mentally agile: *It was a feast for the faster zombies, famine for the slow.*

What is scarier than a zombie? A zombie that can control bees? Maybe. But I think a zombie that can learn is THE SCARIEST ZOMBIE OF ALL!

We've always been able to maintain our domination over the slow, stupid zombies because that's all they were. No comprehension, no ability to understand, no drive to better themselves and advance forward. Just a mindless, base need to eat living flesh. Even Grandma could get in a whack or two at some of these pathetic excuses for preternatural existence.

Now a fast zombie that can understand, learn, and use its brain to figure out better ways to procure fresh meat? That's a zombie I want on my team.

Those are the facts, people.

Scott Ian is that Dude from that Band.

Patton: The case for **SLOW ZOMBIES**:

Fast zombies. Pfffff. Hey, fast zombies, where's the fire? You know what running means to me? Desperation. Neediness. No confidence. No balls.

Okay, so maybe your balls dropped off when you pulled yourself from the loamy earth, but so what? You're dead, doomed to walk the earth as a bloodthirsty ghoul—but you *still* have to hurry? Were you a yuppie before you died? Show me some lurching, some lurking. Tease me, goddammit!

It's very simple — fast zombies are scary for a few seconds, and then you either run or get eaten. Boom.

But the slow, shambling zombies (Old-School Ghouls, I like to call 'em) are a subtle, menacing presence, hovering on the horizon like a stink-pile of horror. If they see you, they come at you... slowly.

And you *can* run away. Unless...

Unless you fall and twist your ankle, and can't move. Accidents happen all the time. There can be a million random reasons why you suddenly can't run. And then...

...you have to wait. Wait in mounting terror as this hungry corpse, this half-finished apocalyptic autopsy, staggers towards you. Maggots writhe in its open maw. Flies buzz around its milky eyeballs. Its belly burst long ago from the death gases. Its skin sloughed off in fist-sized patches from the broiling sun. And yet it moves. Towards you. And after it's done snaggle-toothing your carotid artery out of your neck as you shriek, you'll join him. Another ravenous, walking stiff on an endless, midnight smorgasbord.

Did I get too florid in that last paragraph? That's because you'll have time to dwell as your doom creeps closer. Slow zombies, when they've got your number, give you a chance to imagine your demise before they close the deal, and show you how it's going to be ten times worse than you thought.

You spoiled little punks wouldn't know real terror if it tore your belly out while you were getting your blood pressure checked.

Patton Oswalt plays that Guy on that Show.

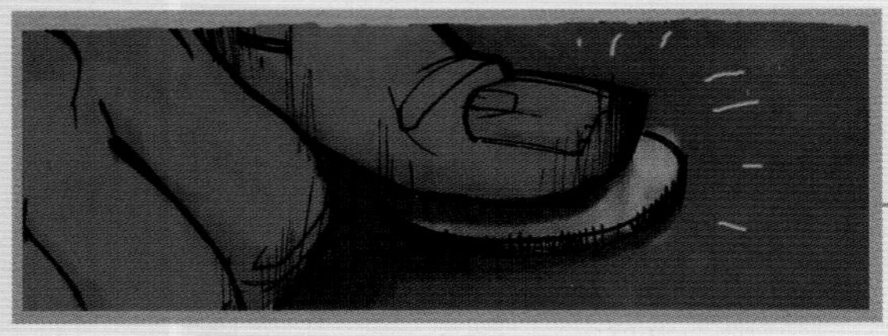

1
chapter

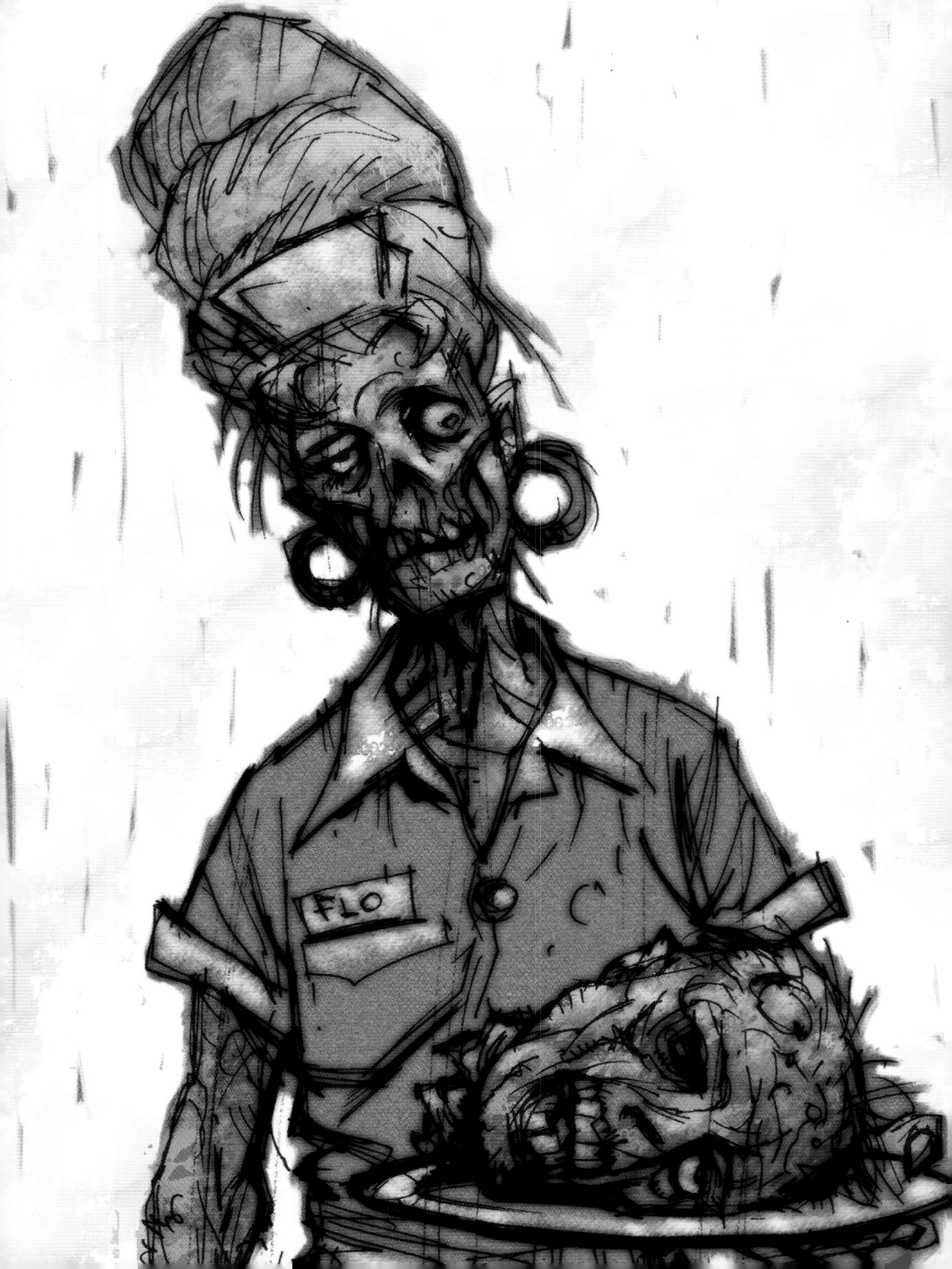
FLO

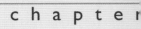

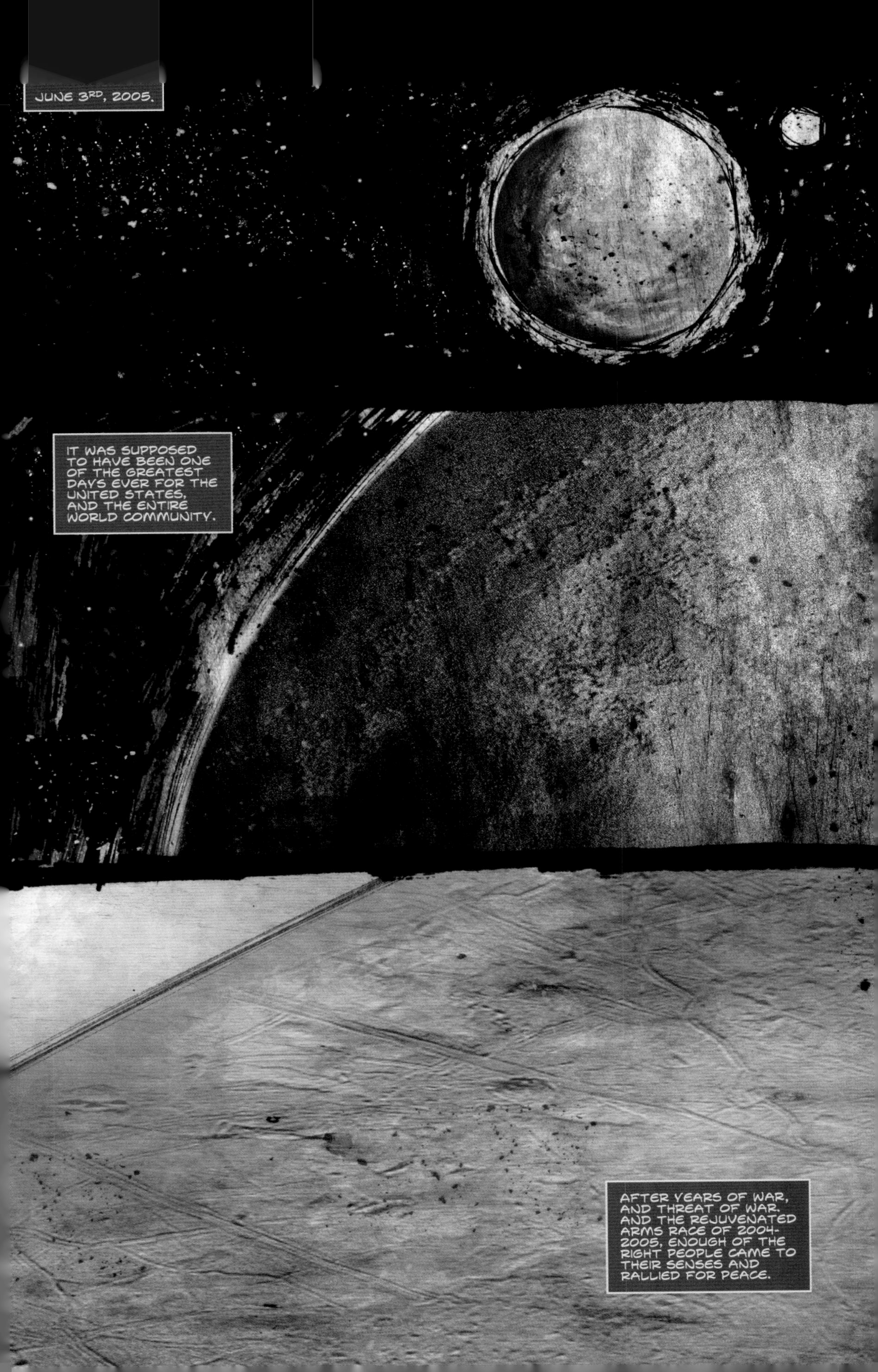
JUNE 3RD, 2005.
IT WAS SUPPOSED TO HAVE BEEN ONE OF THE GREATEST DAYS EVER FOR THE UNITED STATES, AND THE ENTIRE WORLD COMMUNITY.
AFTER YEARS OF WAR, AND THREAT OF WAR, AND THE REJUVENATED ARMS RACE OF 2004-2005, ENOUGH OF THE RIGHT PEOPLE CAME TO THEIR SENSES AND RALLIED FOR PEACE.

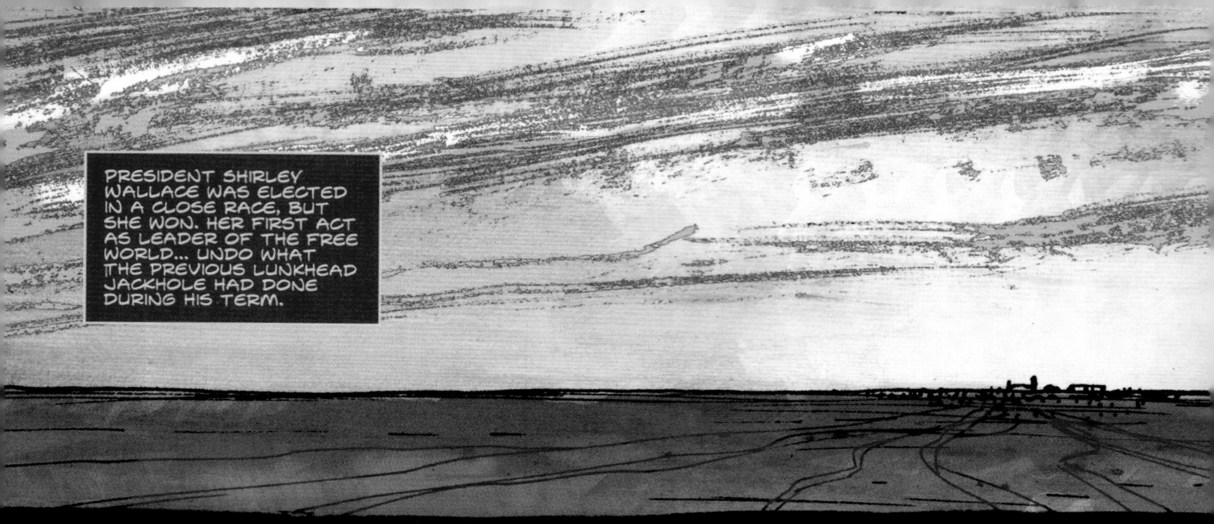
PRESIDENT SHIRLEY WALLACE WAS ELECTED IN A CLOSE RACE, BUT SHE WON. HER FIRST ACT AS LEADER OF THE FREE WORLD... UNDO WHAT THE PREVIOUS LUNKHEAD JACKHOLE HAD DONE DURING HIS TERM.

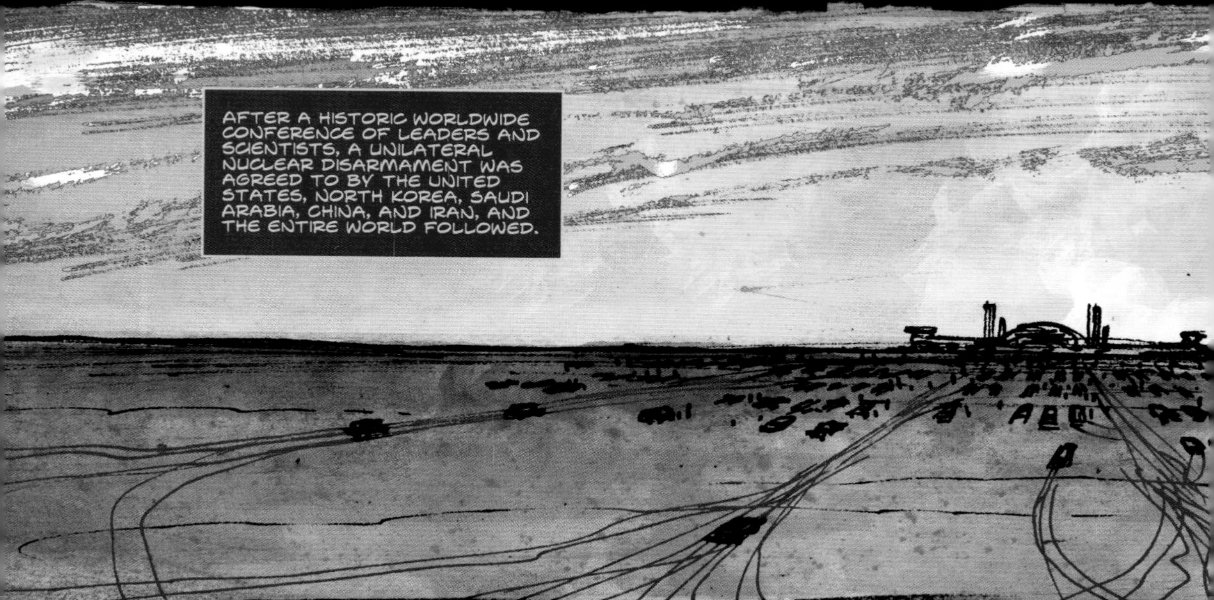
AFTER A HISTORIC WORLDWIDE CONFERENCE OF LEADERS AND SCIENTISTS, A UNILATERAL NUCLEAR DISARMAMENT WAS AGREED TO BY THE UNITED STATES, NORTH KOREA, SAUDI ARABIA, CHINA, AND IRAN, AND THE ENTIRE WORLD FOLLOWED.

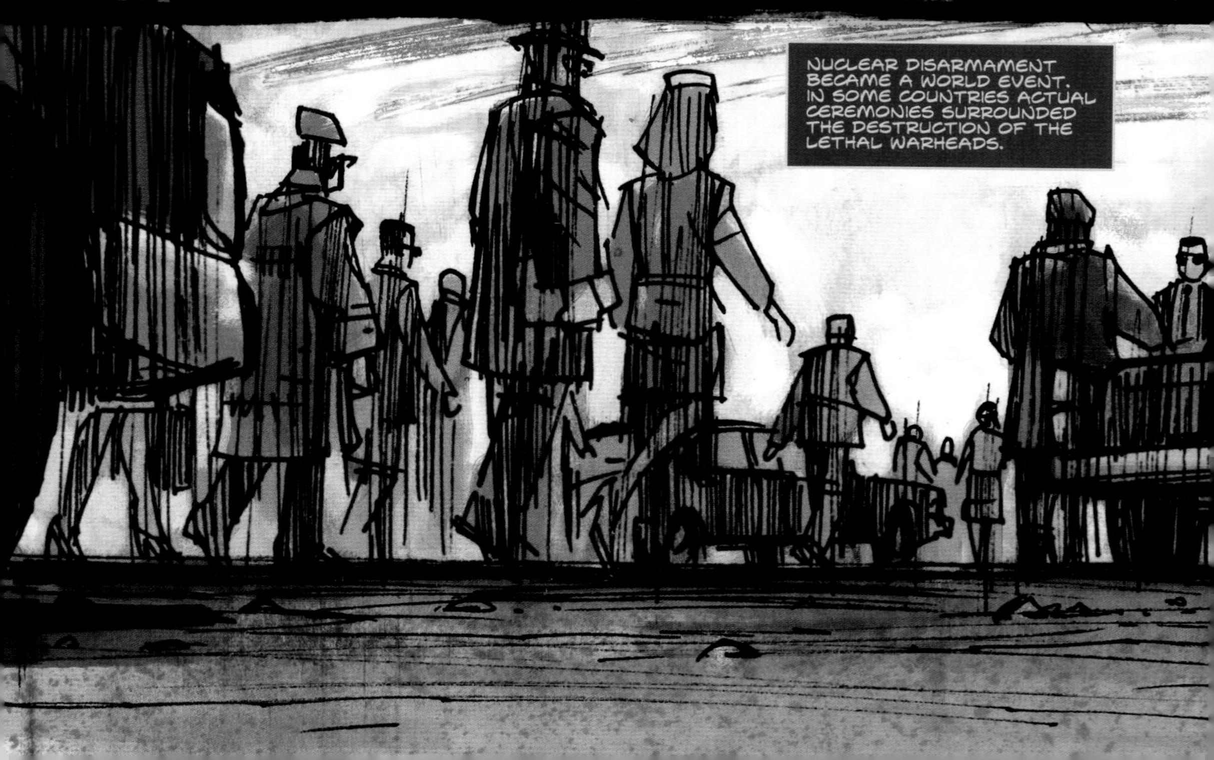
NUCLEAR DISARMAMENT BECAME A WORLD EVENT. IN SOME COUNTRIES ACTUAL CEREMONIES SURROUNDED THE DESTRUCTION OF THE LETHAL WARHEADS.

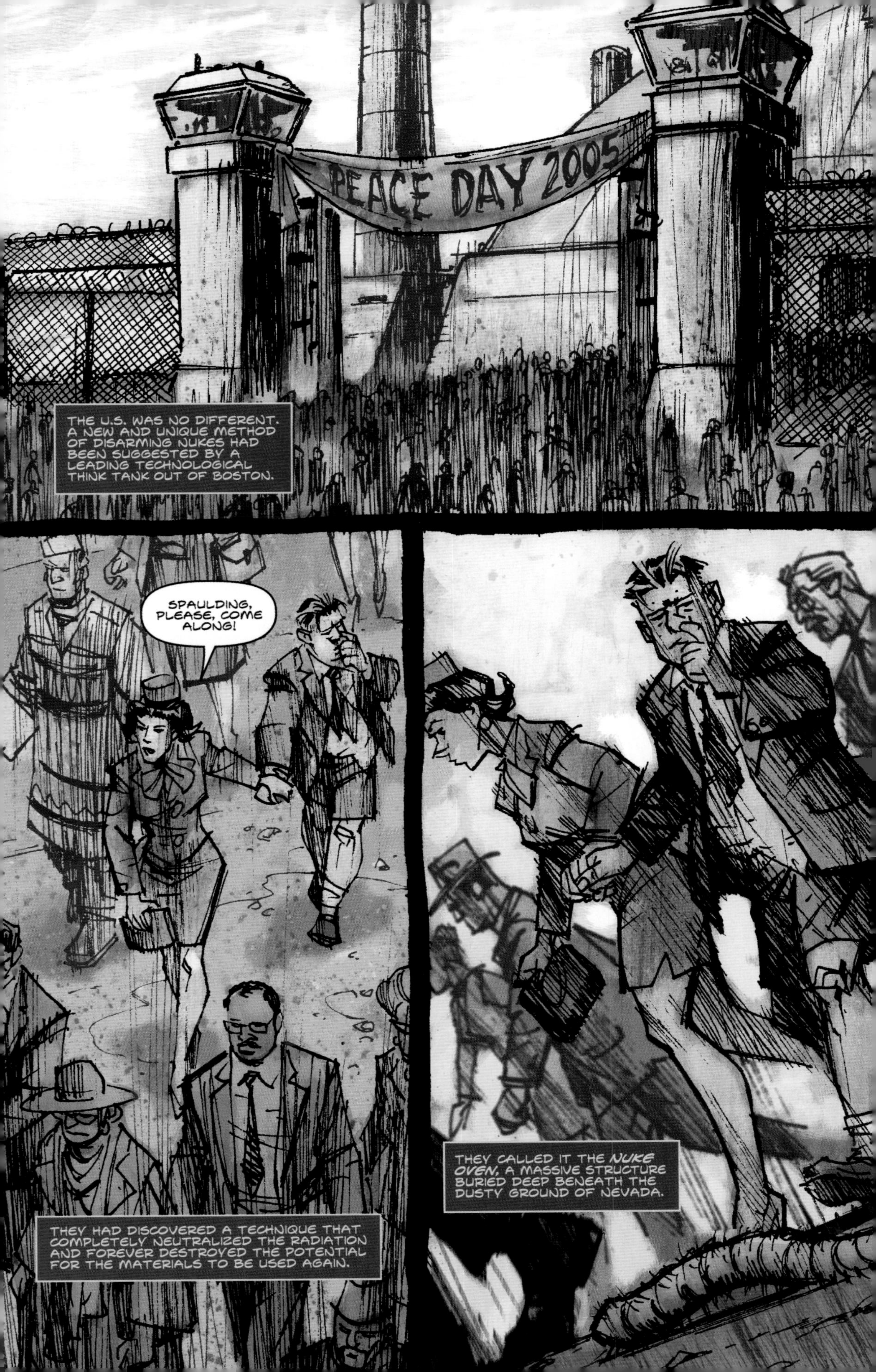
PEACE DAY 2005
THE U.S. WAS NO DIFFERENT. A NEW AND UNIQUE METHOD OF DISARMING NUKES HAD BEEN SUGGESTED BY A LEADING TECHNOLOGICAL THINK TANK OUT OF BOSTON.
SPAULDING, PLEASE, COME ALONG!
THEY HAD DISCOVERED A TECHNIQUE THAT COMPLETELY NEUTRALIZED THE RADIATION AND FOREVER DESTROYED THE POTENTIAL FOR THE MATERIALS TO BE USED AGAIN.
THEY CALLED IT THE *NUKE OVEN*, A MASSIVE STRUCTURE BURIED DEEP BENEATH THE DUSTY GROUND OF NEVADA.

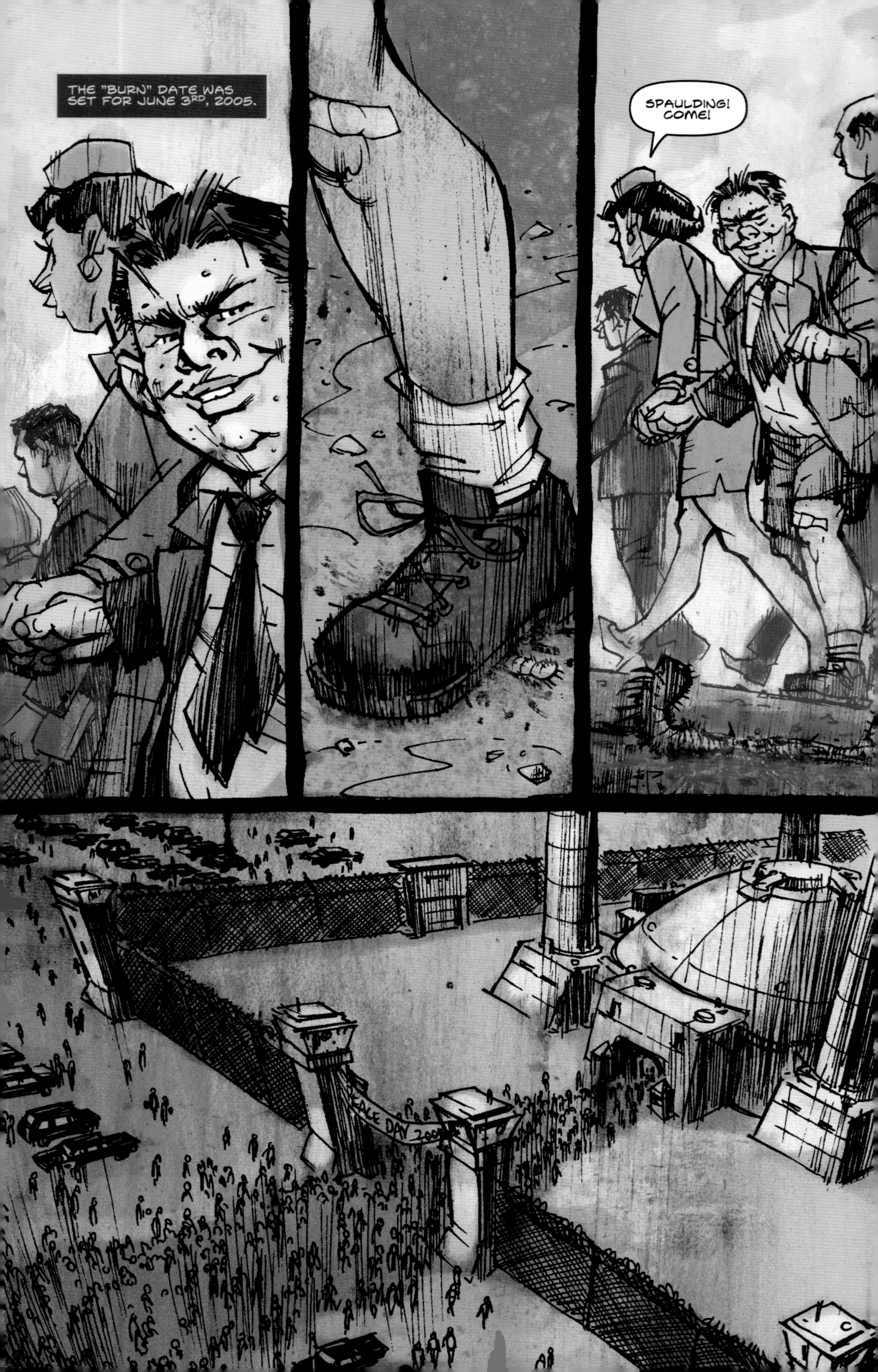
THE "BURN" DATE WAS SET FOR JUNE 3RD, 2005.
SPAULDING! COME!

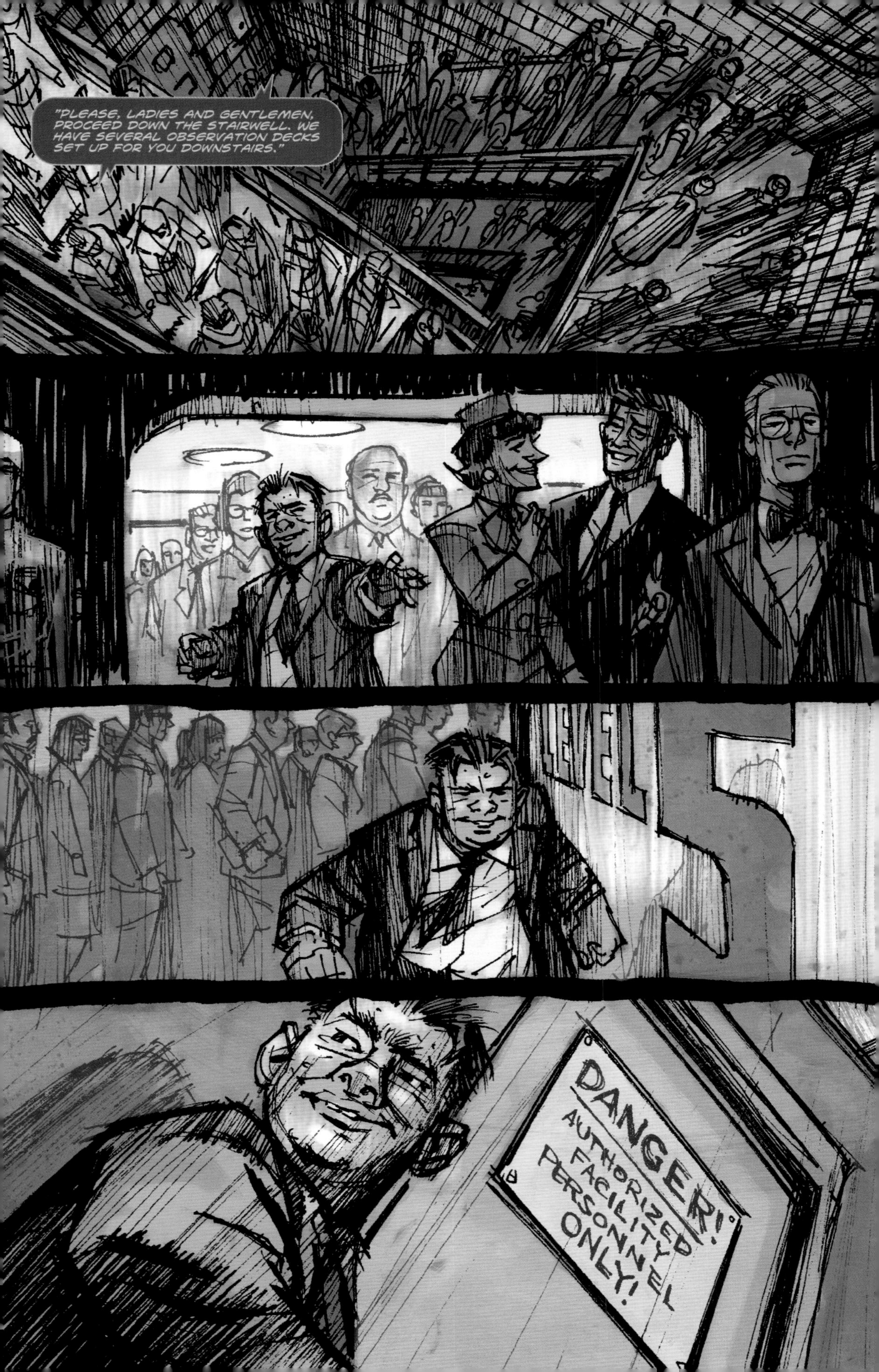
"PLEASE, LADIES AND GENTLEMEN, PROCEED DOWN THE STAIRWELL. WE HAVE SEVERAL OBSERVATION DECKS SET UP FOR YOU DOWNSTAIRS."
LEVEL
DANGER!
AUTHORIZED FACILITY PERSONNEL ONLY!

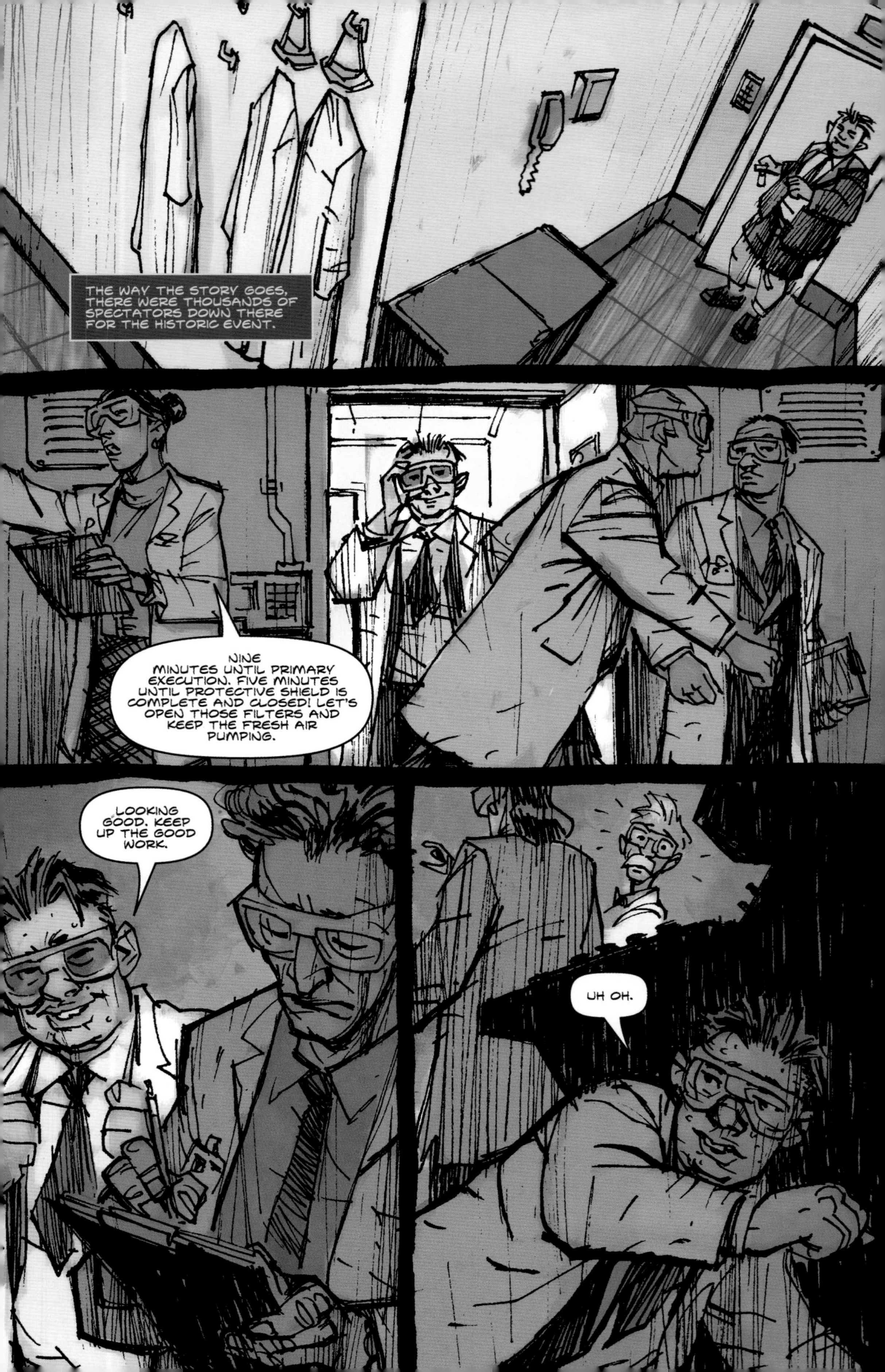
THE WAY THE STORY GOES, THERE WERE THOUSANDS OF SPECTATORS DOWN THERE FOR THE HISTORIC EVENT.
NINE MINUTES UNTIL PRIMARY EXECUTION. FIVE MINUTES UNTIL PROTECTIVE SHIELD IS COMPLETE AND CLOSED! LET'S OPEN THOSE FILTERS AND KEEP THE FRESH AIR PUMPING.
LOOKING GOOD. KEEP UP THE GOOD WORK.
UH OH.

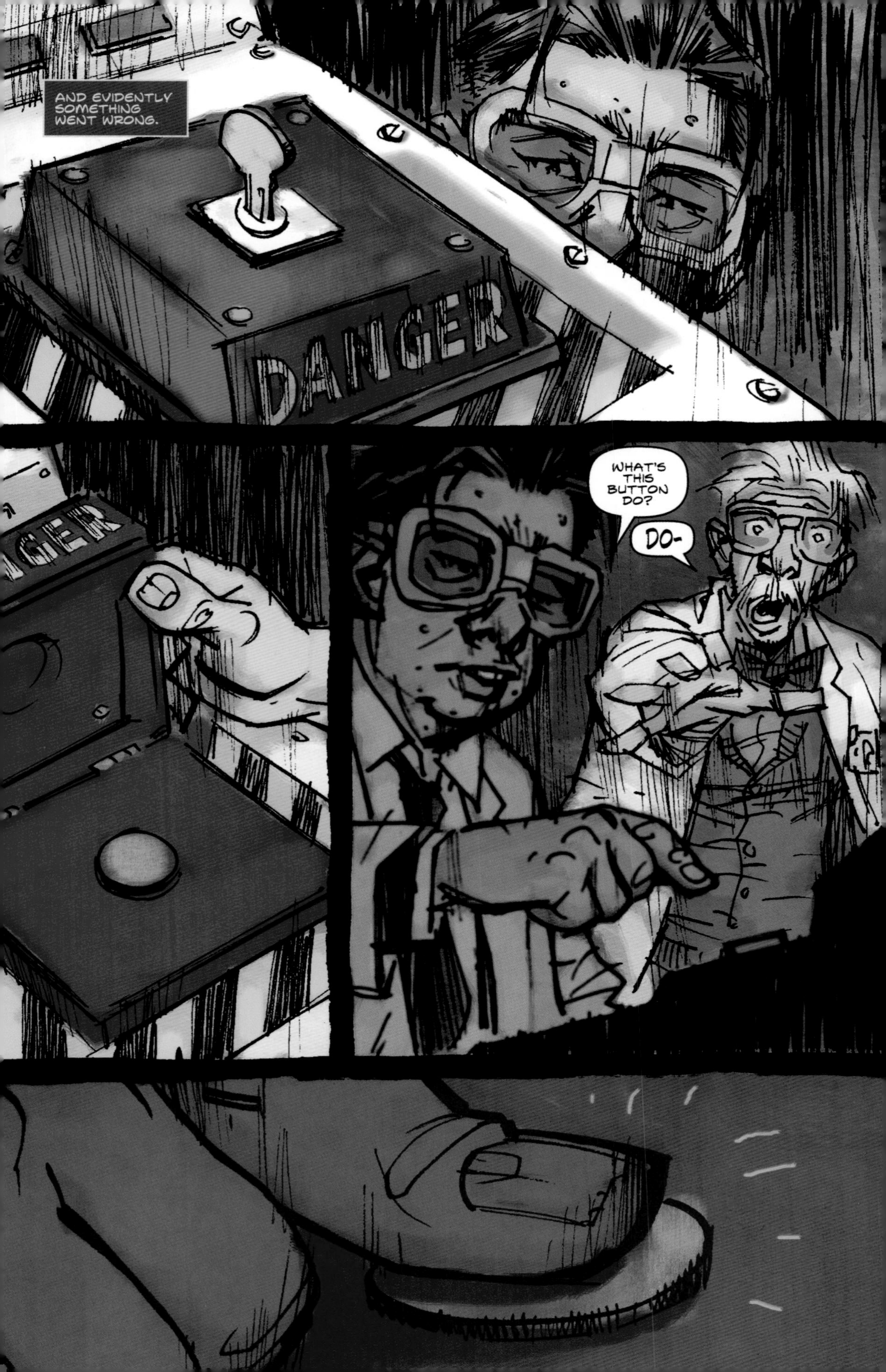
AND EVIDENTLY SOMETHING WENT WRONG.
DANGER
GER
WHAT'S THIS BUTTON DO?
DO-

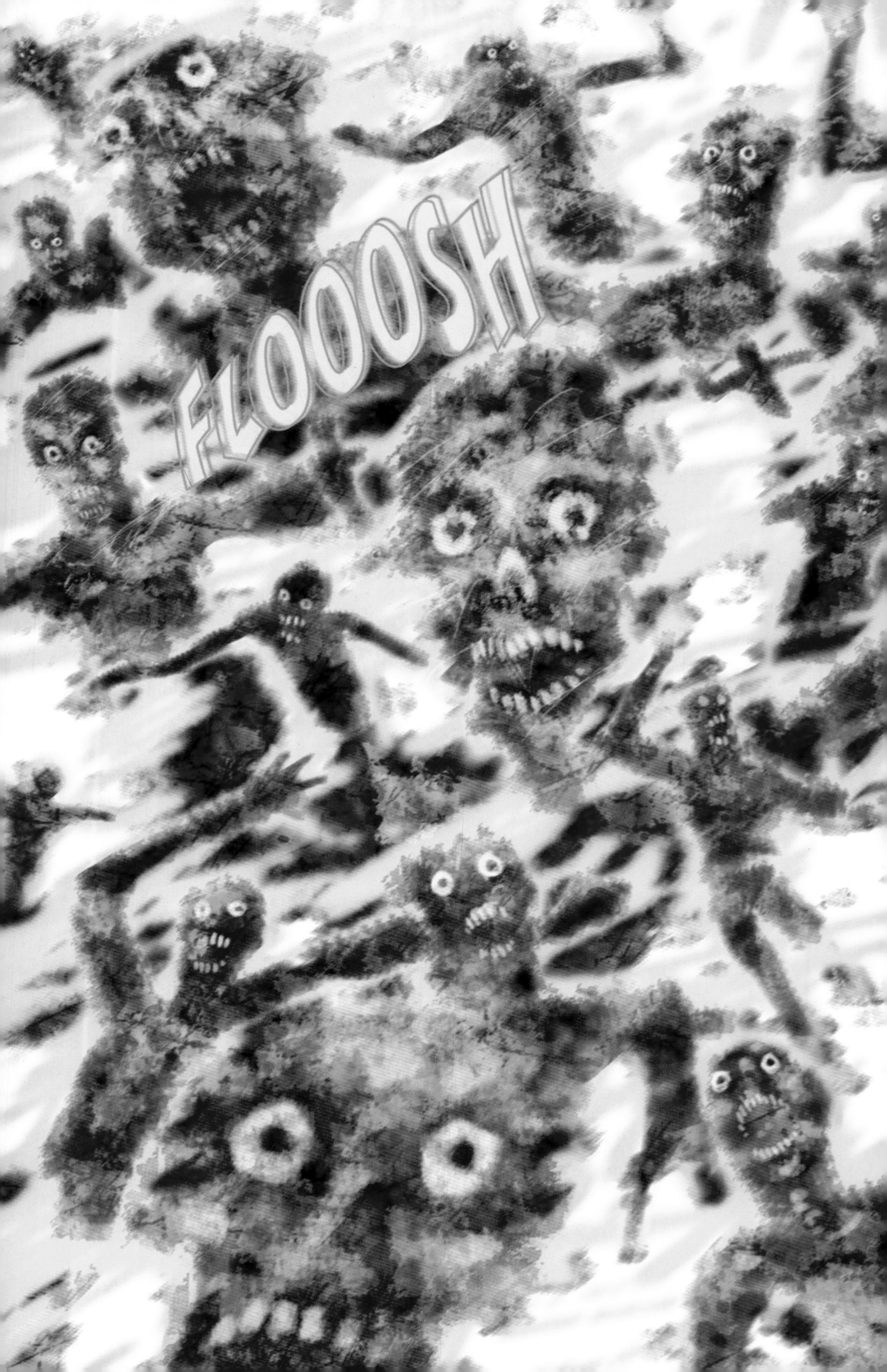
FLOOOSH

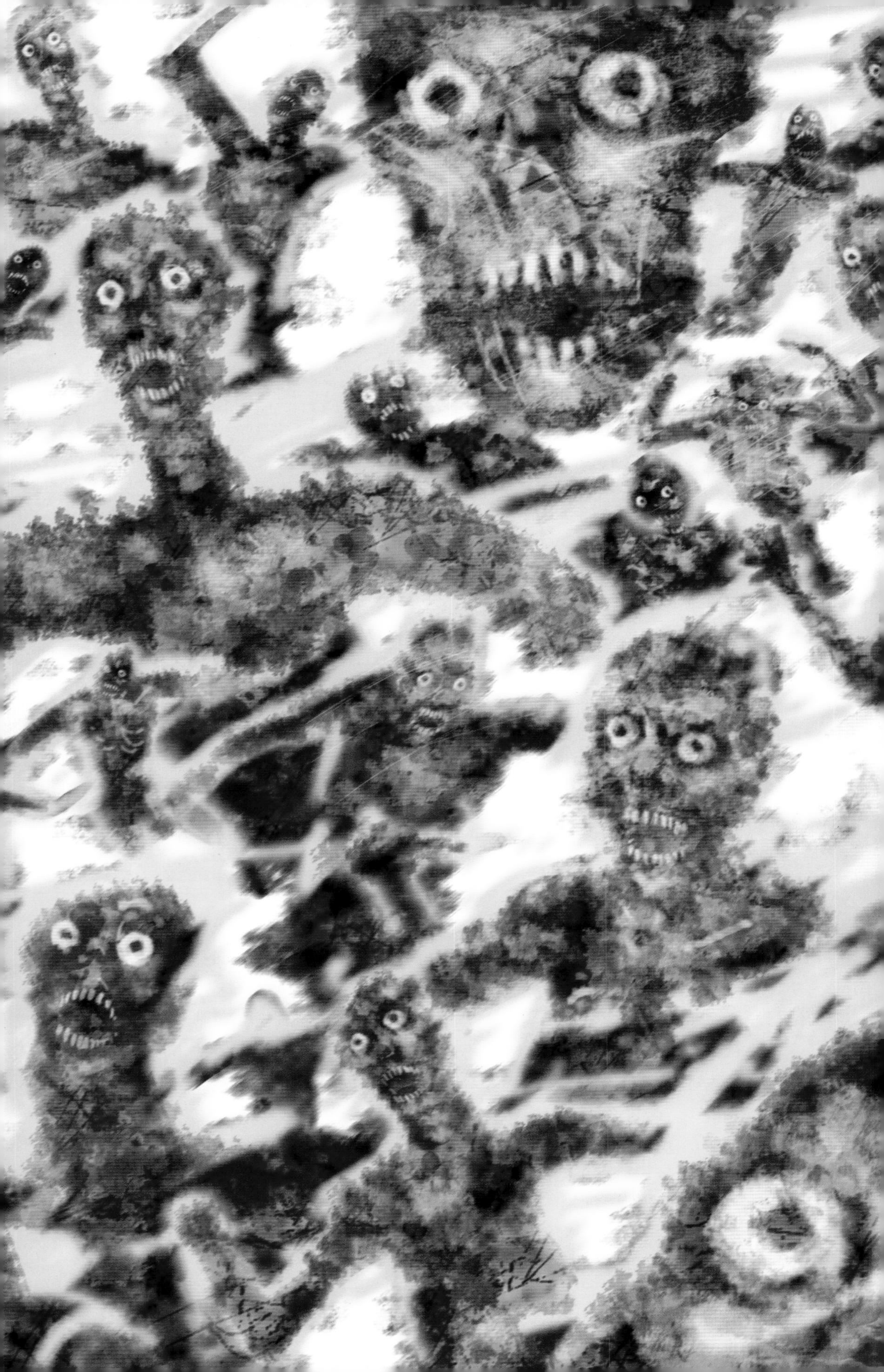

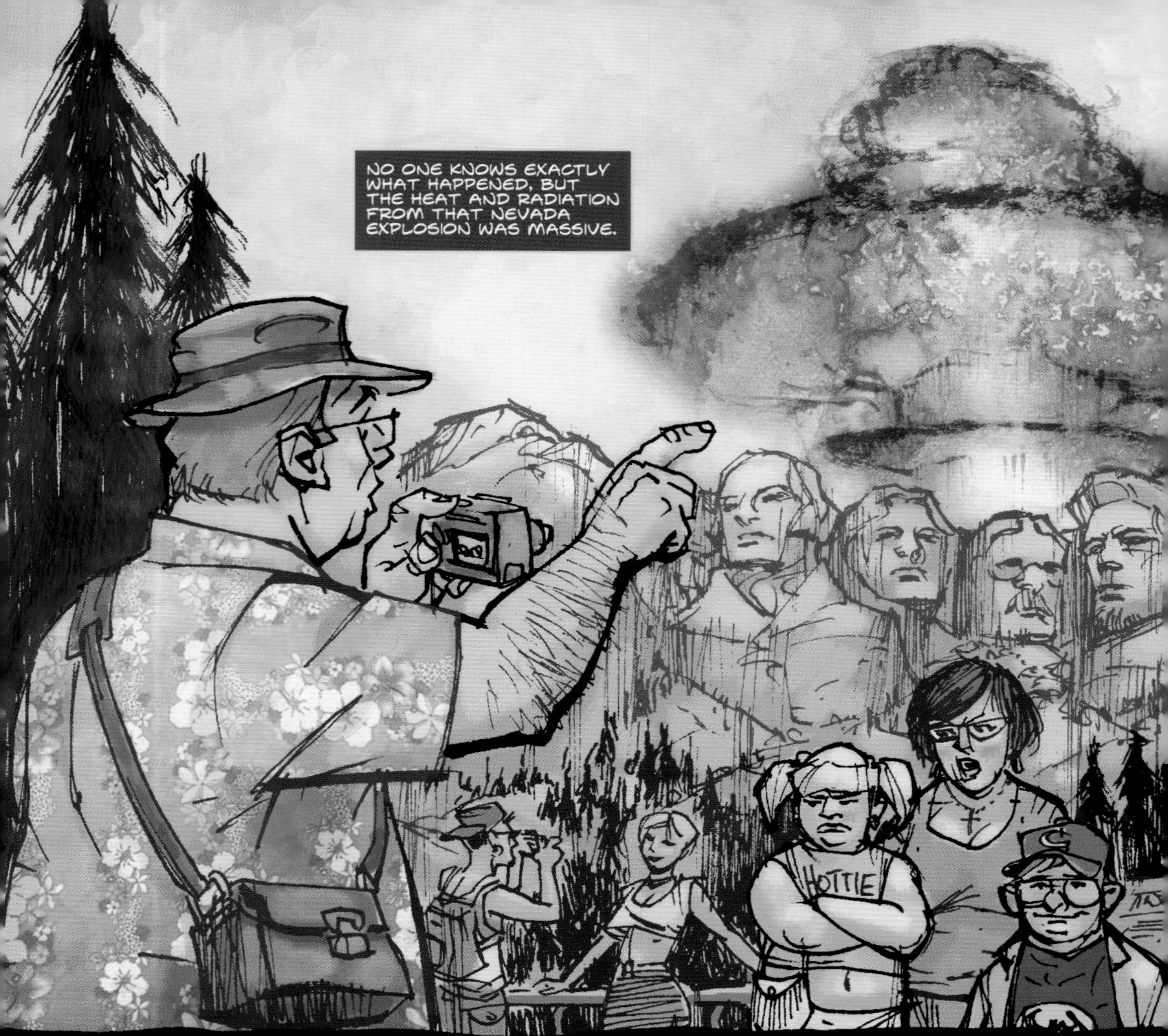
NO ONE KNOWS EXACTLY WHAT HAPPENED, BUT THE HEAT AND RADIATION FROM THAT NEVADA EXPLOSION WAS MASSIVE.
HOTTIE

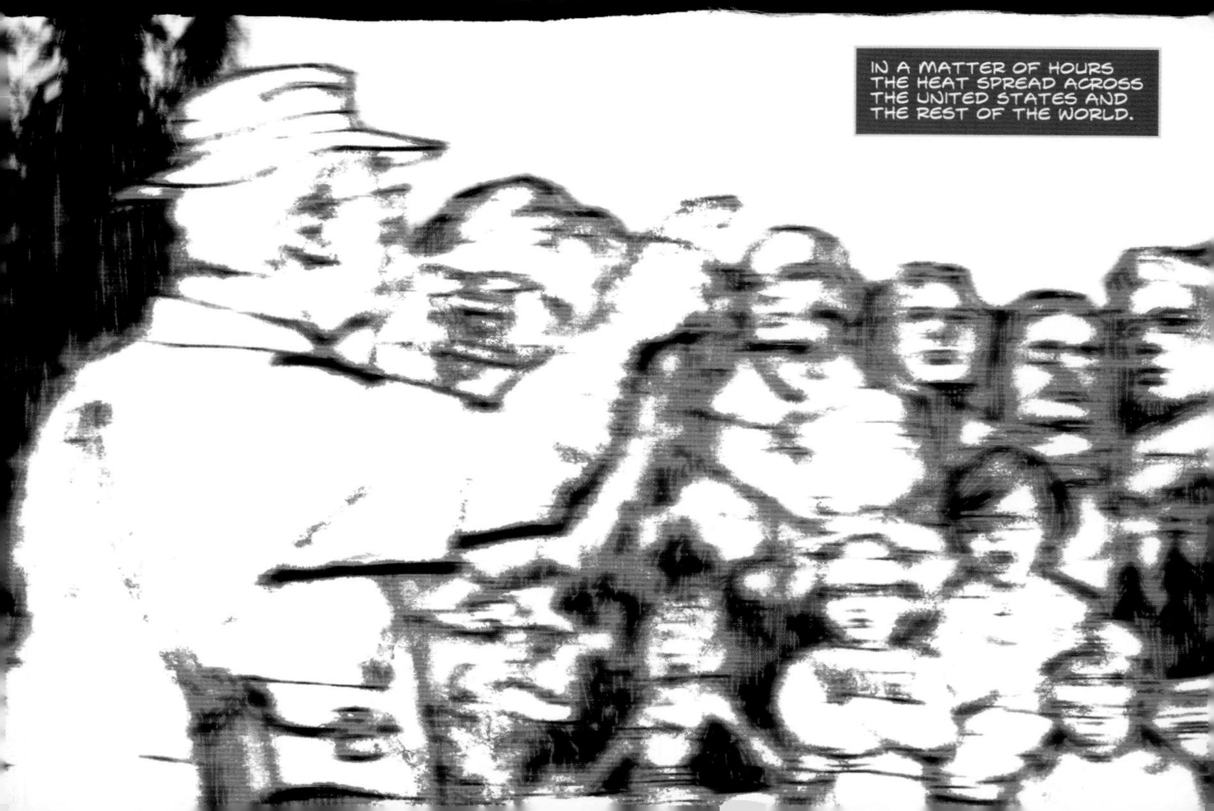
IN A MATTER OF HOURS THE HEAT SPREAD ACROSS THE UNITED STATES AND THE REST OF THE WORLD.

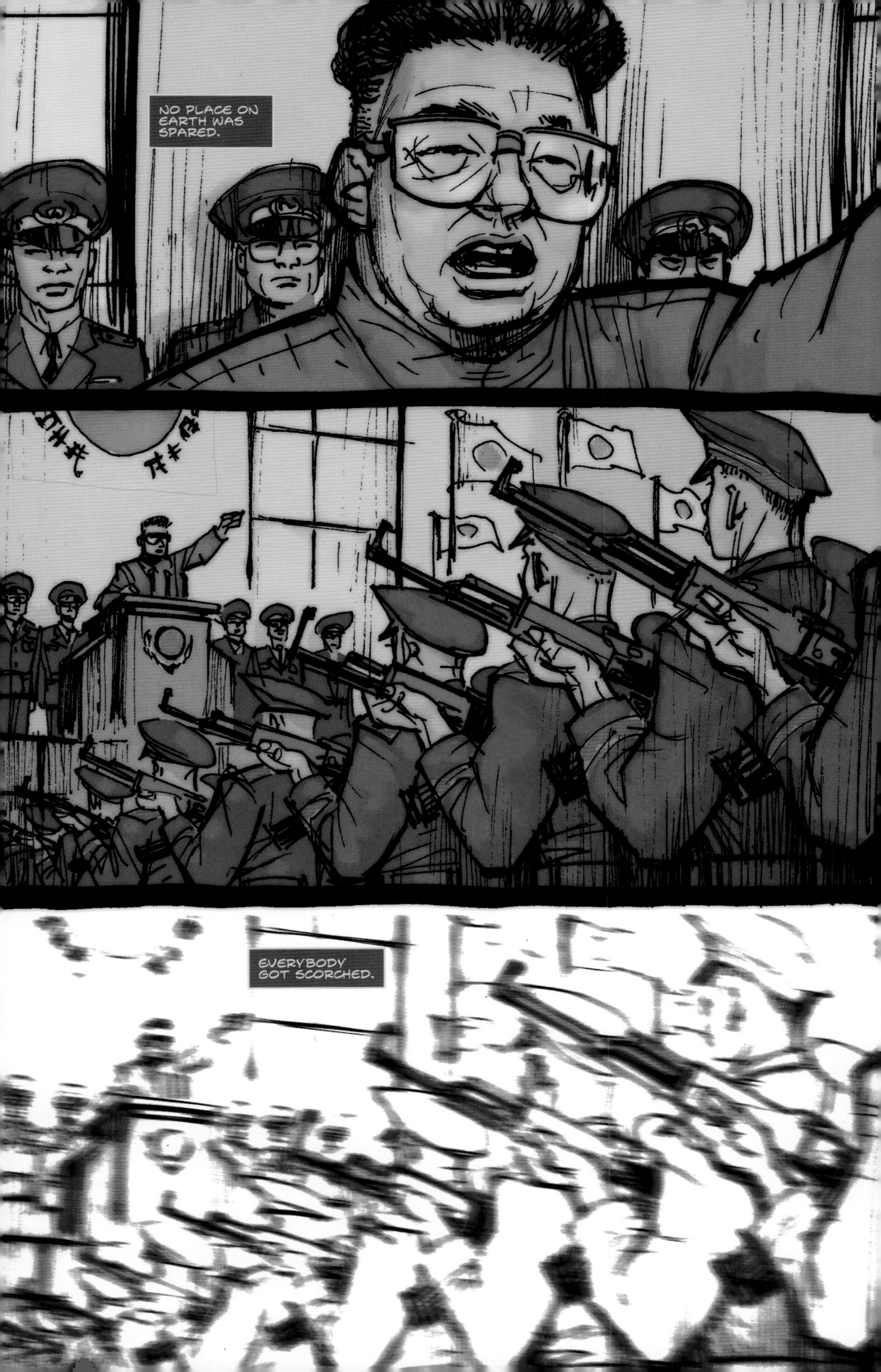
NO PLACE ON EARTH WAS SPARED.
EVERYBODY GOT SCORCHED.

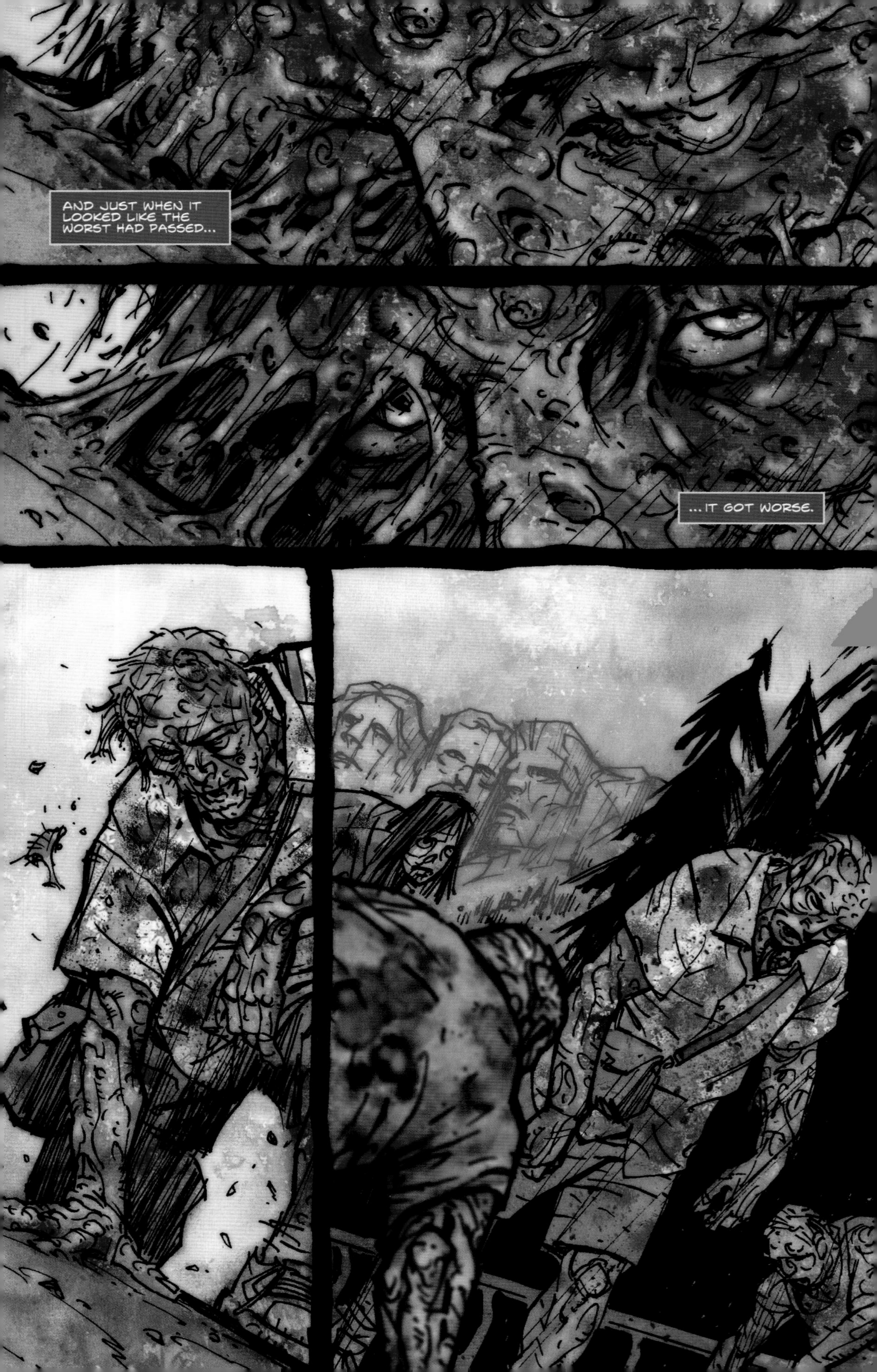
AND JUST WHEN IT LOOKED LIKE THE WORST HAD PASSED...
...IT GOT WORSE.

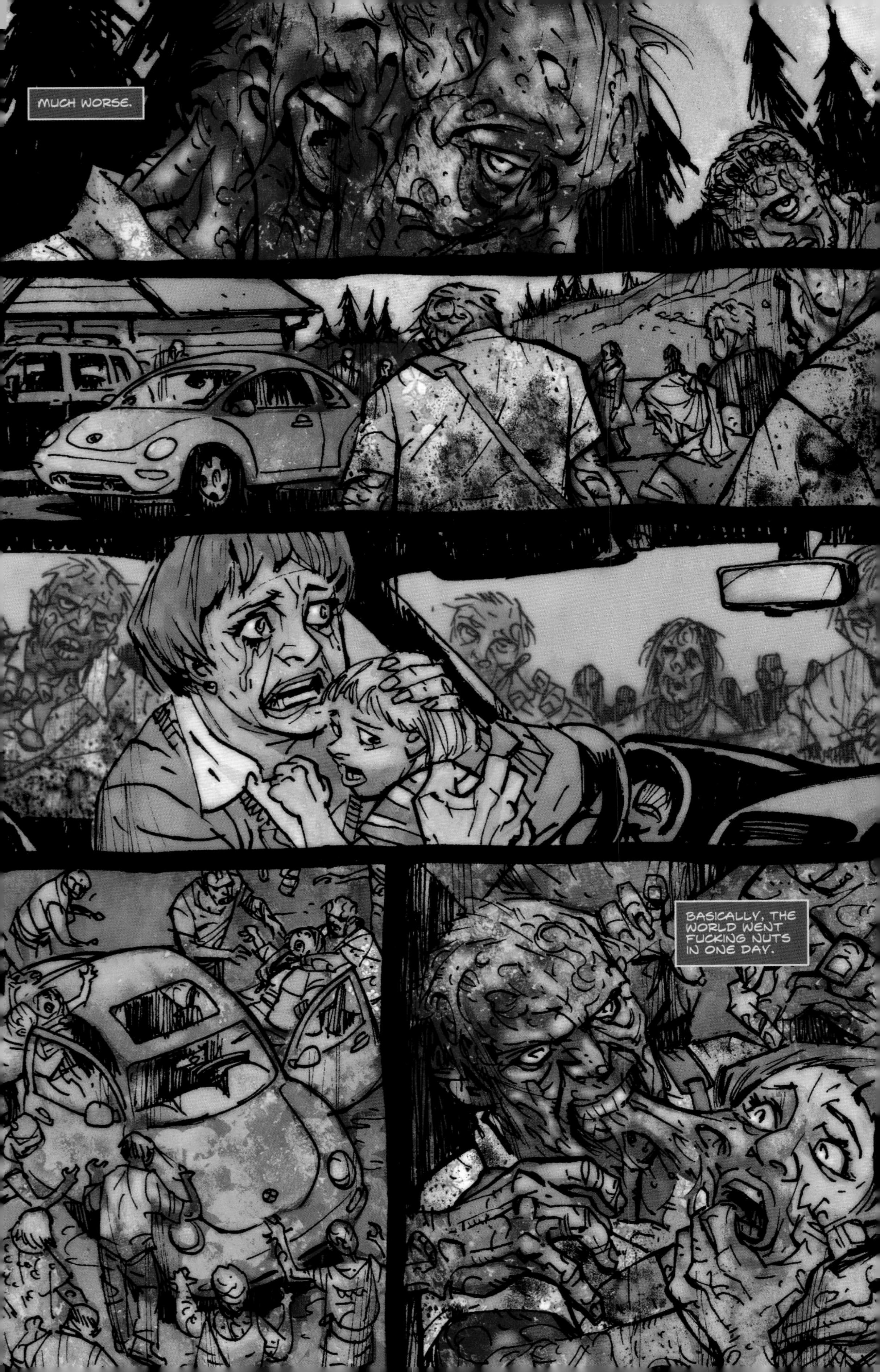
MUCH WORSE.
BASICALLY, THE WORLD WENT FUCKING NUTS IN ONE DAY.

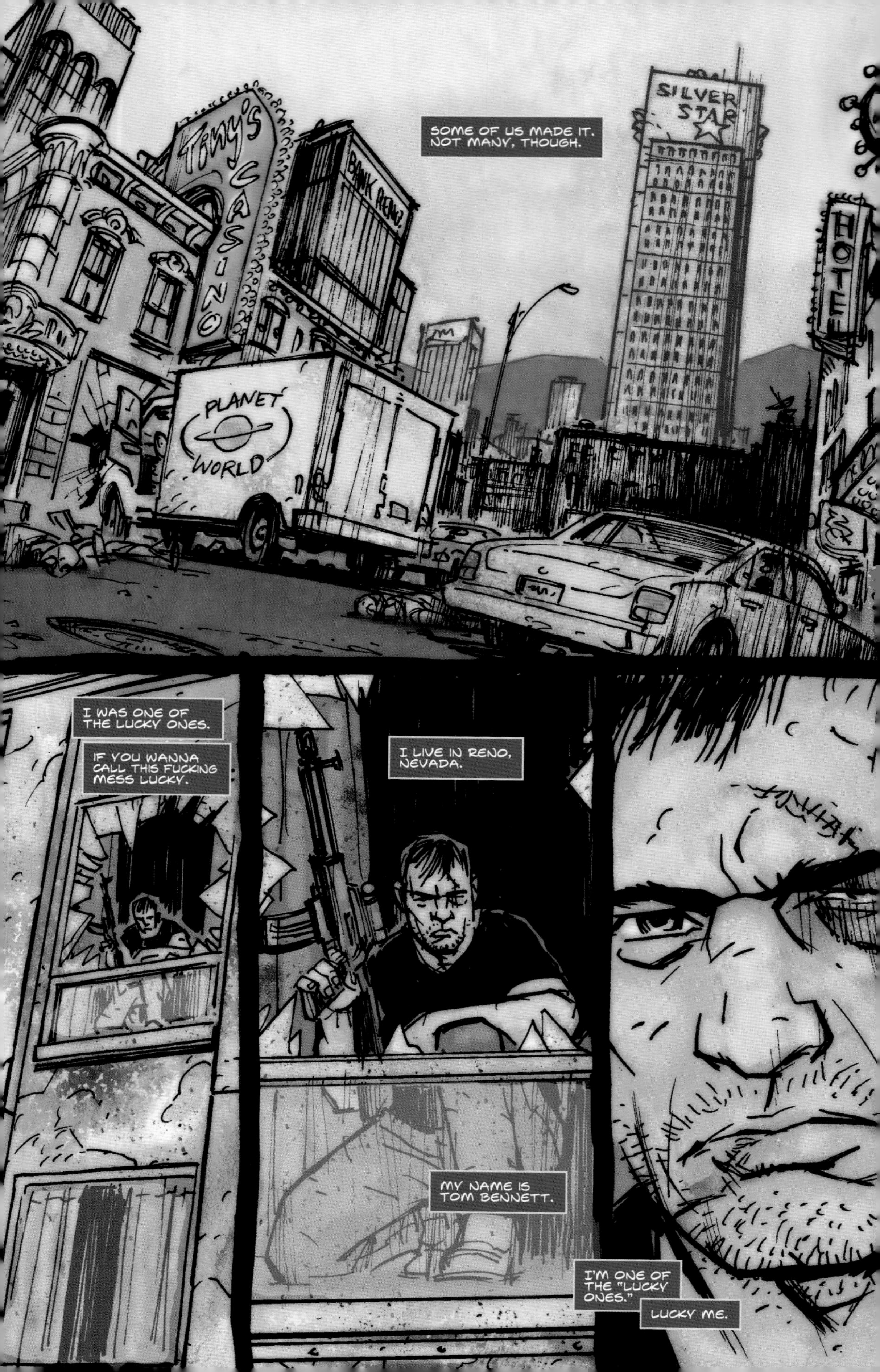
SOME OF US MADE IT. NOT MANY, THOUGH.
SILVER STAR
TINY'S CASINO
BANK RENO
HOTE
PLANET WORLD
I WAS ONE OF THE LUCKY ONES.
IF YOU WANNA CALL THIS FUCKING MESS LUCKY.
I LIVE IN RENO, NEVADA.
MY NAME IS TOM BENNETT.
I'M ONE OF THE "LUCKY ONES."
LUCKY ME.

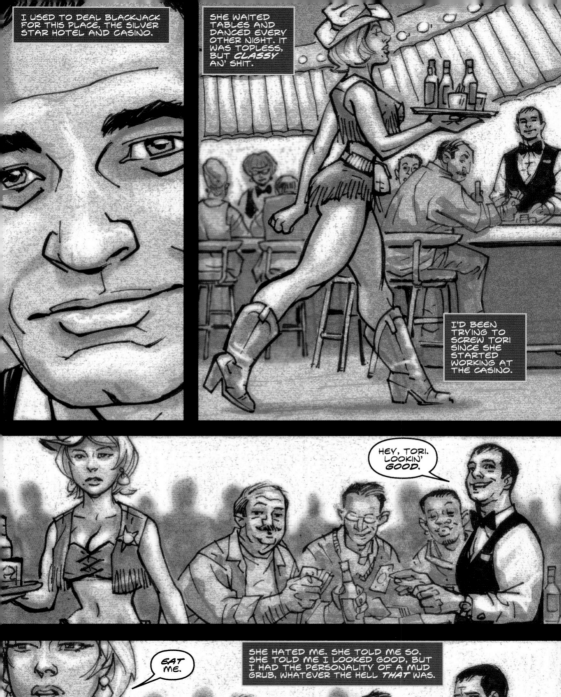

I USED TO DEAL BLACKJACK FOR THIS PLACE, THE SILVER STAR HOTEL AND CASINO.

SHE WAITED TABLES AND DANCED EVERY OTHER NIGHT. IT WAS TOPLESS, BUT *CLASSY* AN' SHIT.

I'D BEEN TRYING TO SCREW TORI SINCE SHE STARTED WORKING AT THE CASINO.

HEY, TORI. LOOKIN' *GOOD.*

EAT ME.

SHE HATED ME. SHE TOLD ME SO. SHE TOLD ME I LOOKED GOOD, BUT I HAD THE PERSONALITY OF A MUD GRUB, WHATEVER THE HELL *THAT* WAS.

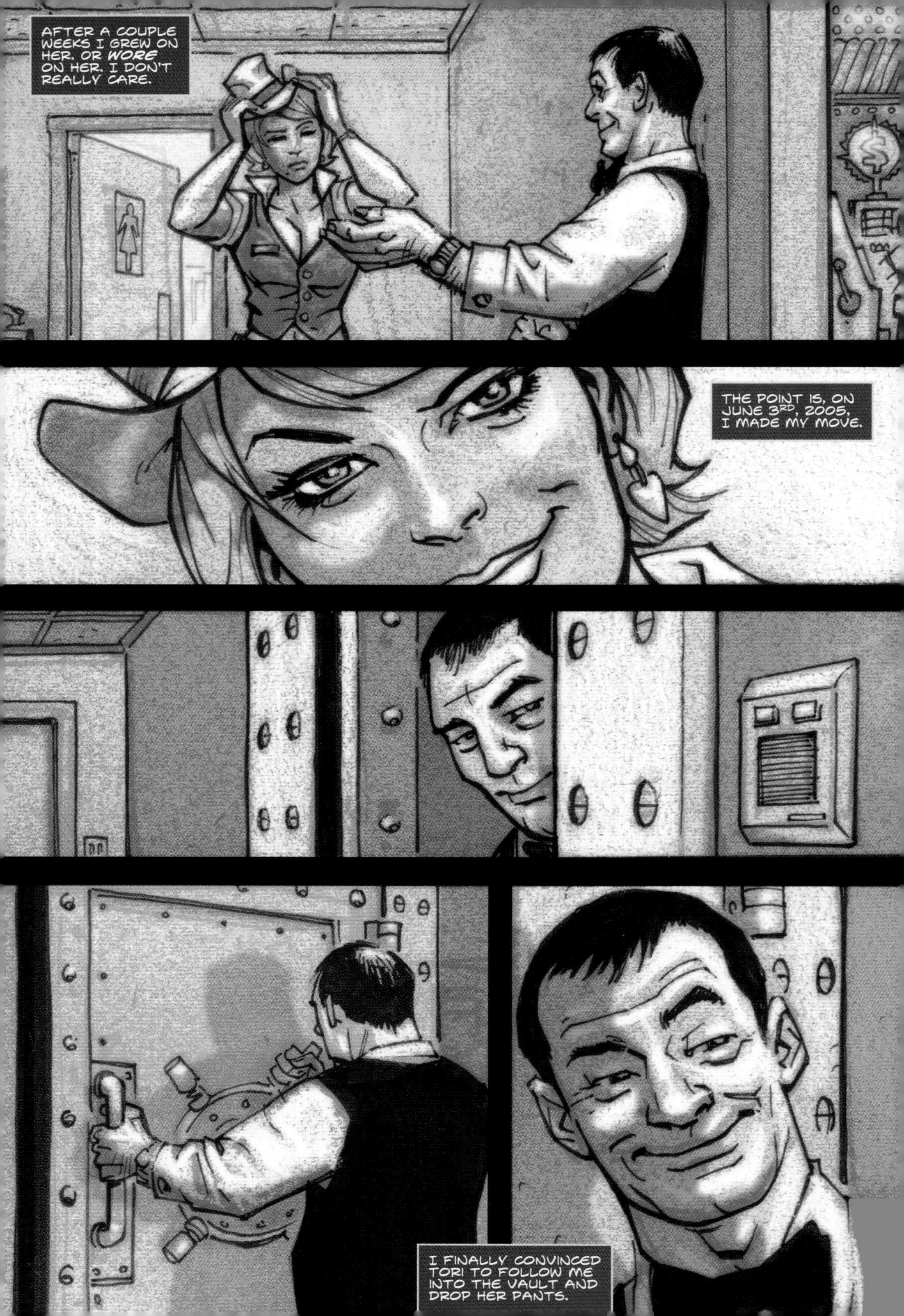
AFTER A COUPLE WEEKS I GREW ON HER. OR *WORE* ON HER. I DON'T REALLY CARE.
THE POINT IS, ON JUNE 3RD, 2005, I MADE MY MOVE.
I FINALLY CONVINCED TORI TO FOLLOW ME INTO THE VAULT AND DROP HER PANTS.

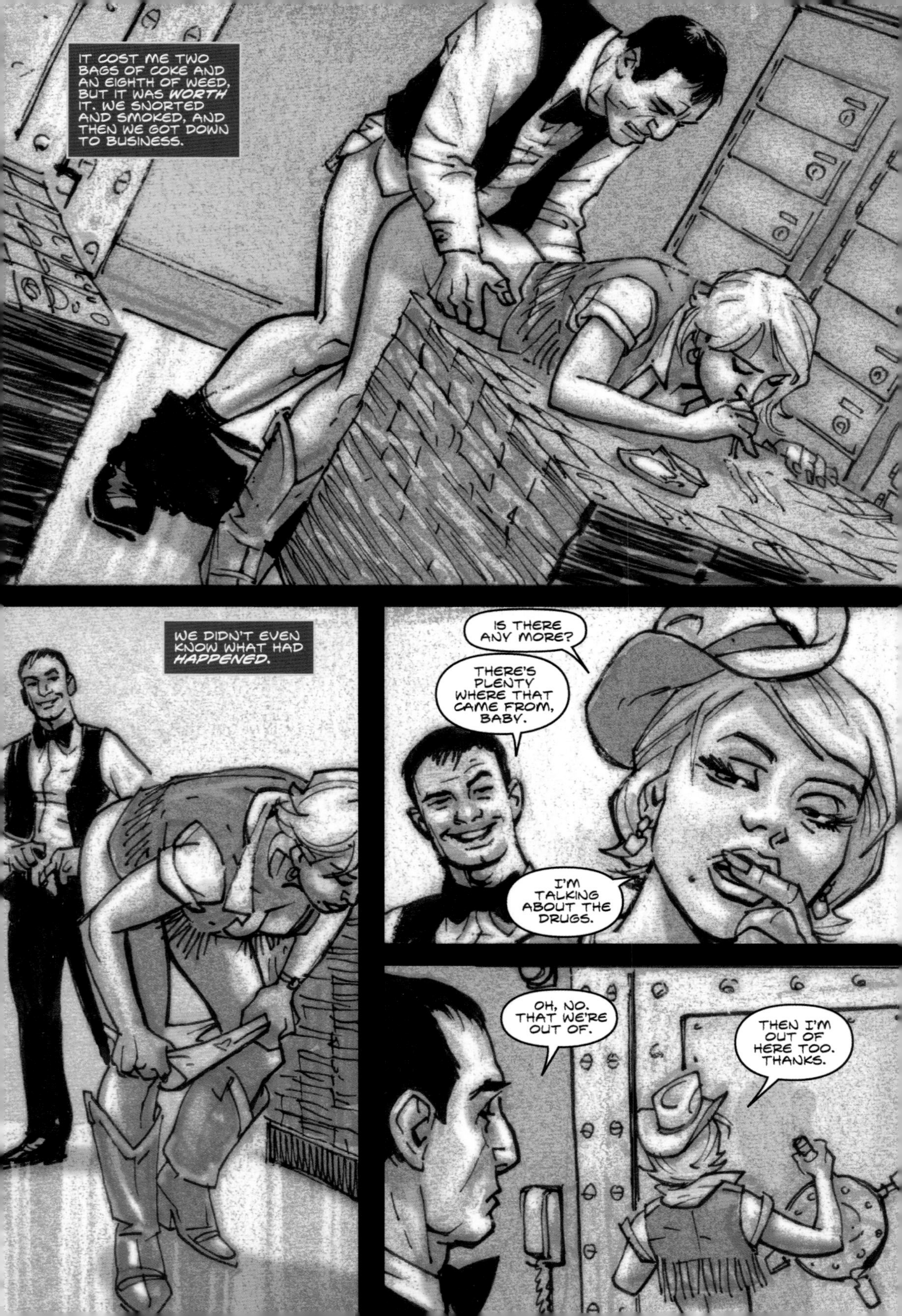
IT COST ME TWO BAGS OF COKE AND AN EIGHTH OF WEED, BUT IT WAS *WORTH* IT. WE SNORTED AND SMOKED, AND THEN WE GOT DOWN TO BUSINESS.
WE DIDN'T EVEN KNOW WHAT HAD *HAPPENED*.
IS THERE ANY MORE?
THERE'S PLENTY WHERE THAT CAME FROM, BABY.
I'M TALKING ABOUT THE DRUGS.
OH, NO. THAT WE'RE OUT OF.
THEN I'M OUT OF HERE TOO. THANKS.

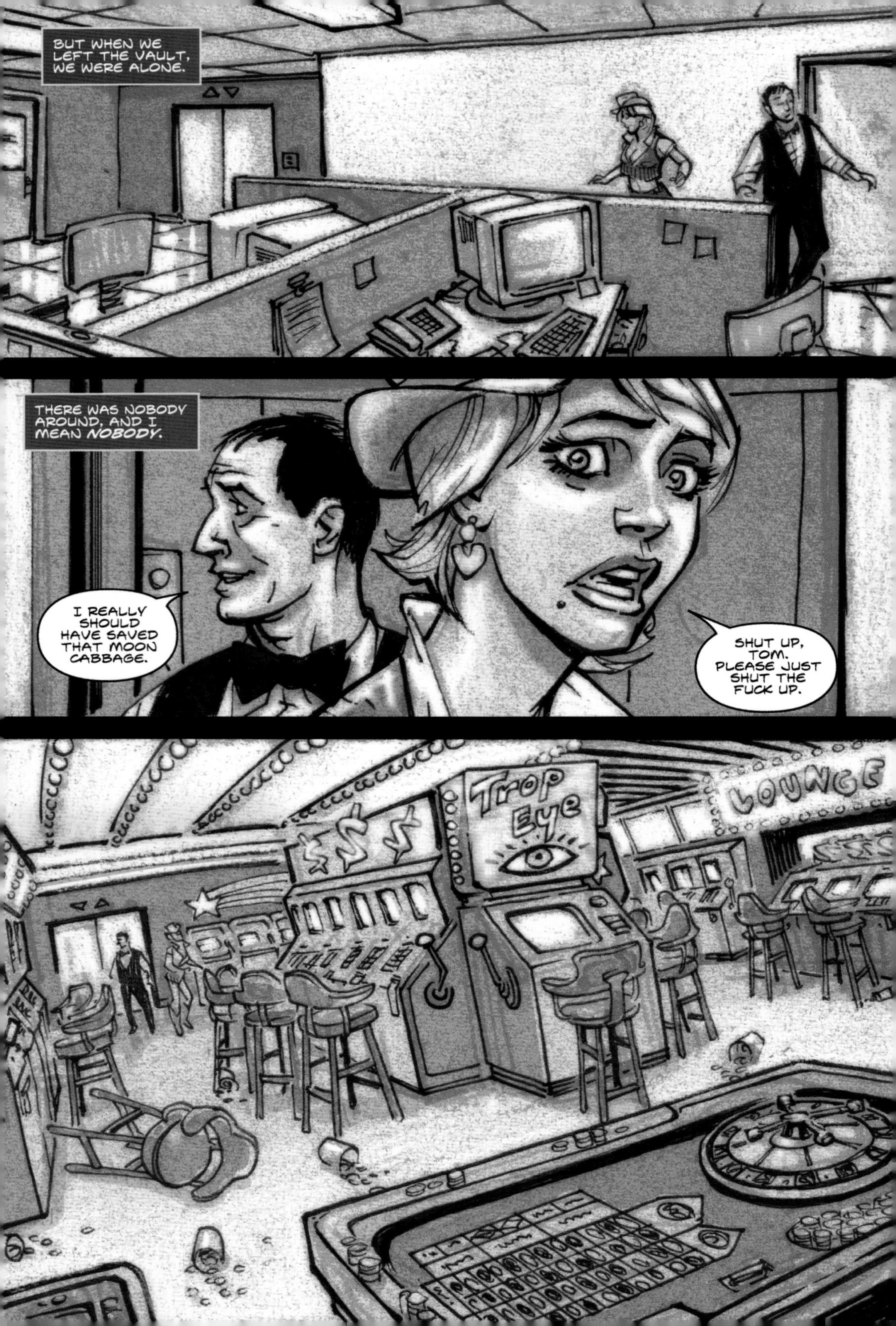
BUT WHEN WE LEFT THE VAULT, WE WERE ALONE.
THERE WAS NOBODY AROUND, AND I MEAN *NOBODY*.
I REALLY SHOULD HAVE SAVED THAT MOON CABBAGE.
SHUT UP, TOM. PLEASE JUST SHUT THE FUCK UP.
Trop Eye
LOUNGE

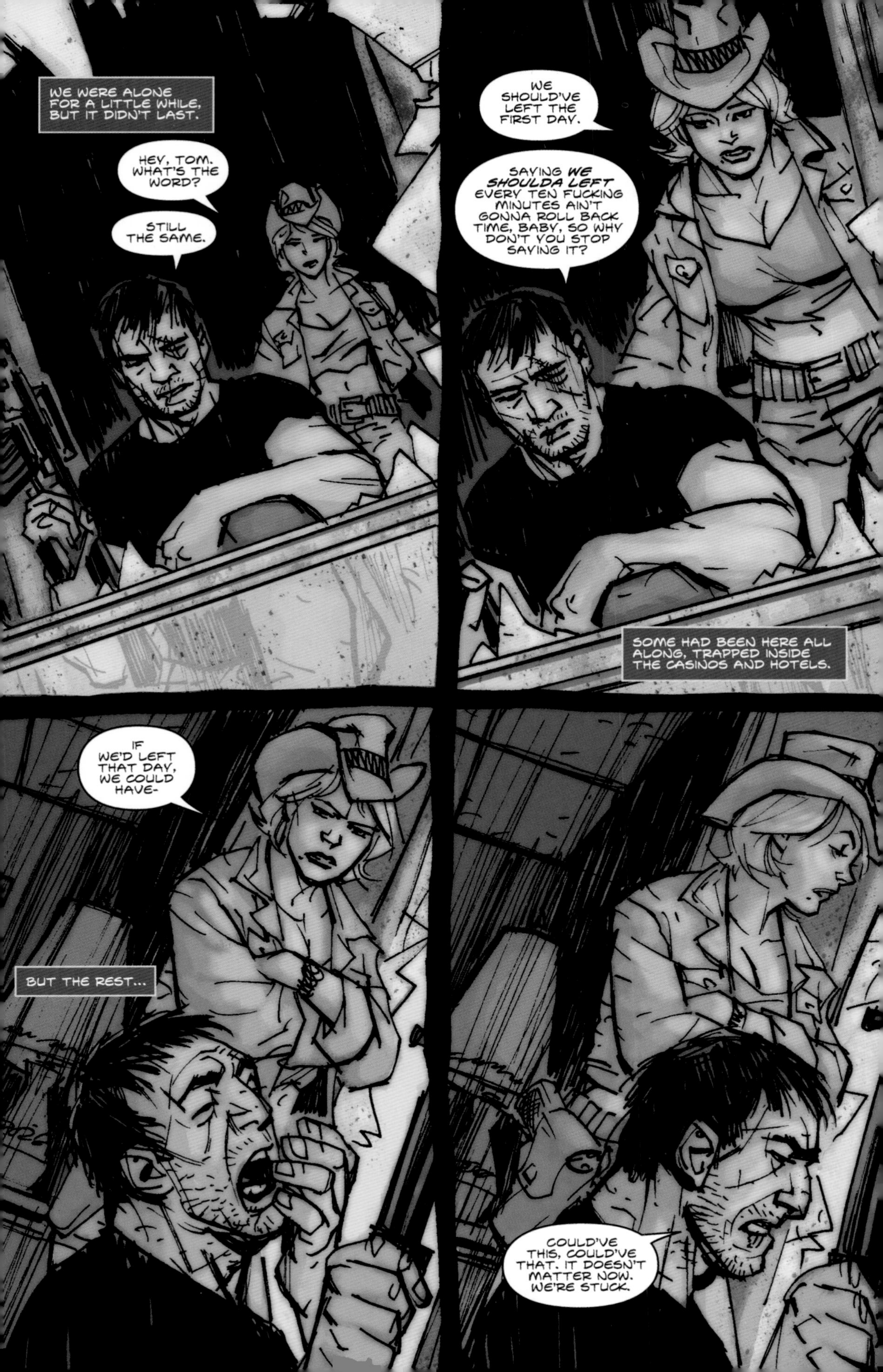
WE WERE ALONE FOR A LITTLE WHILE, BUT IT DIDN'T LAST.
HEY, TOM. WHAT'S THE WORD?
STILL THE SAME.
WE SHOULD'VE LEFT THE FIRST DAY.
SAYING WE SHOULDA LEFT EVERY TEN FUCKING MINUTES AIN'T GONNA ROLL BACK TIME, BABY, SO WHY DON'T YOU STOP SAYING IT?
SOME HAD BEEN HERE ALL ALONG, TRAPPED INSIDE THE CASINOS AND HOTELS.
IF WE'D LEFT THAT DAY, WE COULD HAVE-
BUT THE REST...
COULD'VE THIS, COULD'VE THAT. IT DOESN'T MATTER NOW. WE'RE STUCK.

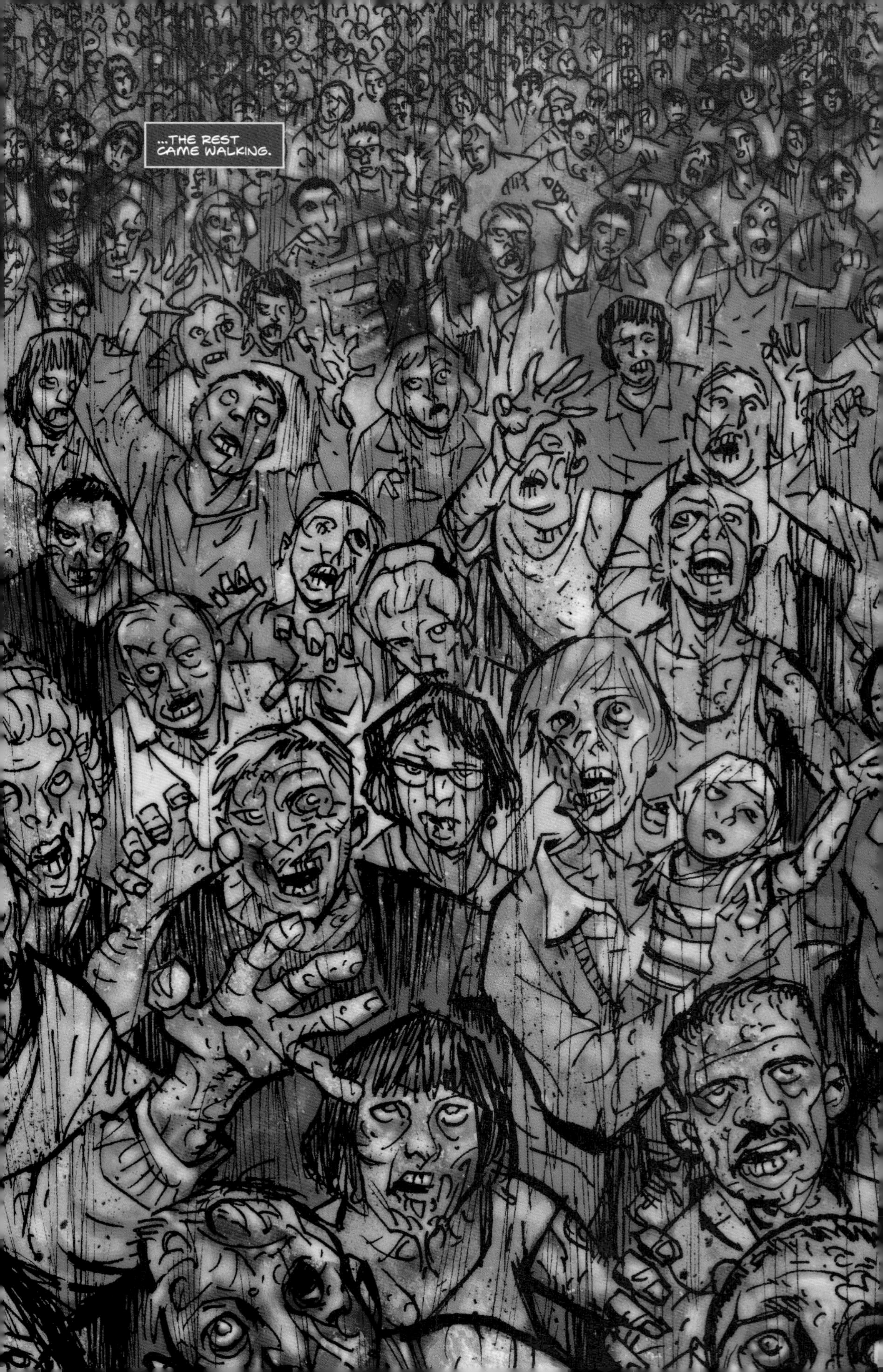
...THE REST
CAME WALKING.

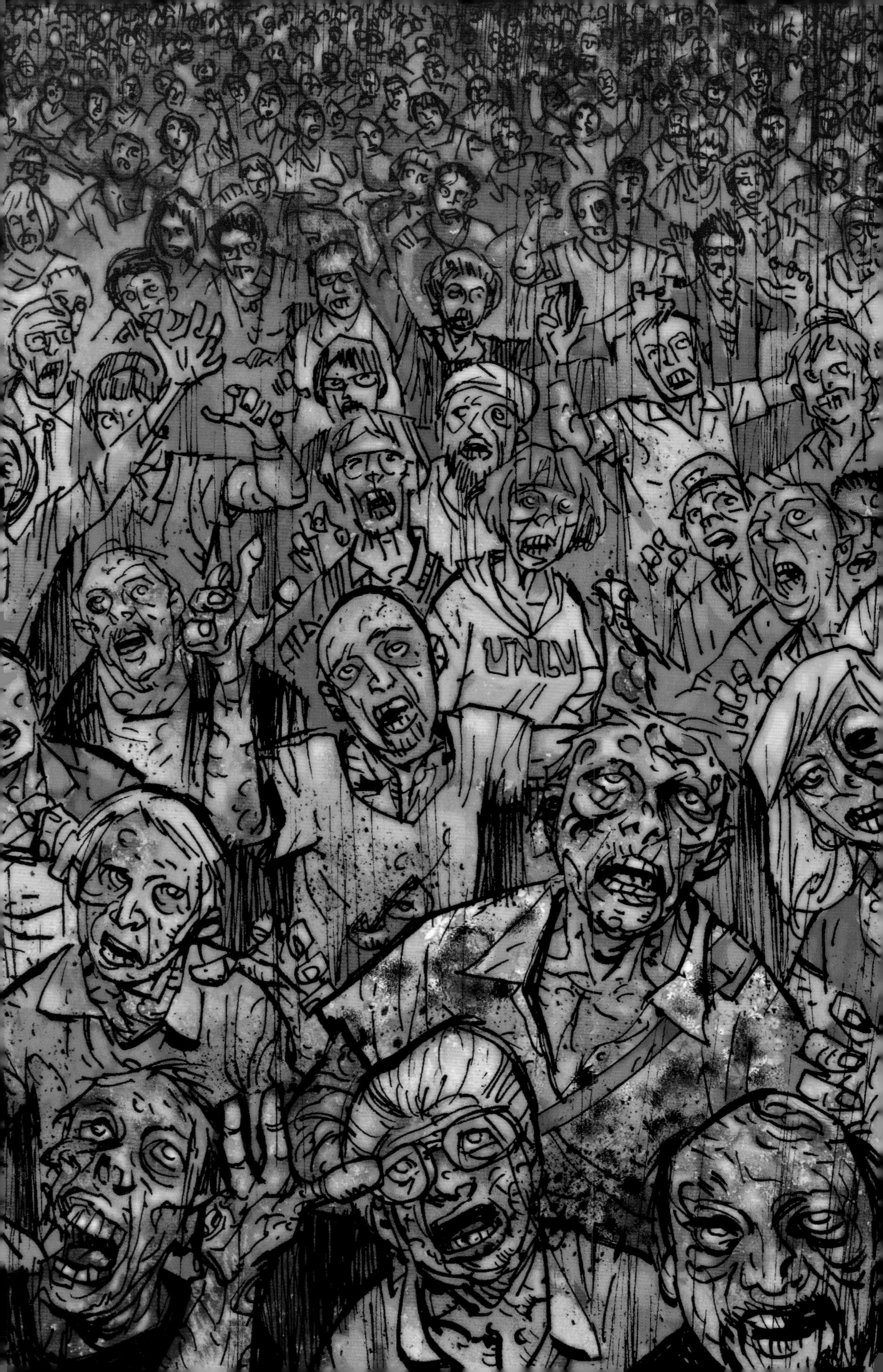
UNLV

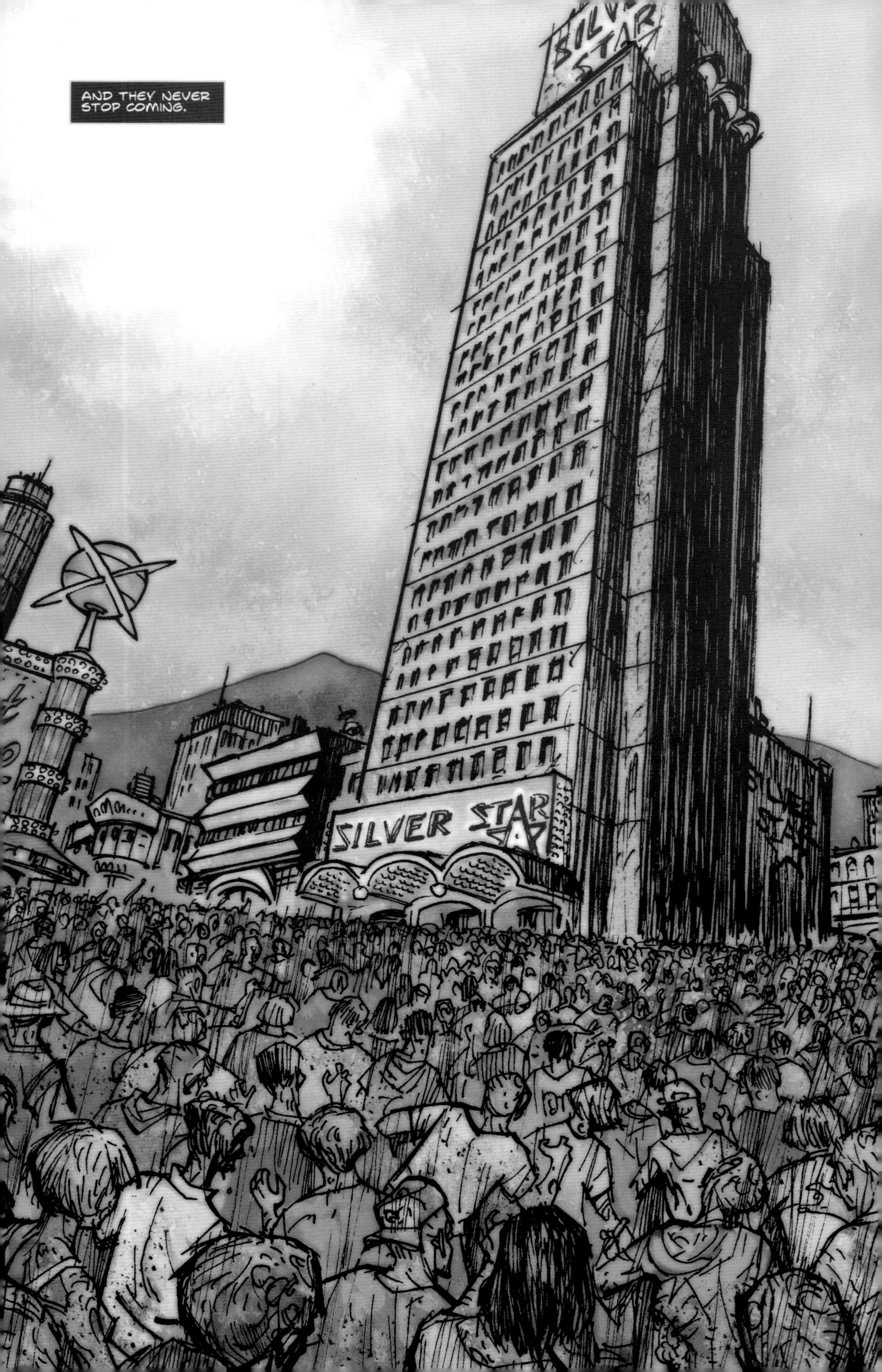
AND THEY NEVER STOP COMING.
SILVER STAR
SILVER STAR

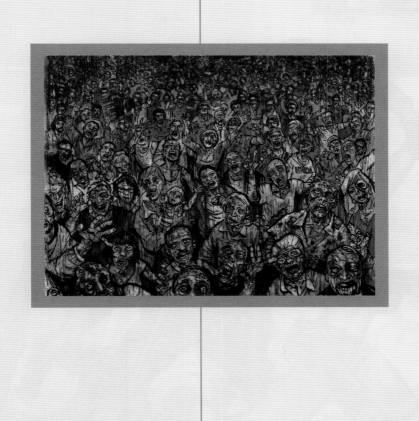

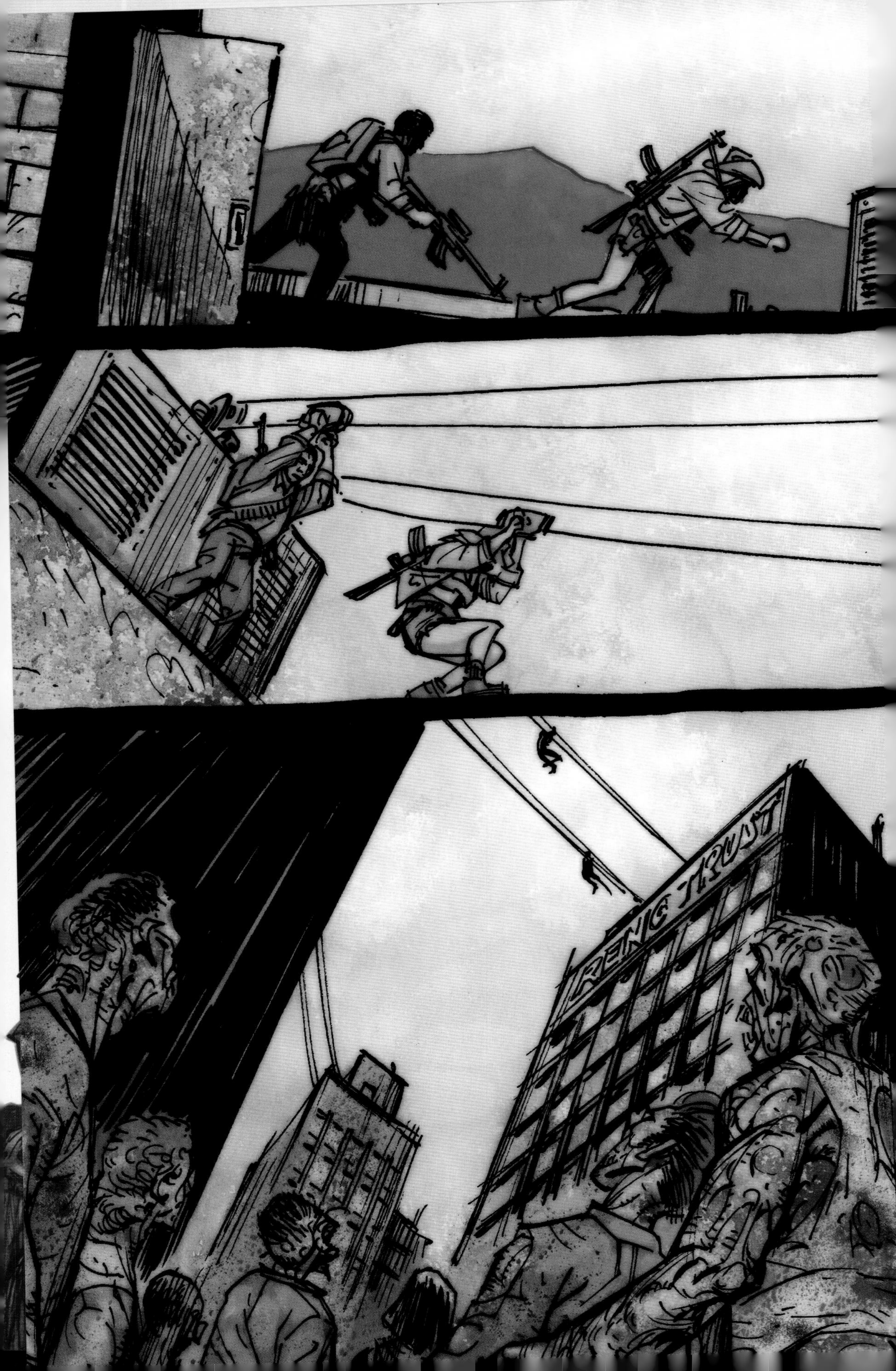
RENO TRUST

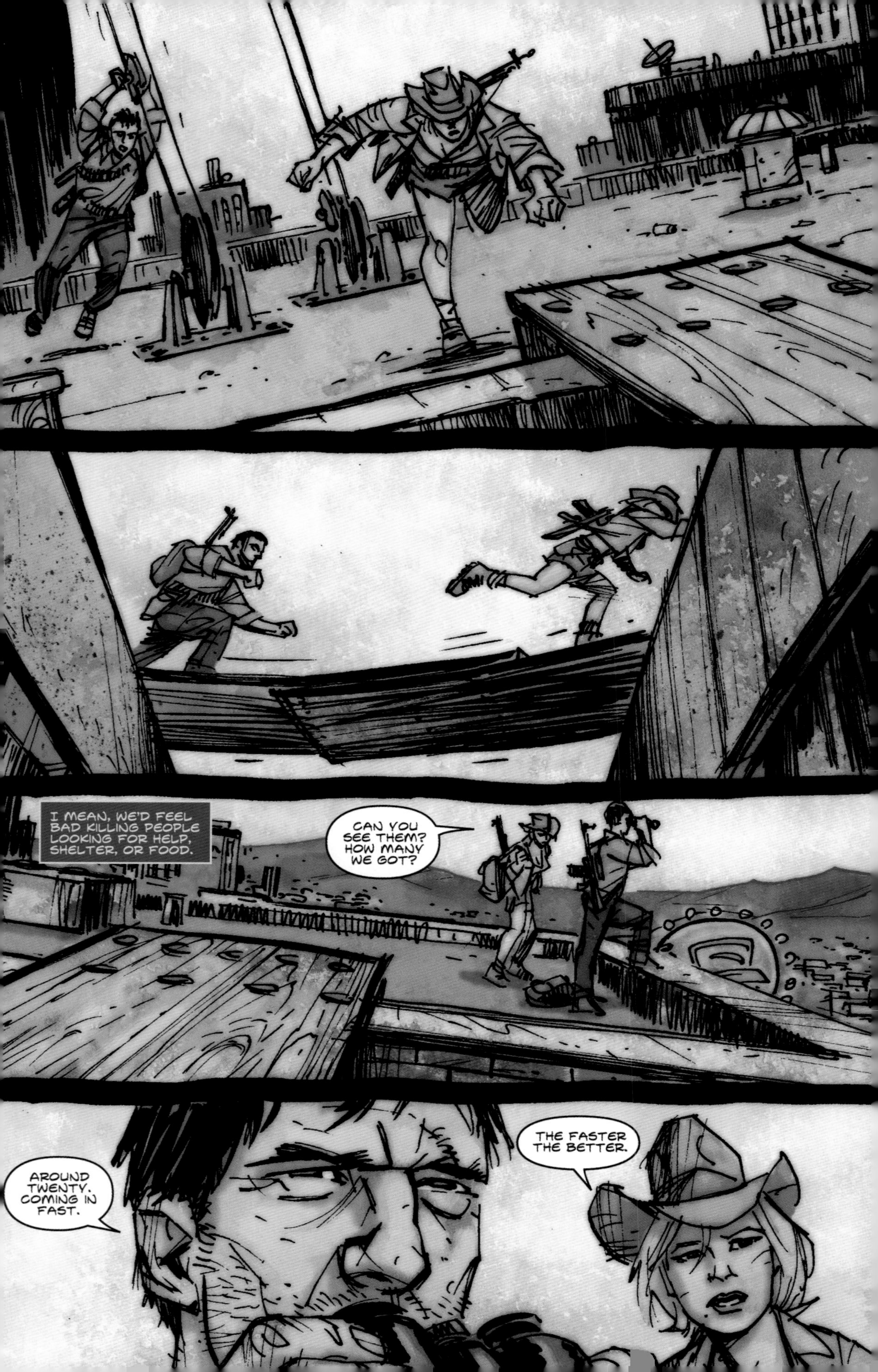
I MEAN, WE'D FEEL BAD KILLING PEOPLE LOOKING FOR HELP, SHELTER, OR FOOD.
CAN YOU SEE THEM? HOW MANY WE GOT?
AROUND TWENTY. COMING IN FAST.
THE FASTER THE BETTER.

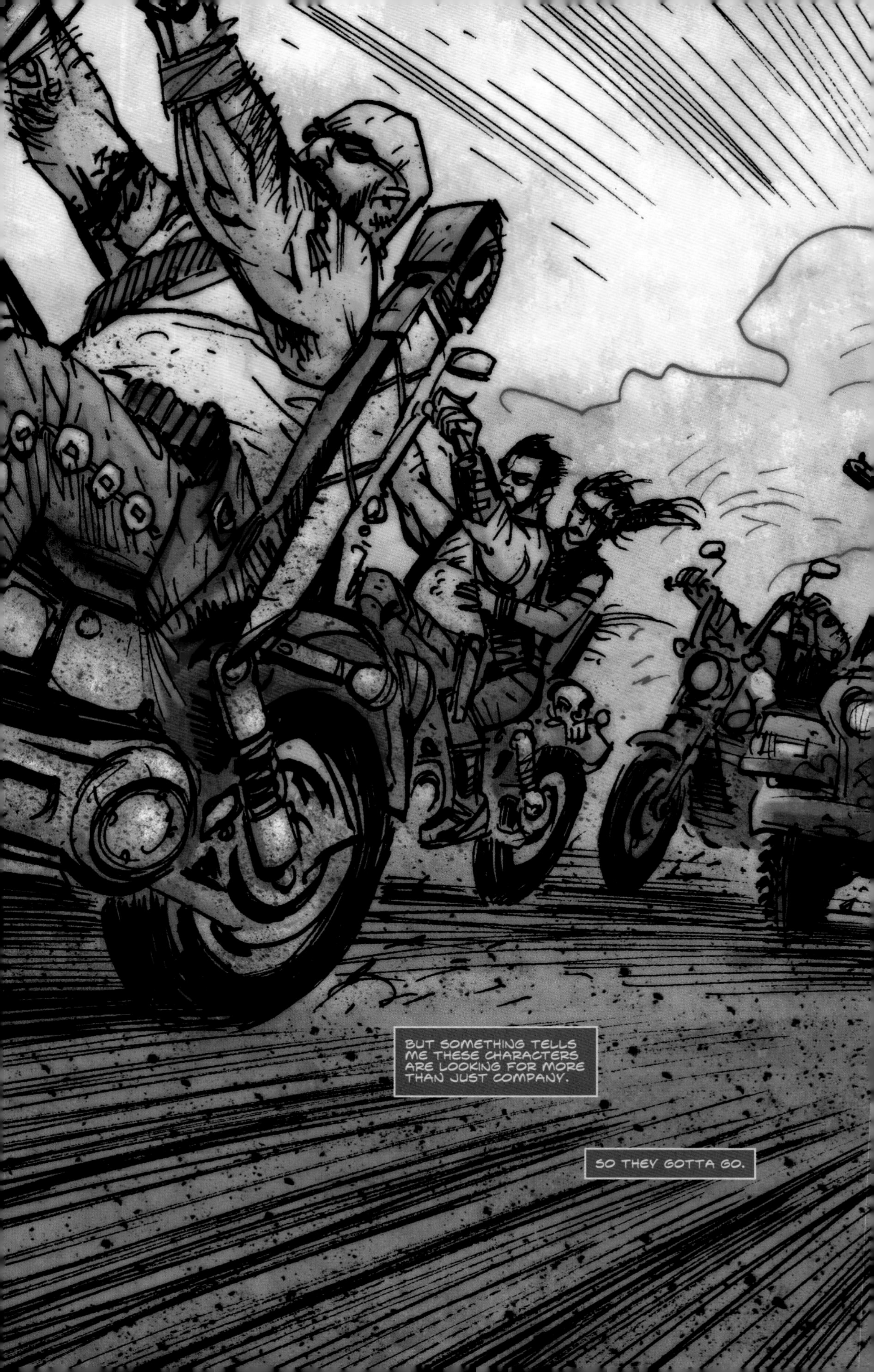
BUT SOMETHING TELLS ME THESE CHARACTERS ARE LOOKING FOR MORE THAN JUST COMPANY.
SO THEY GOTTA GO.

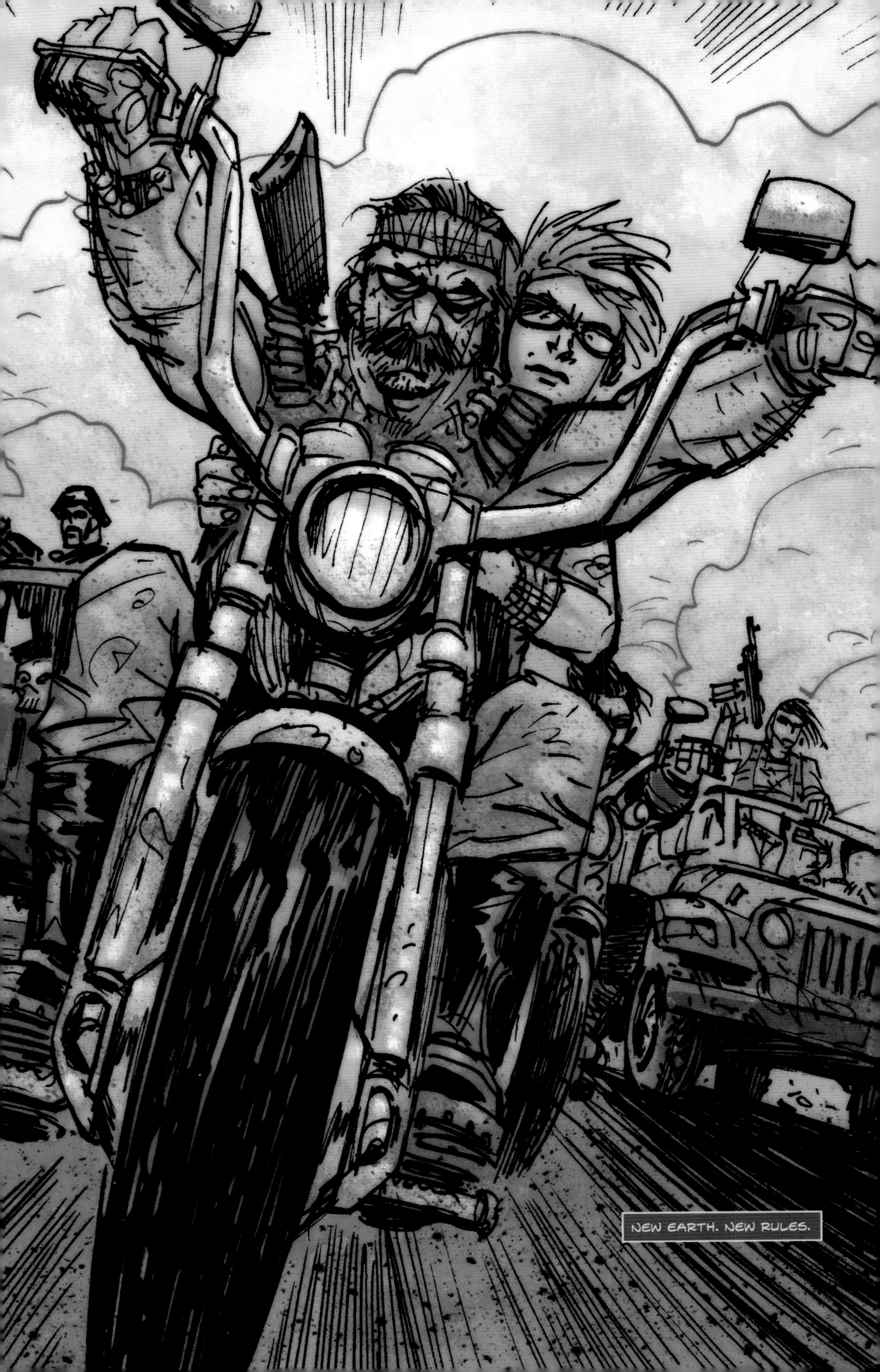
NEW EARTH. NEW RULES.

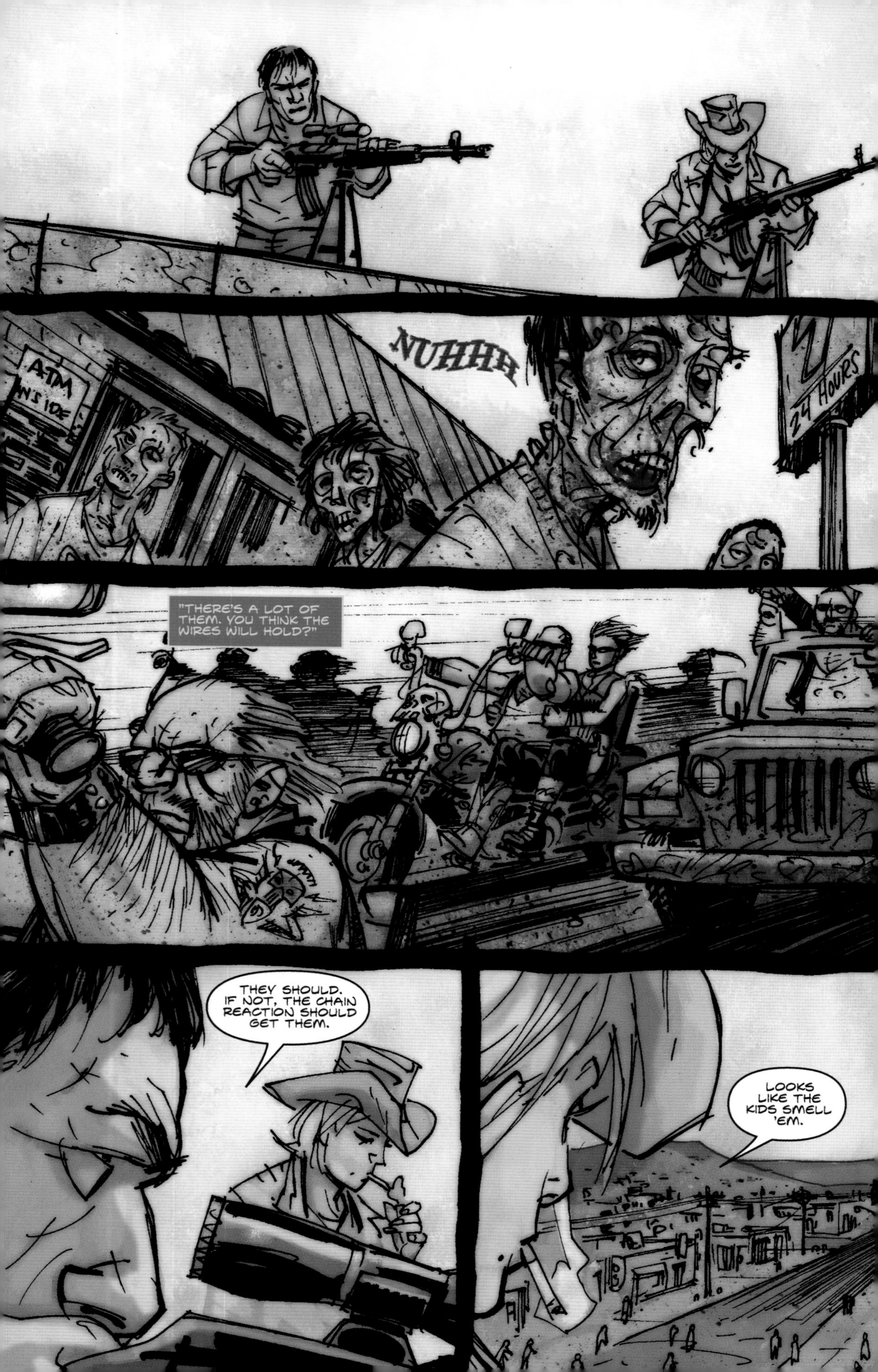

NUHHH
ATM
INSIDE
24 HOURS
"THERE'S A LOT OF THEM. YOU THINK THE WIRES WILL HOLD?"
THEY SHOULD. IF NOT, THE CHAIN REACTION SHOULD GET THEM.
LOOKS LIKE THE KIDS SMELL 'EM.

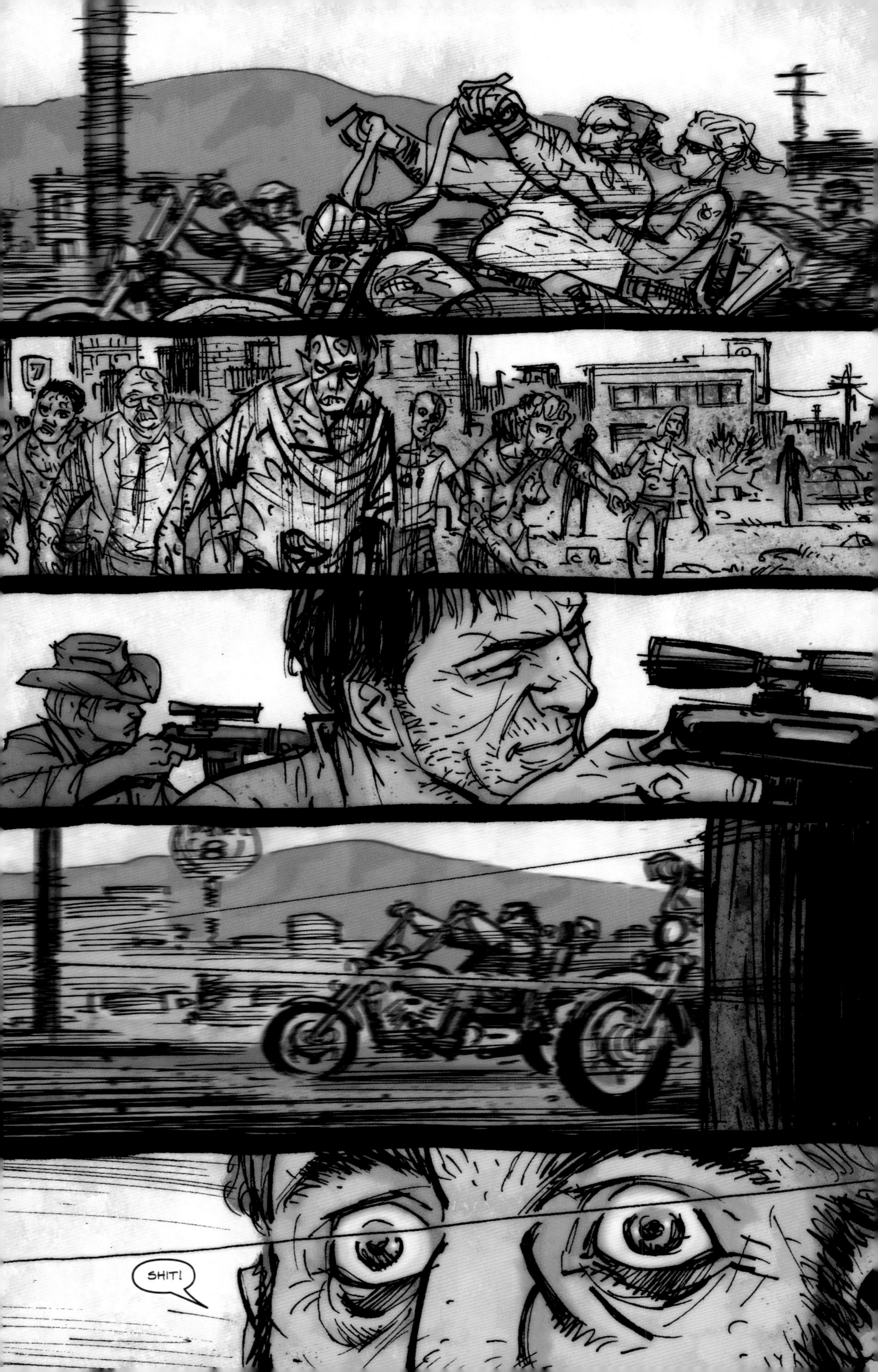
SHIT!

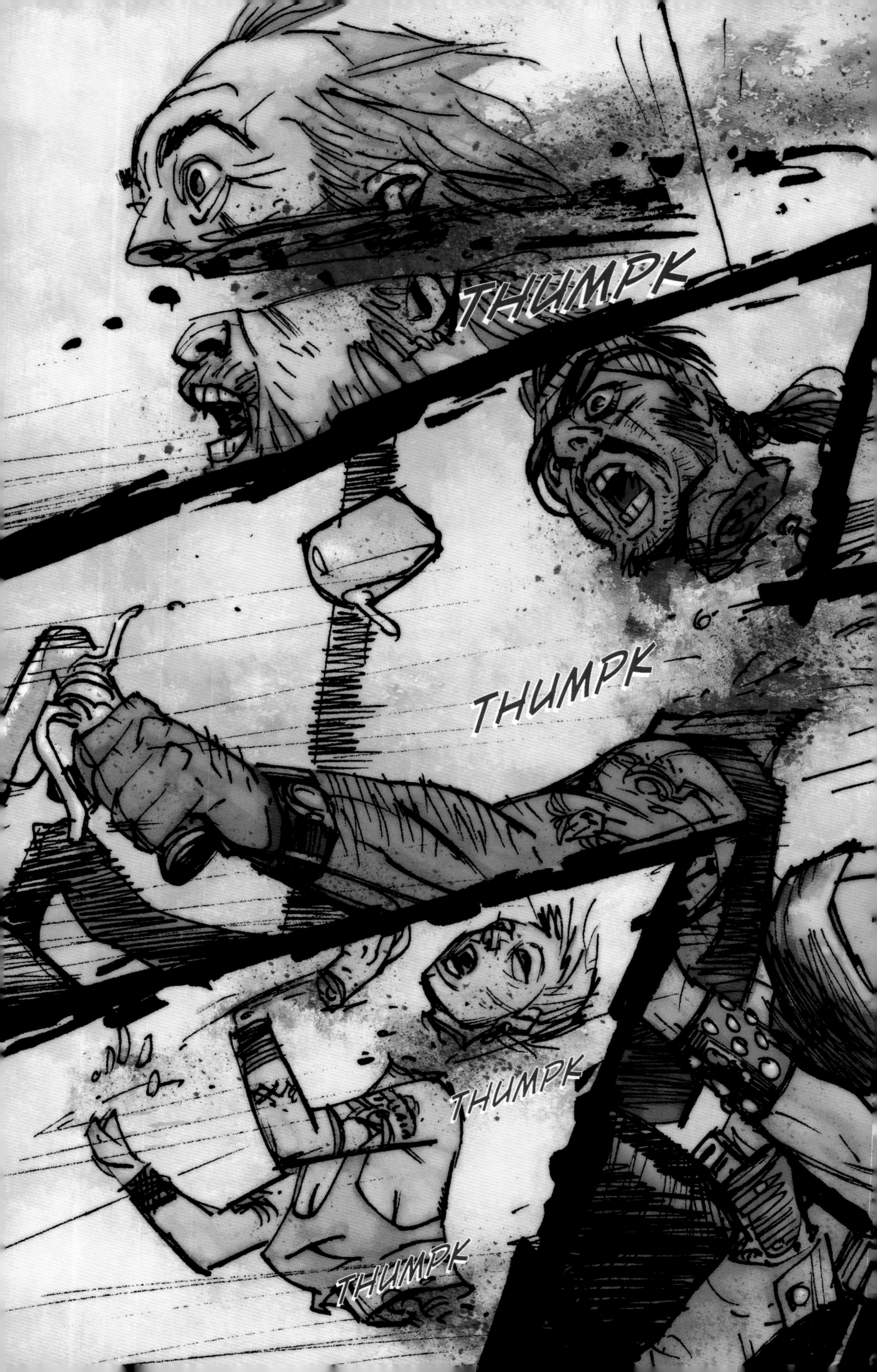
THUMPK
THUMPK
THUMPK
THUMPK

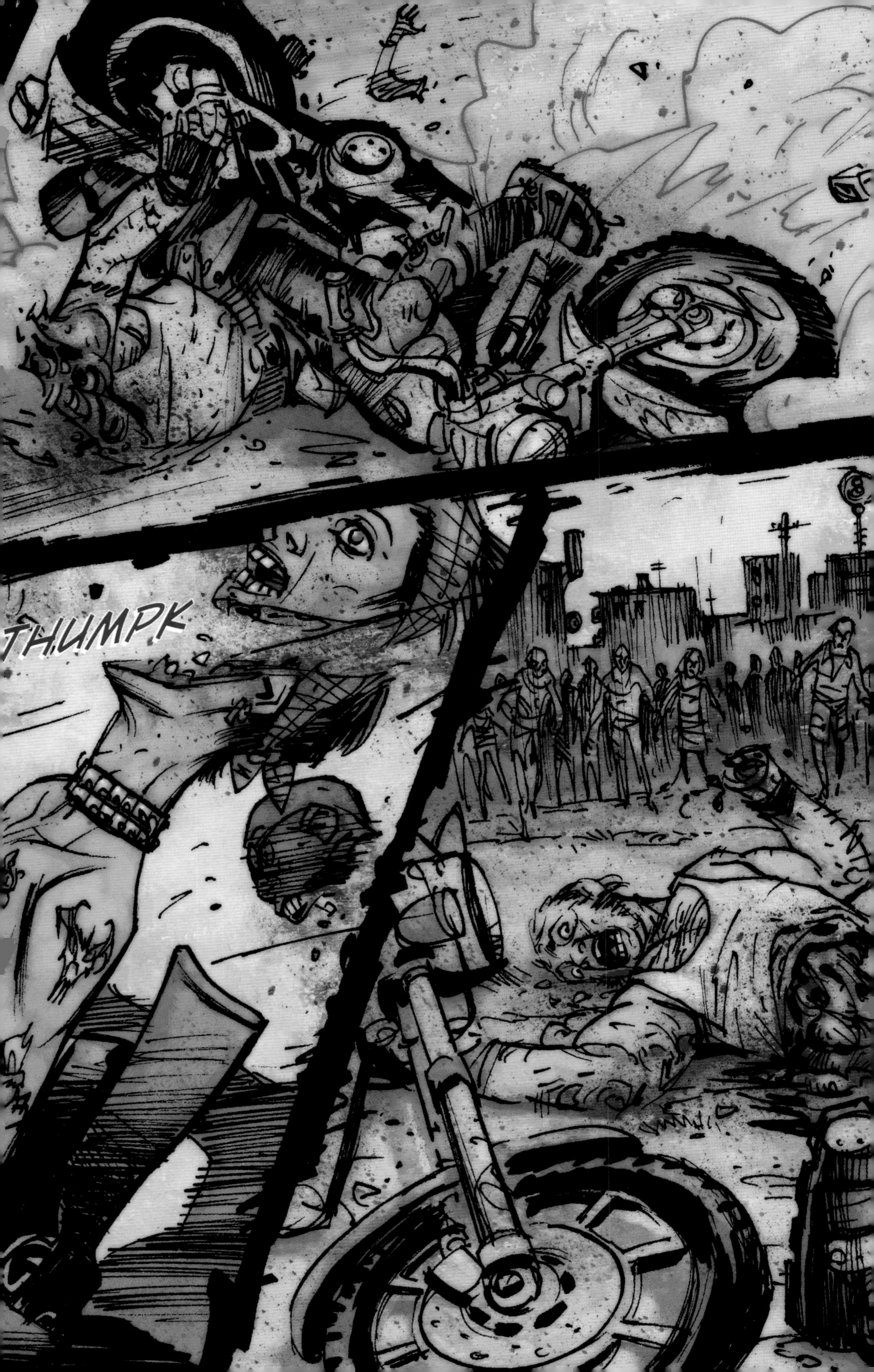
THUMPK

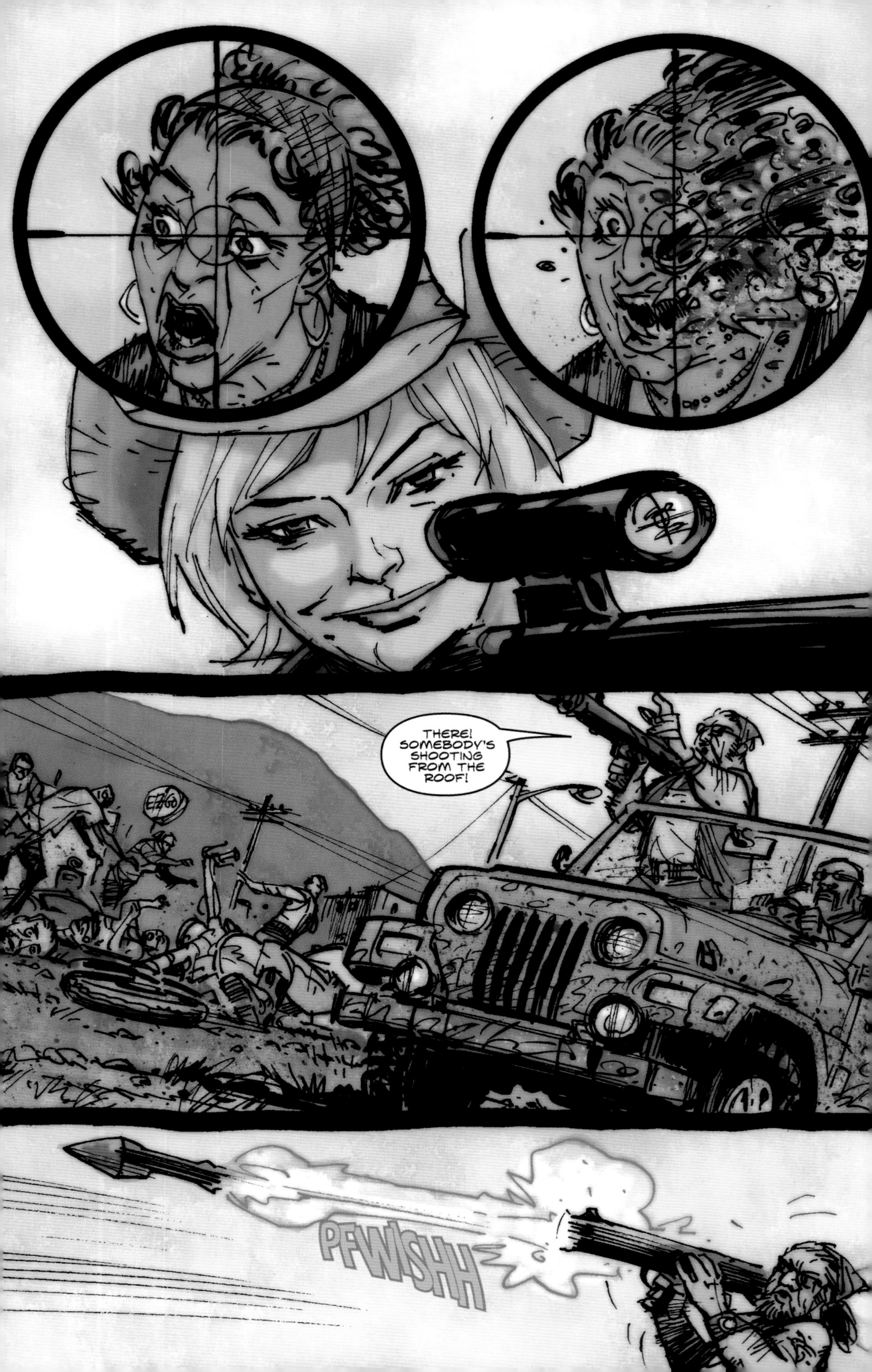
THERE! SOMEBODY'S SHOOTING FROM THE ROOF!
PFWISHH

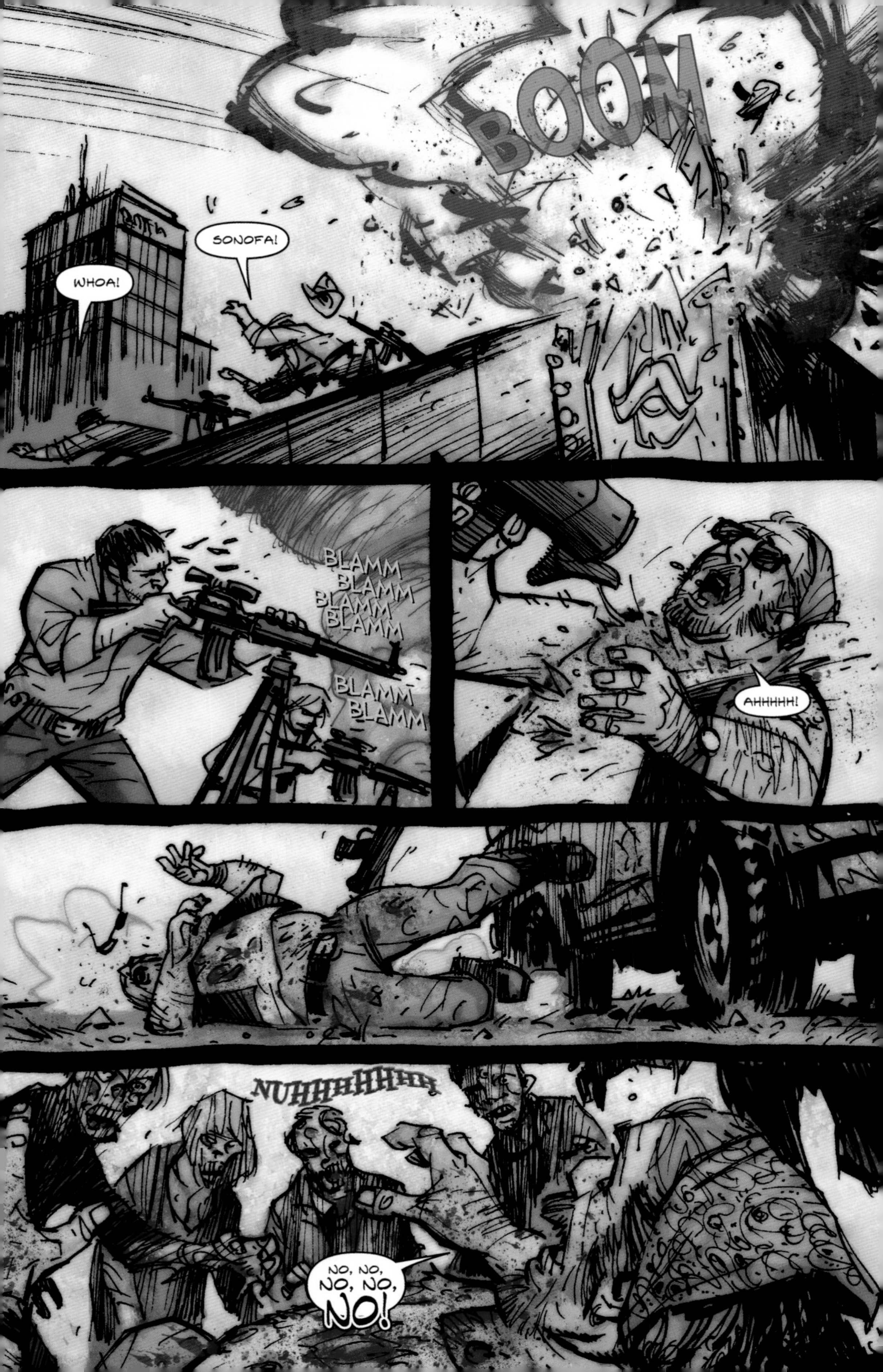
BOOM
SONOFA!
WHOA!
BLAMM BLAMM BLAMM BLAMM
BLAMM BLAMM
AHHHHH!
NUHHHHHHH
NO, NO, NO, NO, NO!

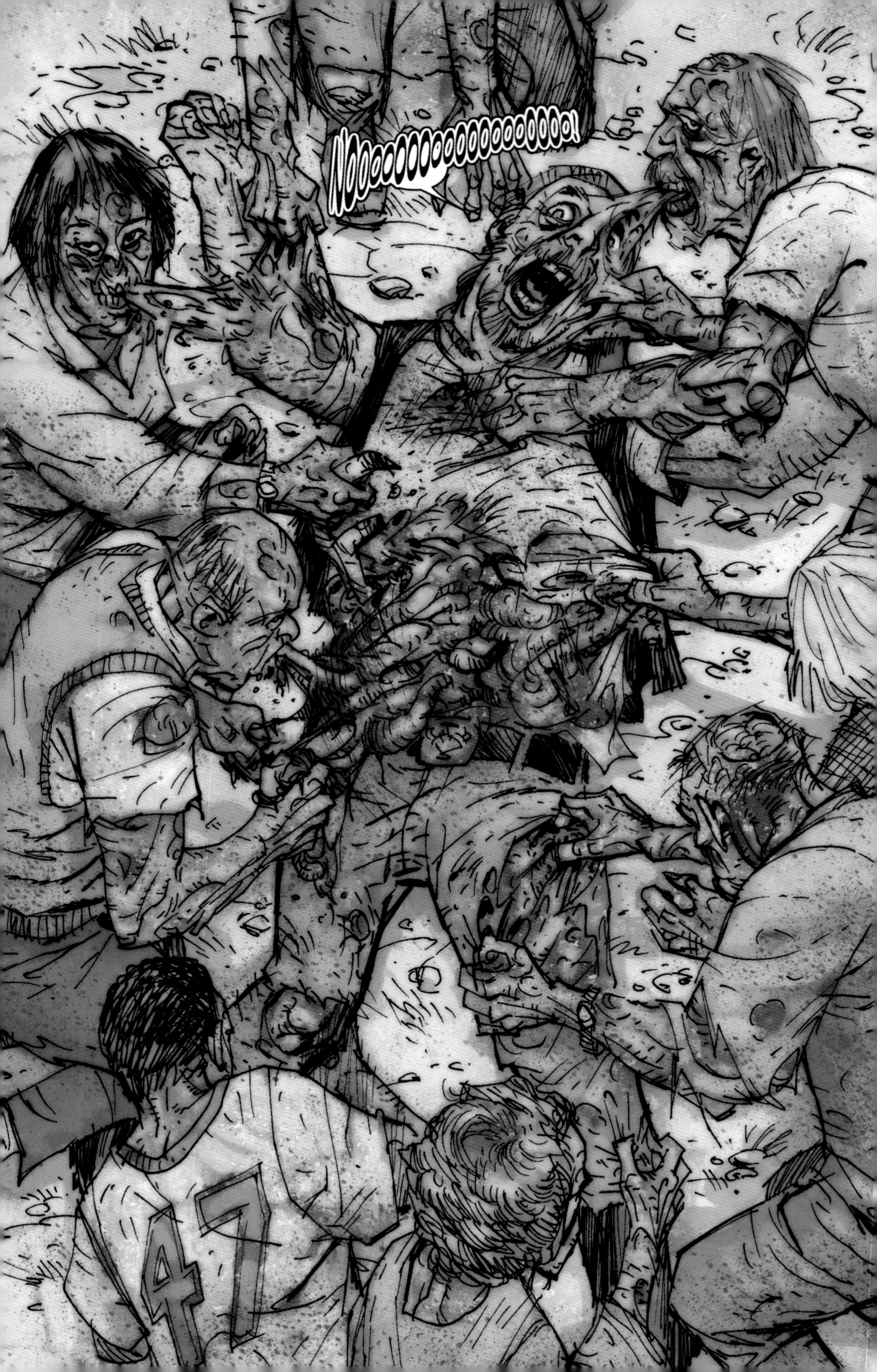
NOOOOOOOOOOOOOOOOOOO!
47

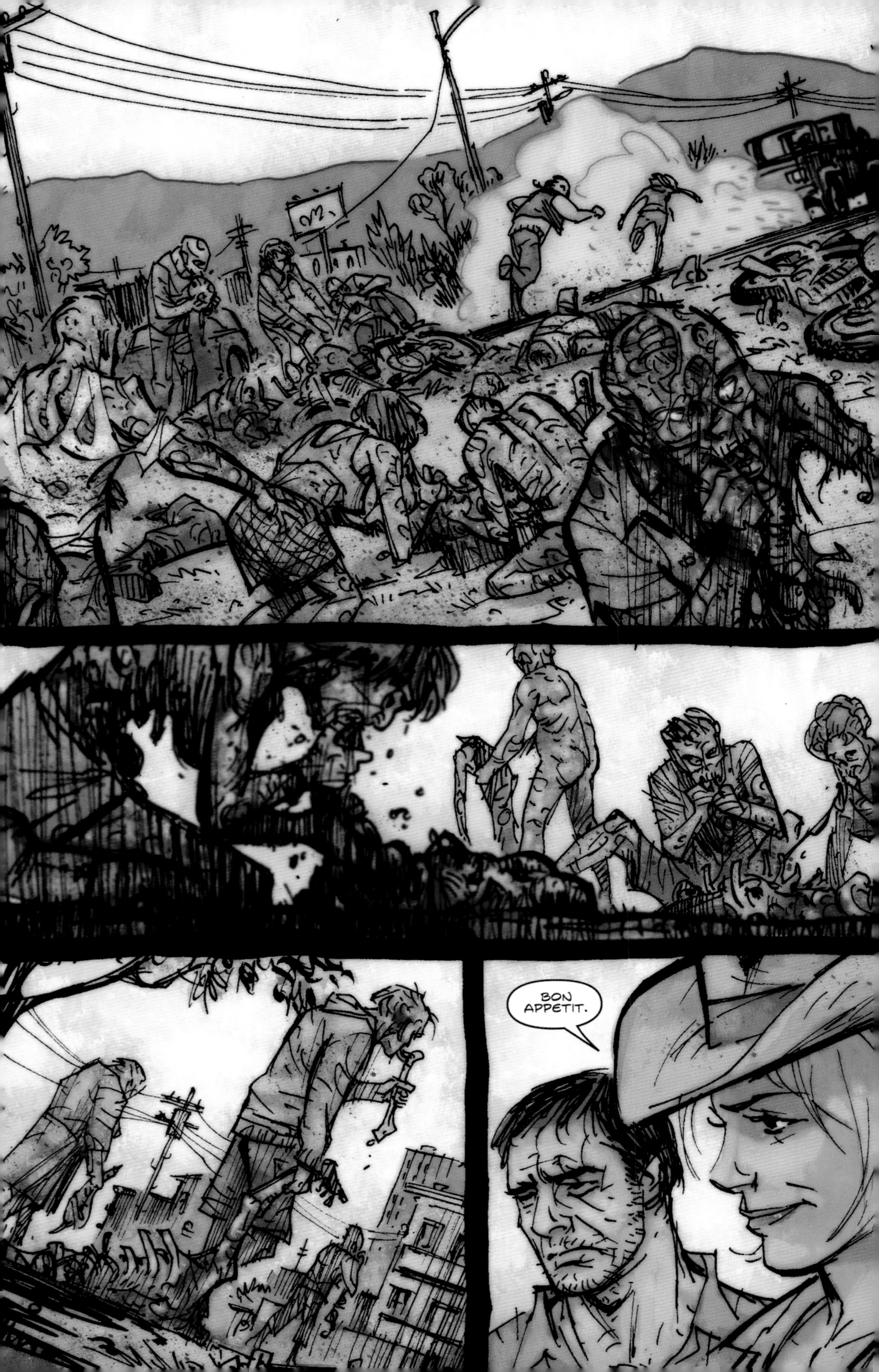
BON APPETIT.

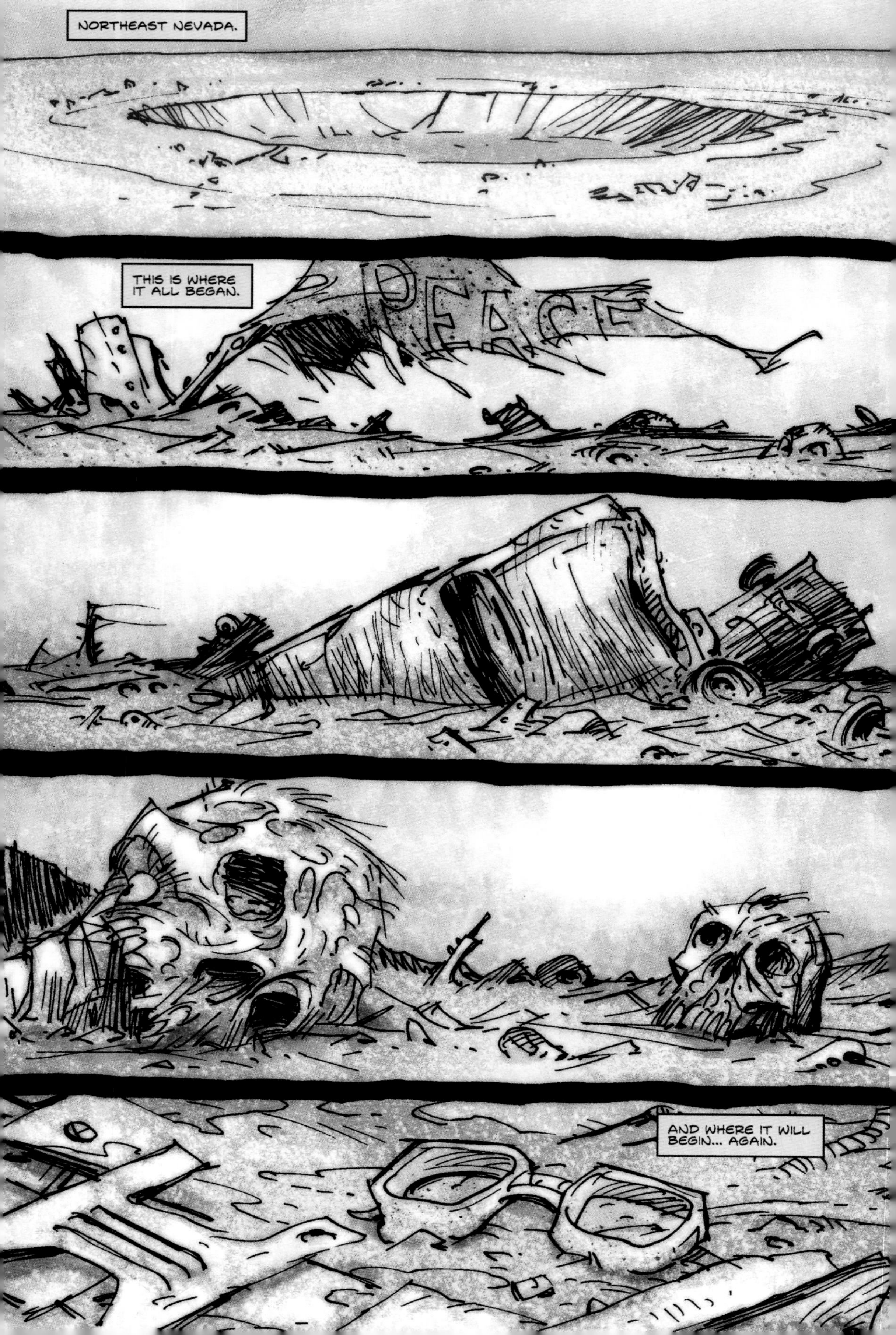
NORTHEAST NEVADA.
THIS IS WHERE IT ALL BEGAN.
PEACE
AND WHERE IT WILL BEGIN... AGAIN.

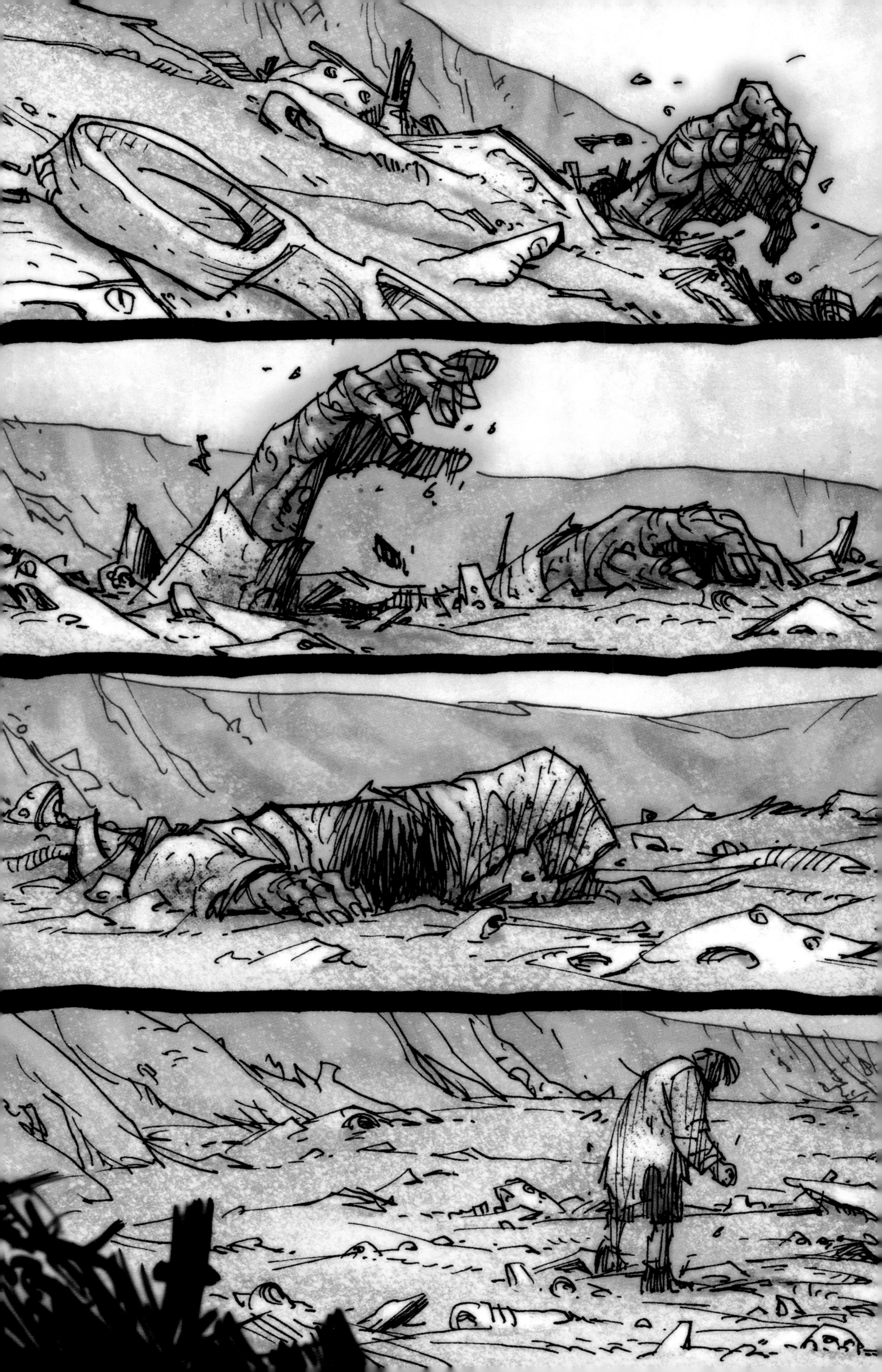

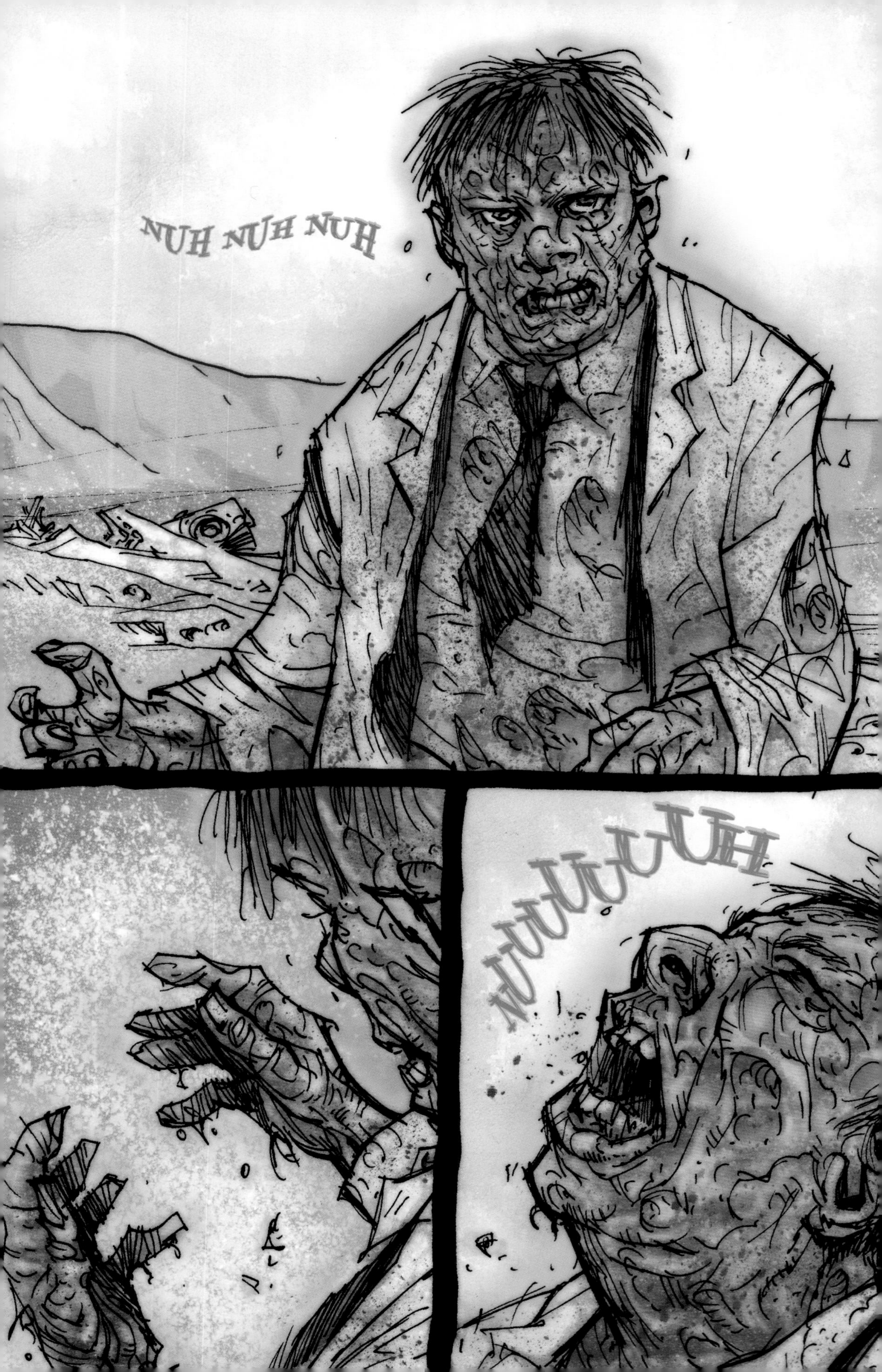
NUH NUH NUH
NUUUUUUUH

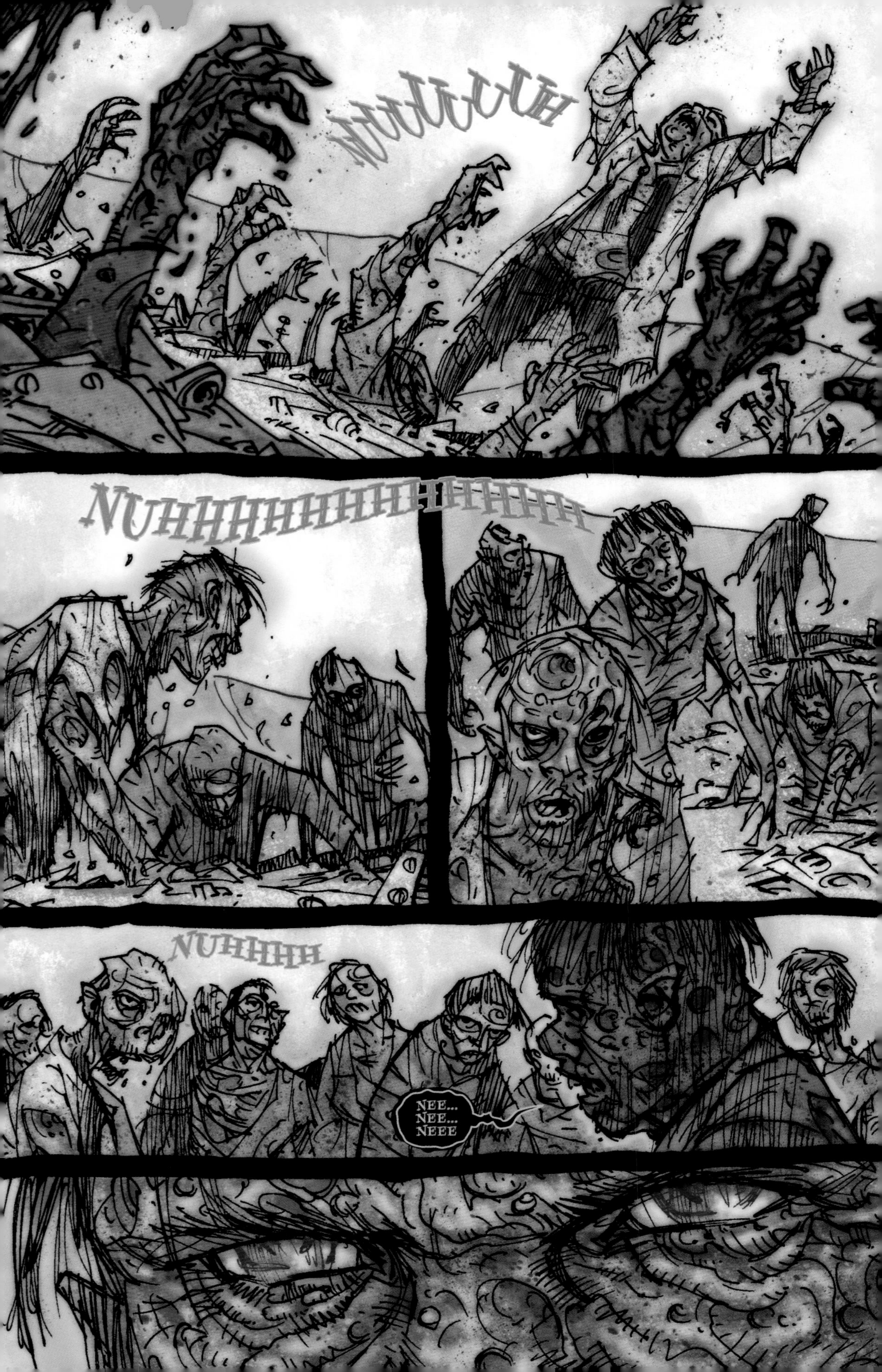
MUUUUUH
NUHHHHHHHHHHHHHH
NUHHHH
NEE... NEE... NEEE

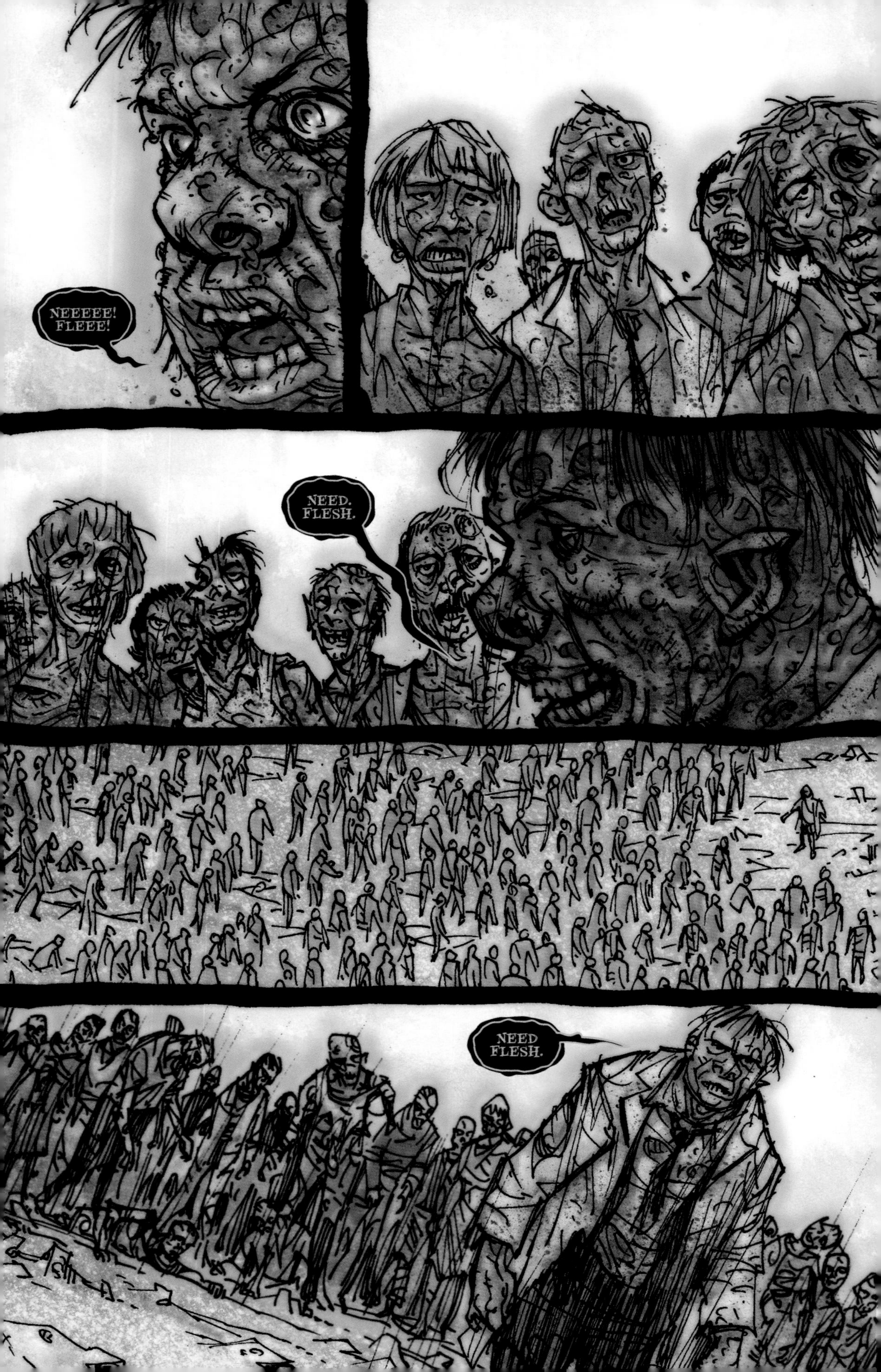
NEEEEE! FLEEE!
NEED. FLESH.
NEED FLESH.

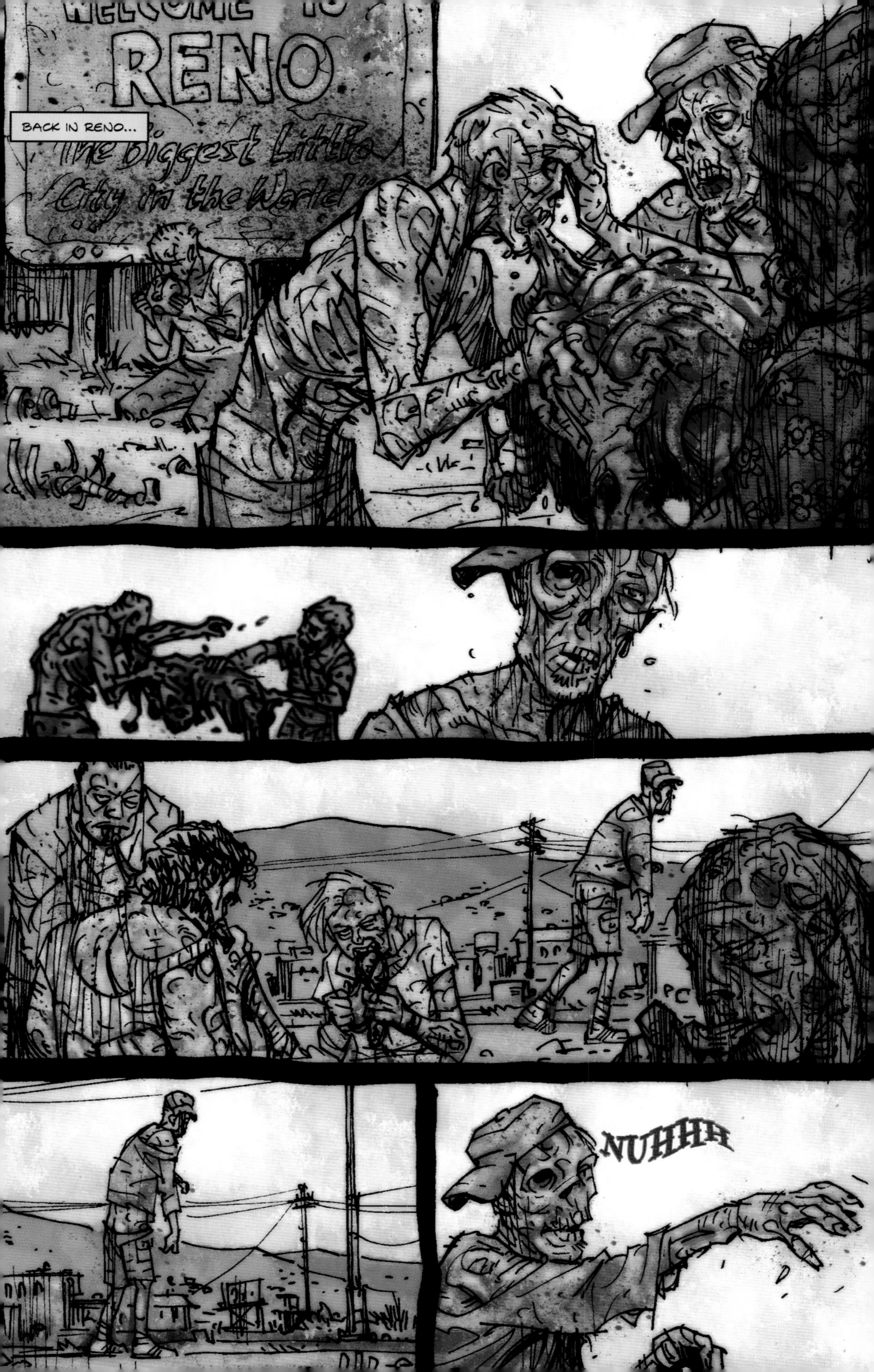
WELCOME TO
RENO
BACK IN RENO...
"The Biggest Little City in the World"
NUHHH

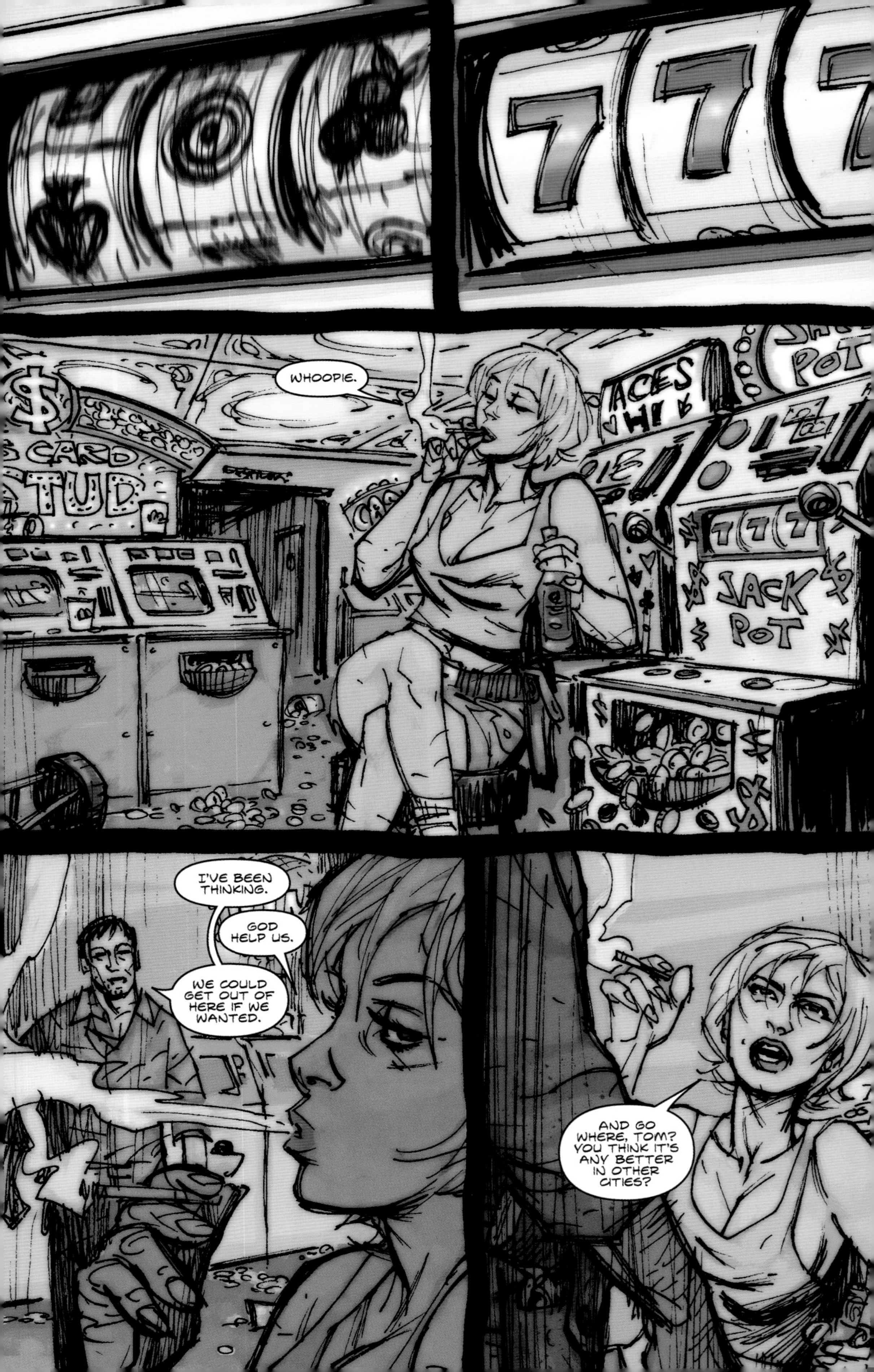
WHOOPIE.
ACES HI!
JACK POT
I'VE BEEN THINKING.
GOD HELP US.
WE COULD GET OUT OF HERE IF WE WANTED.
AND GO WHERE, TOM? YOU THINK IT'S ANY BETTER IN OTHER CITIES?

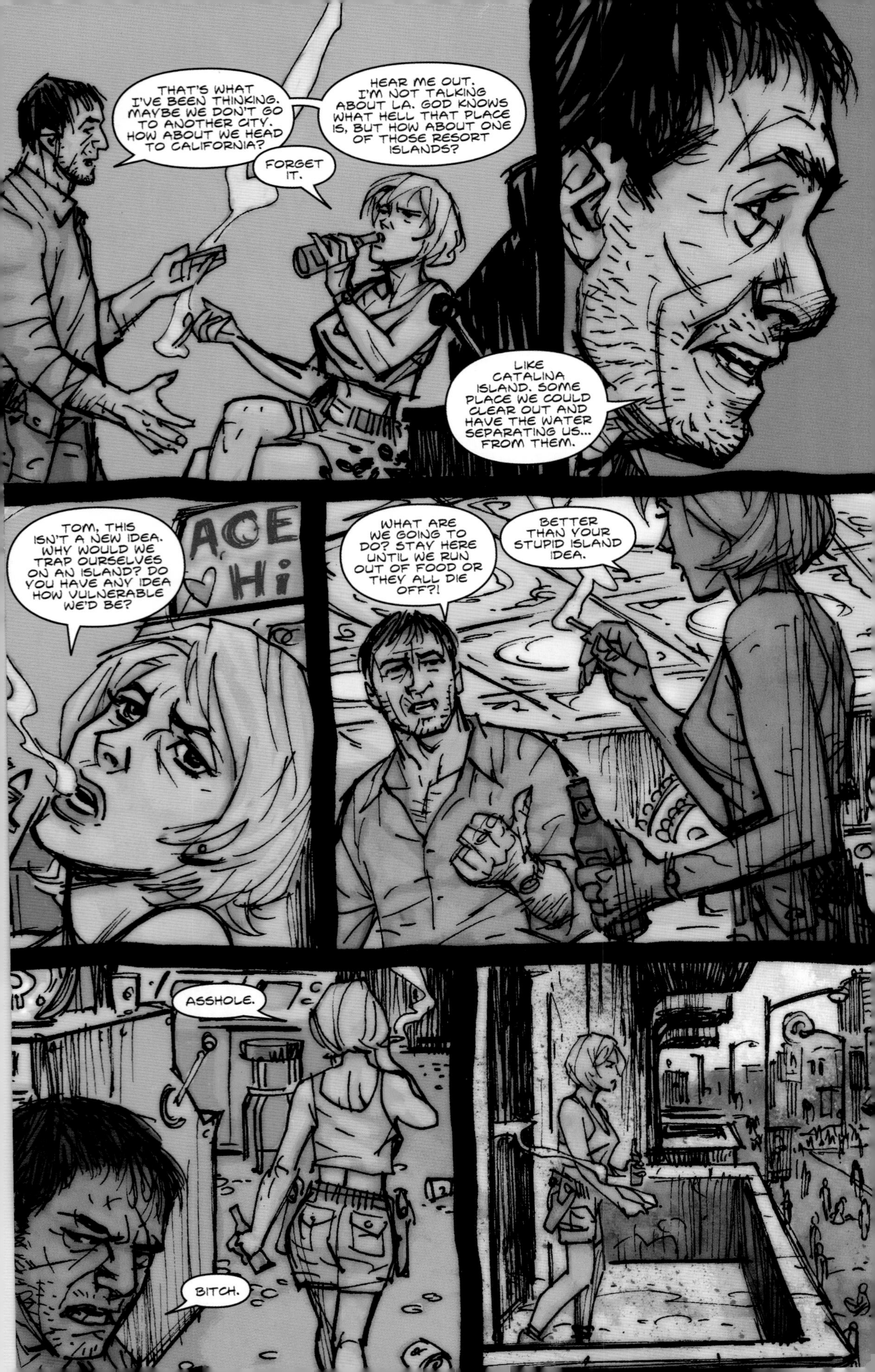
THAT'S WHAT I'VE BEEN THINKING. MAYBE WE DON'T GO TO ANOTHER CITY. HOW ABOUT WE HEAD TO CALIFORNIA?
FORGET IT.
HEAR ME OUT. I'M NOT TALKING ABOUT LA. GOD KNOWS WHAT HELL THAT PLACE IS, BUT HOW ABOUT ONE OF THOSE RESORT ISLANDS?
LIKE CATALINA ISLAND. SOME PLACE WE COULD CLEAR OUT AND HAVE THE WATER SEPARATING US... FROM THEM.
ACE
Hi
TOM, THIS ISN'T A NEW IDEA. WHY WOULD WE TRAP OURSELVES ON AN ISLAND? DO YOU HAVE ANY IDEA HOW VULNERABLE WE'D BE?
WHAT ARE WE GOING TO DO? STAY HERE UNTIL WE RUN OUT OF FOOD OR THEY ALL DIE OFF?!
BETTER THAN YOUR STUPID ISLAND IDEA.
ASSHOLE.
BITCH.

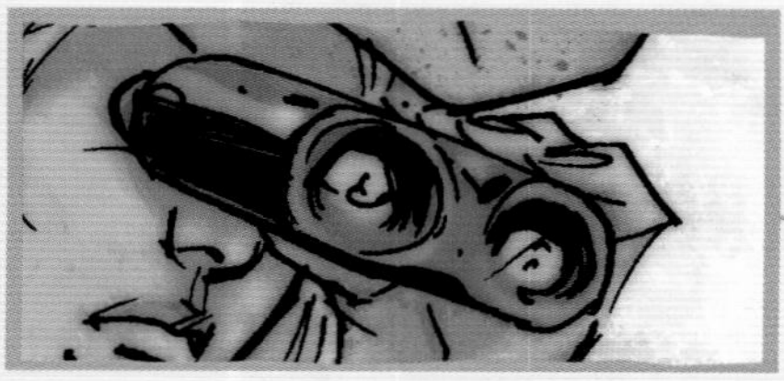

3 chapter

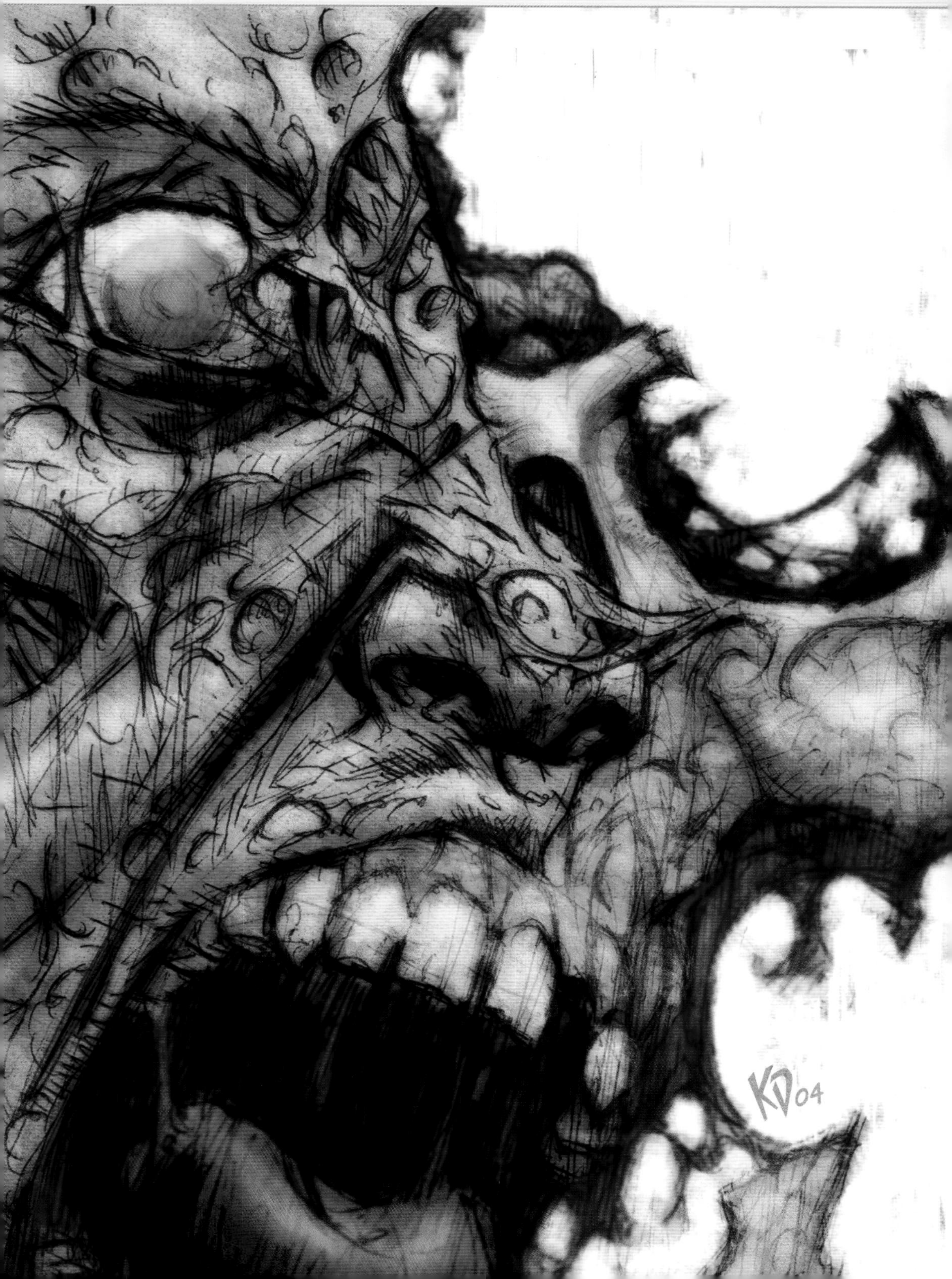
KD04

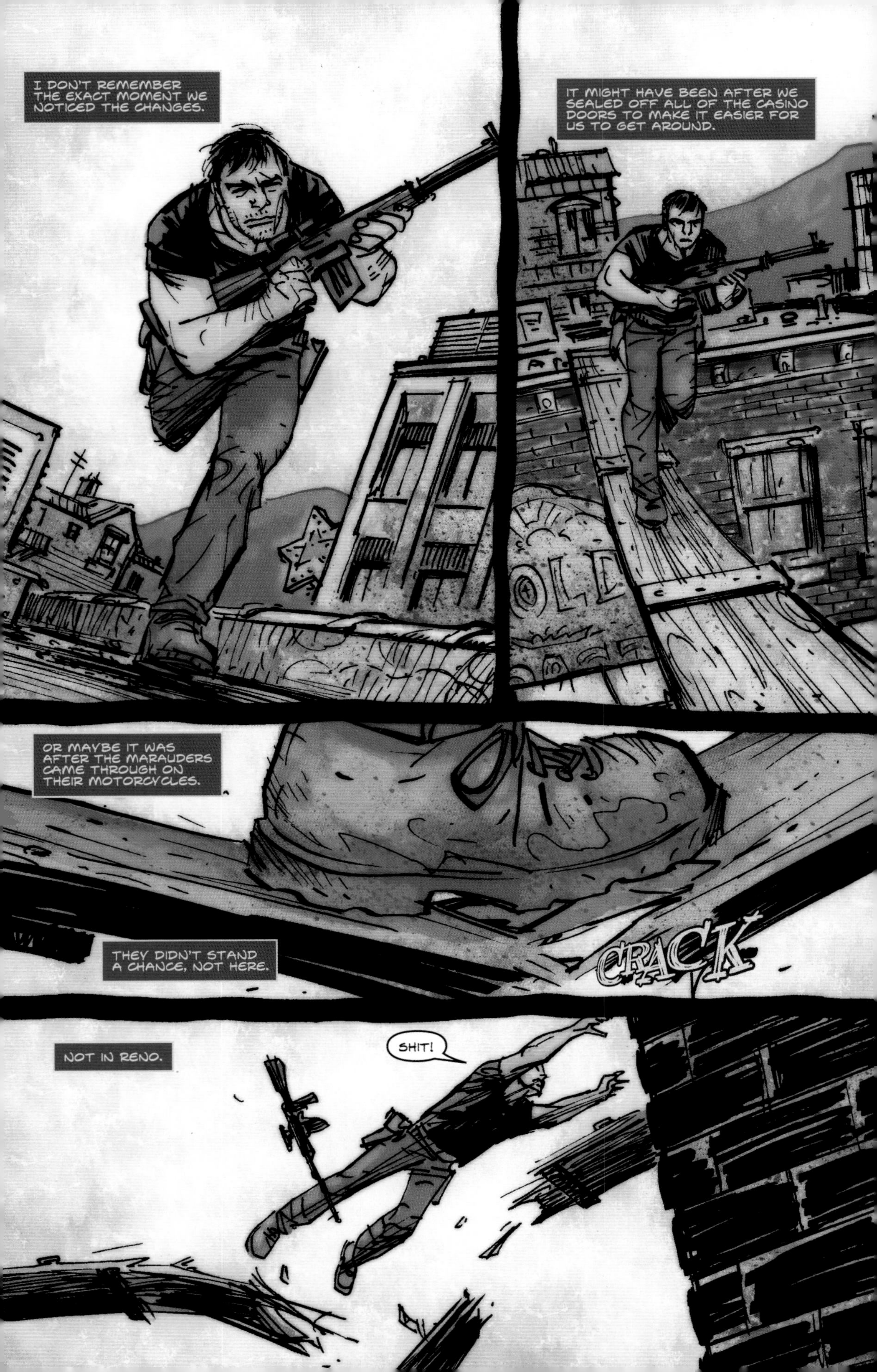
I DON'T REMEMBER THE EXACT MOMENT WE NOTICED THE CHANGES.
IT MIGHT HAVE BEEN AFTER WE SEALED OFF ALL OF THE CASINO DOORS TO MAKE IT EASIER FOR US TO GET AROUND.
OLD
OR MAYBE IT WAS AFTER THE MARAUDERS CAME THROUGH ON THEIR MOTORCYCLES.
THEY DIDN'T STAND A CHANCE, NOT HERE.
CRACK
NOT IN RENO.
SHIT!

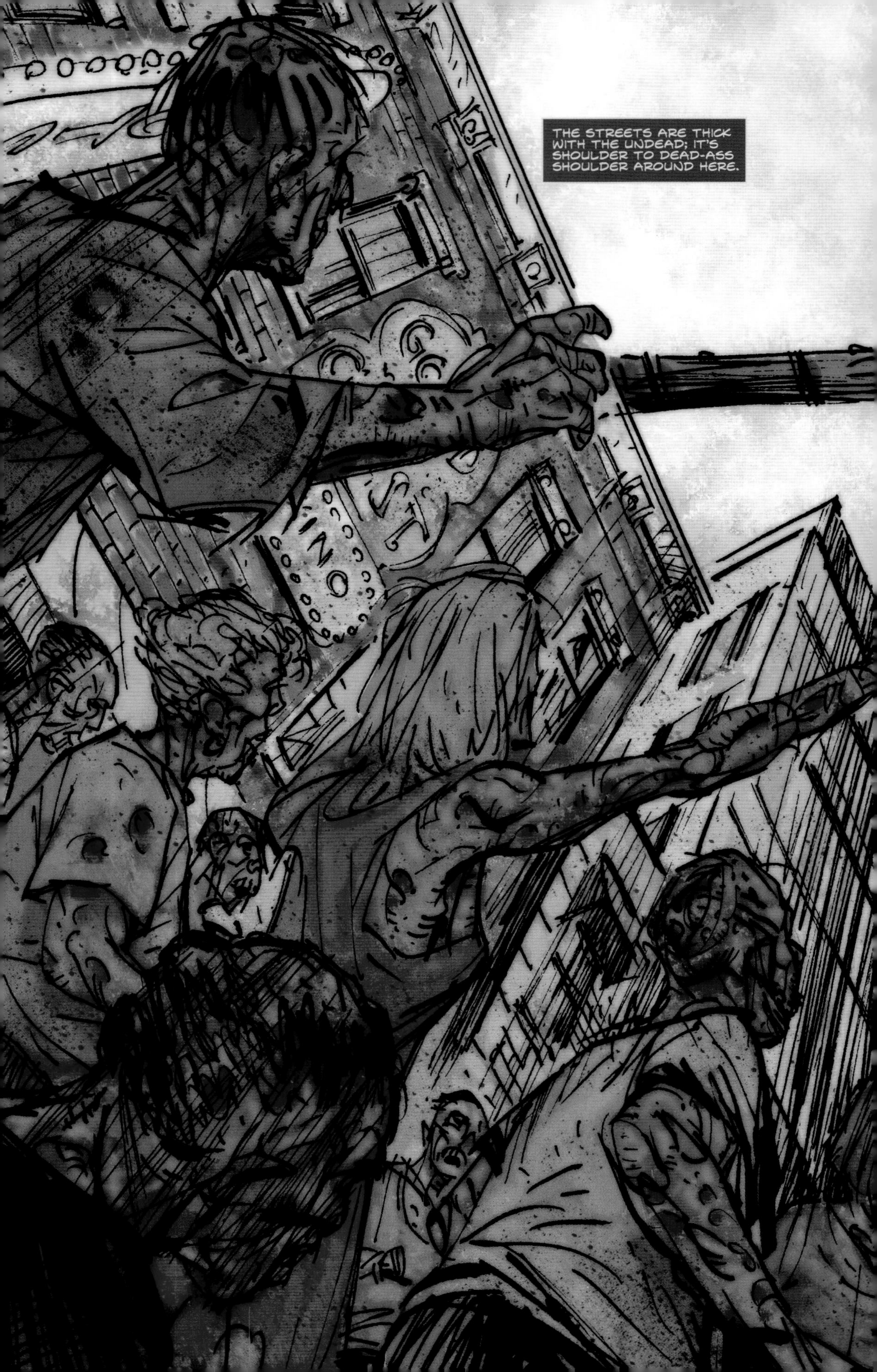
THE STREETS ARE THICK WITH THE UNDEAD; IT'S SHOULDER TO DEAD-ASS SHOULDER AROUND HERE.

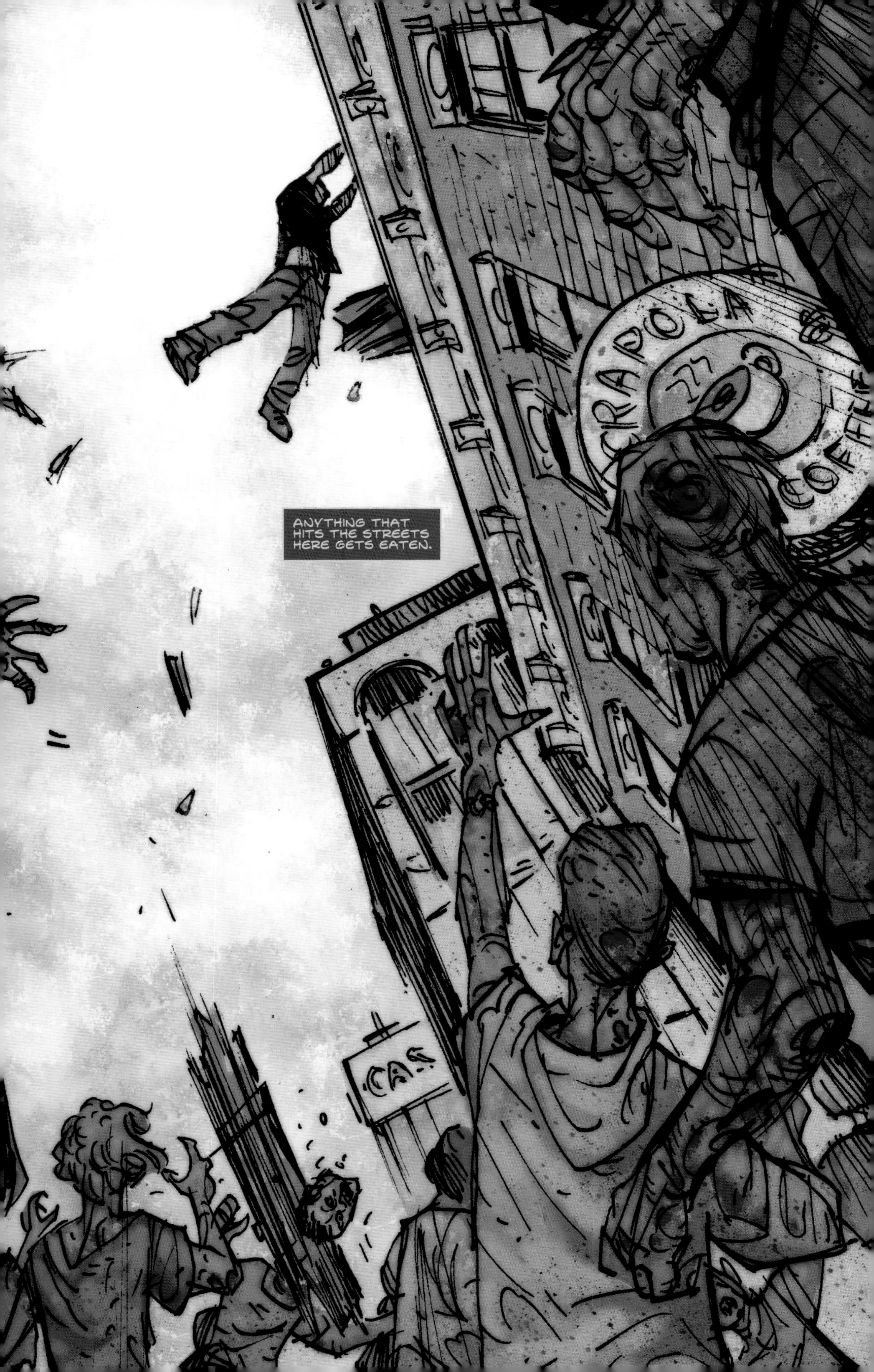
ANYTHING THAT HITS THE STREETS HERE GETS EATEN.
CRAPOLA
COFFEE
CAS

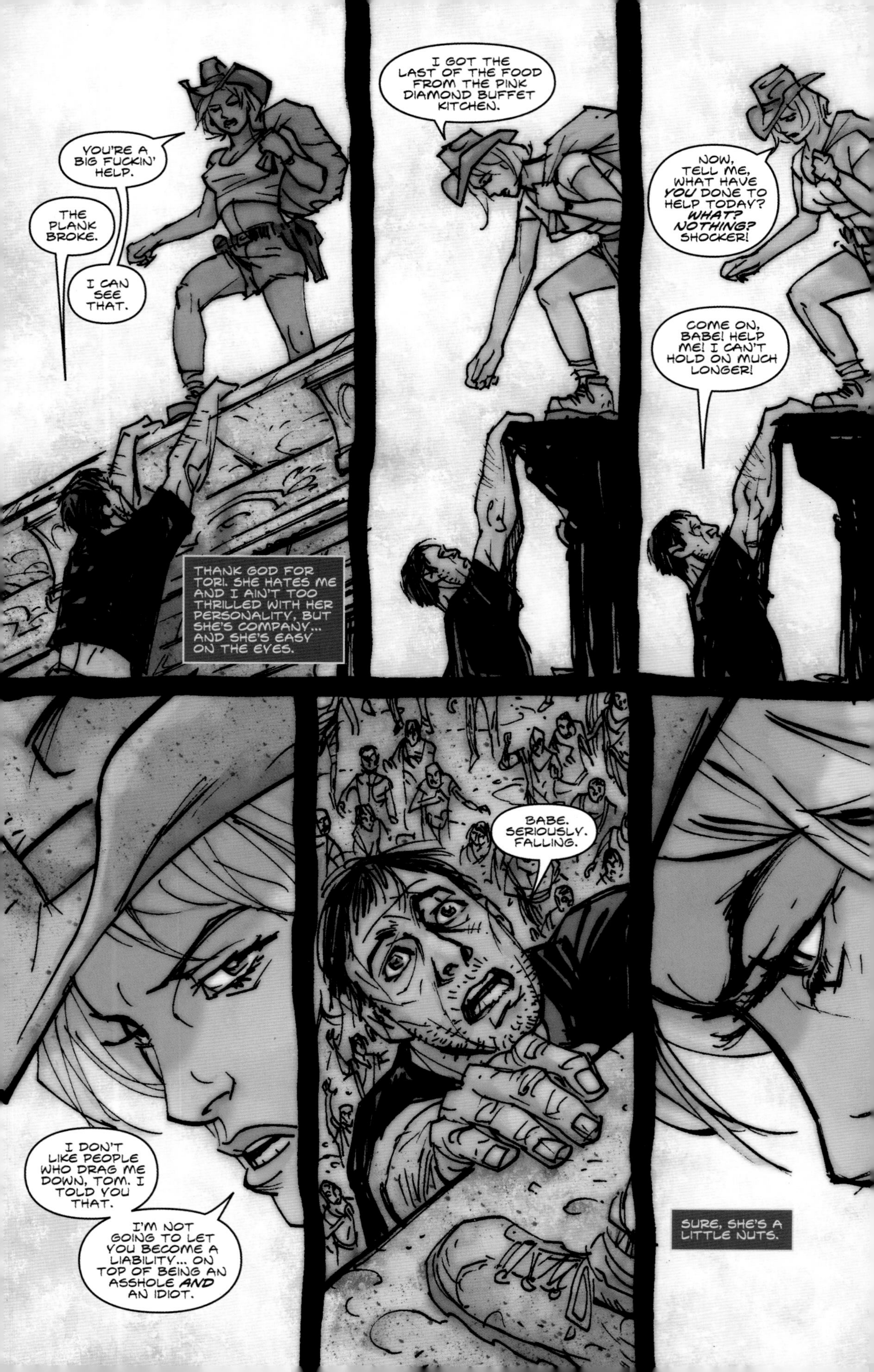
YOU'RE A BIG FUCKIN' HELP.
THE PLANK BROKE.
I CAN SEE THAT.
THANK GOD FOR TORI. SHE HATES ME AND I AIN'T TOO THRILLED WITH HER PERSONALITY, BUT SHE'S COMPANY... AND SHE'S EASY ON THE EYES.
I GOT THE LAST OF THE FOOD FROM THE PINK DIAMOND BUFFET KITCHEN.
NOW, TELL ME, WHAT HAVE YOU DONE TO HELP TODAY? WHAT? NOTHING? SHOCKER!
COME ON, BABE! HELP ME! I CAN'T HOLD ON MUCH LONGER!
I DON'T LIKE PEOPLE WHO DRAG ME DOWN, TOM. I TOLD YOU THAT.
I'M NOT GOING TO LET YOU BECOME A LIABILITY... ON TOP OF BEING AN ASSHOLE AND AN IDIOT.
BABE. SERIOUSLY. FALLING.
SURE, SHE'S A LITTLE NUTS.

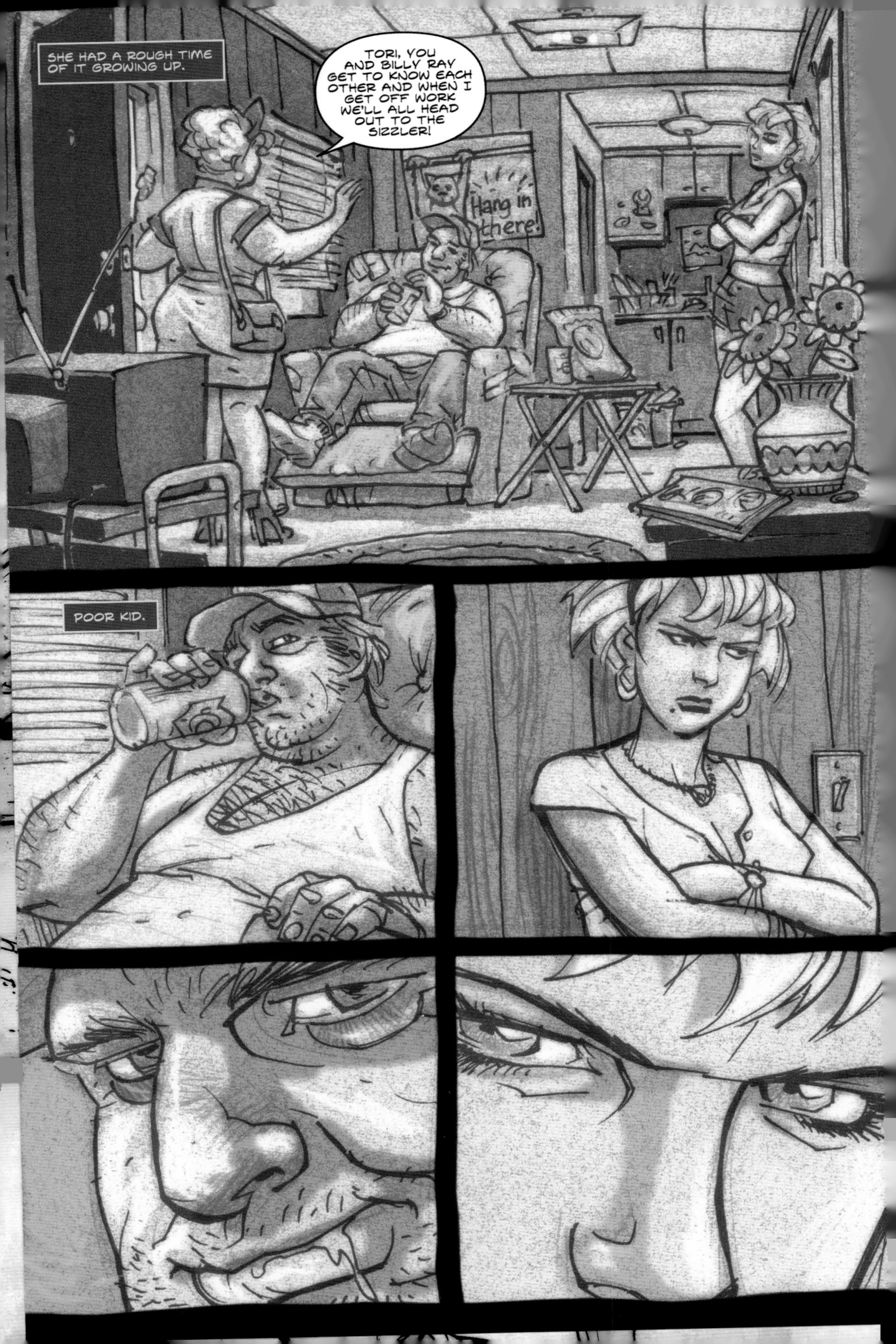
SHE HAD A ROUGH TIME OF IT GROWING UP.
TORI, YOU AND BILLY RAY GET TO KNOW EACH OTHER AND WHEN I GET OFF WORK WE'LL ALL HEAD OUT TO THE SIZZLER!
Hang in there!
POOR KID.

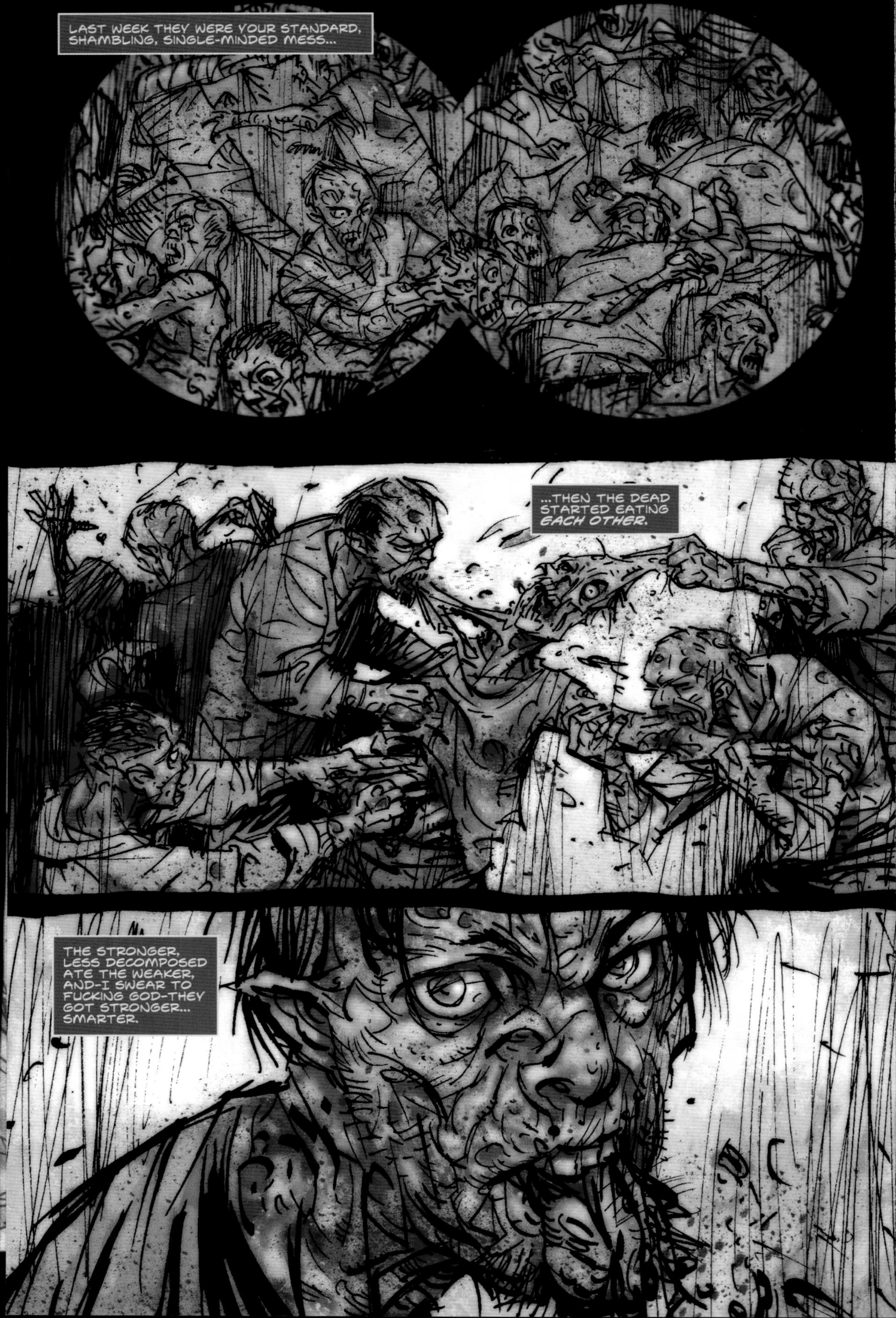
LAST WEEK THEY WERE YOUR STANDARD, SHAMBLING, SINGLE-MINDED MESS...
...THEN THE DEAD STARTED EATING *EACH OTHER*.
THE STRONGER, LESS DECOMPOSED ATE THE WEAKER, AND-I SWEAR TO FUCKING GOD-THEY GOT STRONGER... SMARTER.

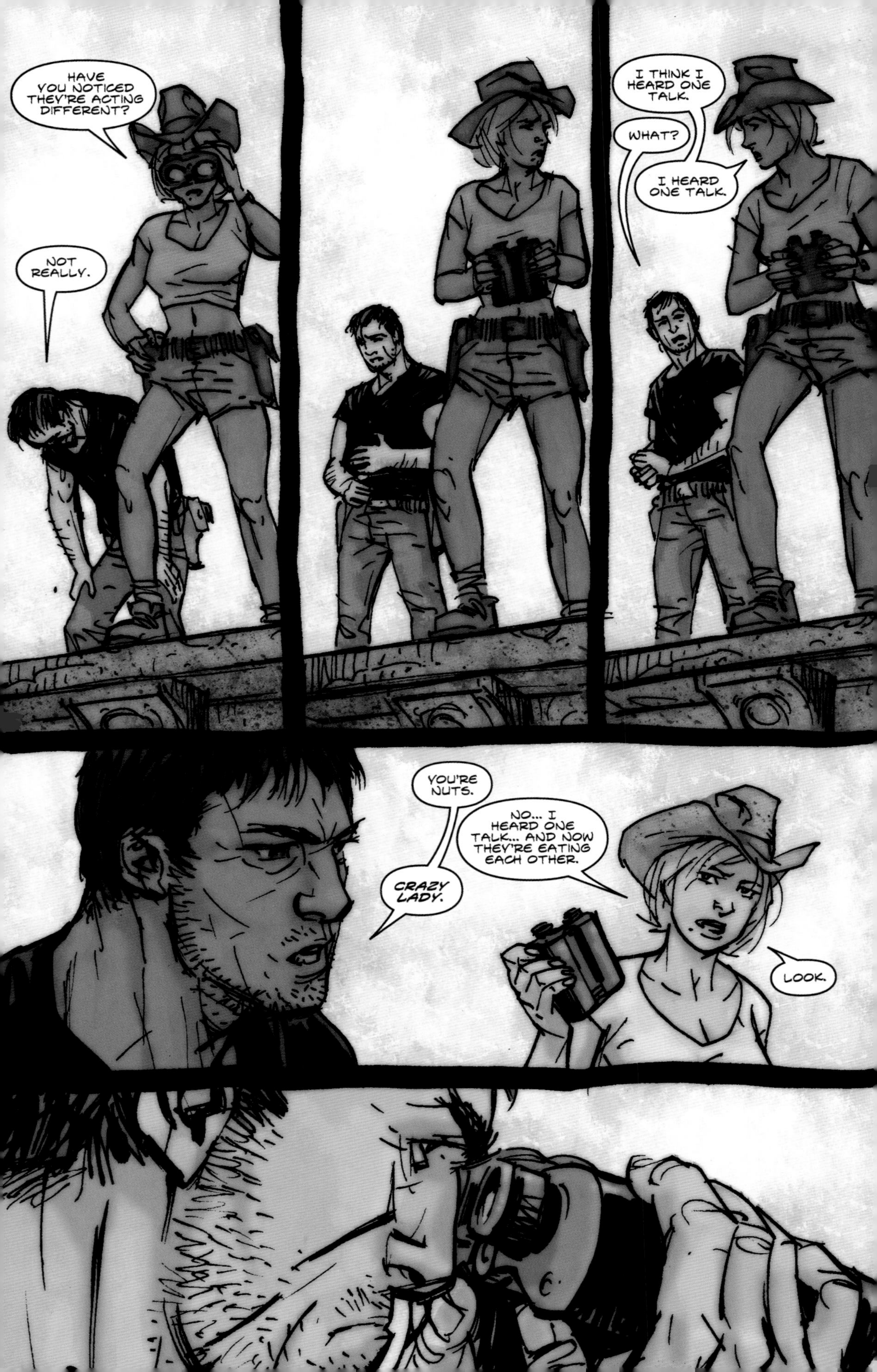
HAVE YOU NOTICED THEY'RE ACTING DIFFERENT?
NOT REALLY.
I THINK I HEARD ONE TALK.
WHAT?
I HEARD ONE TALK.
YOU'RE NUTS.
NO... I HEARD ONE TALK... AND NOW THEY'RE EATING EACH OTHER.
CRAZY LADY.
LOOK.

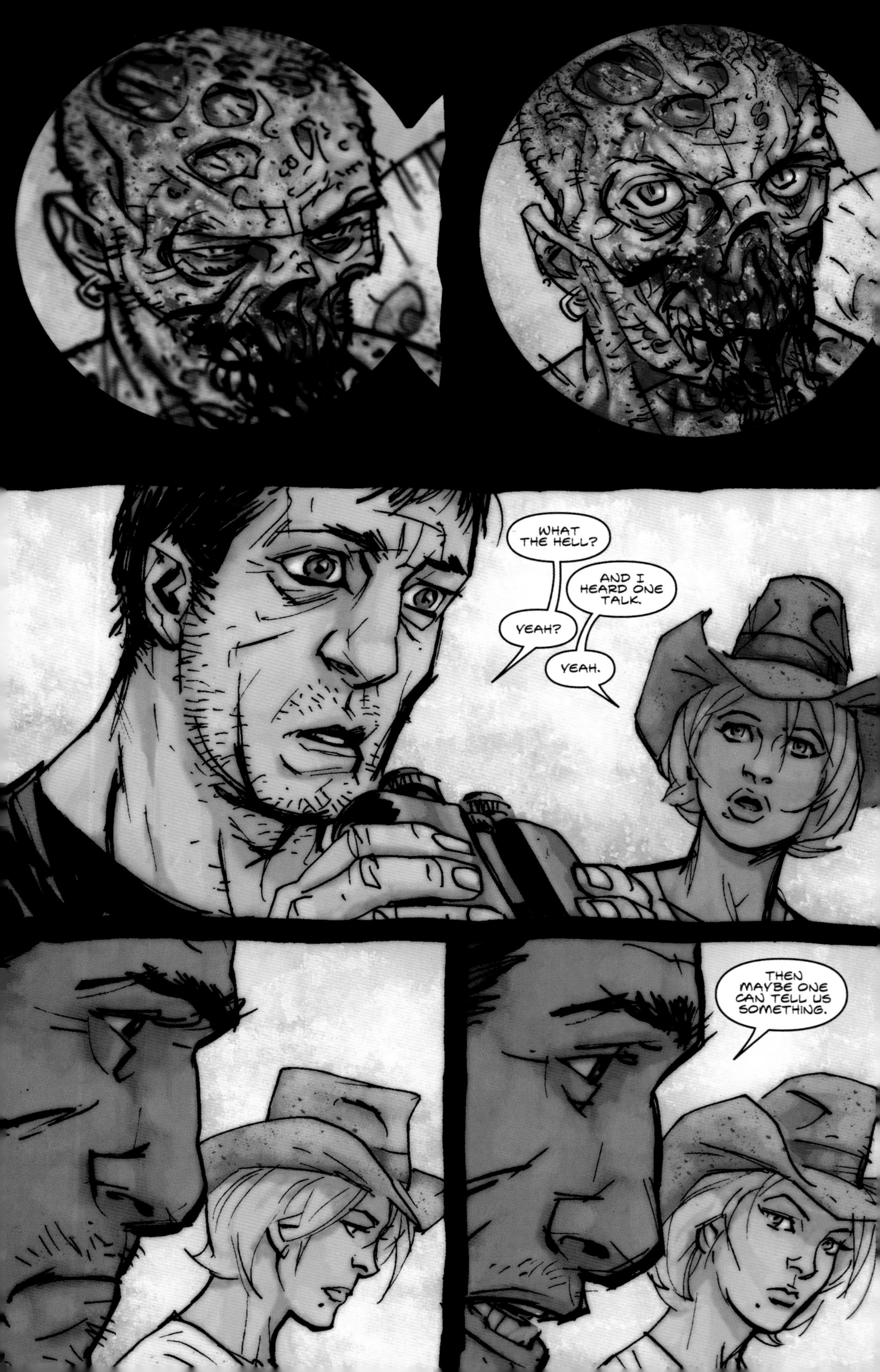

WHAT THE HELL?
AND I HEARD ONE TALK.
YEAH?
YEAH.
THEN MAYBE ONE CAN TELL US SOMETHING.

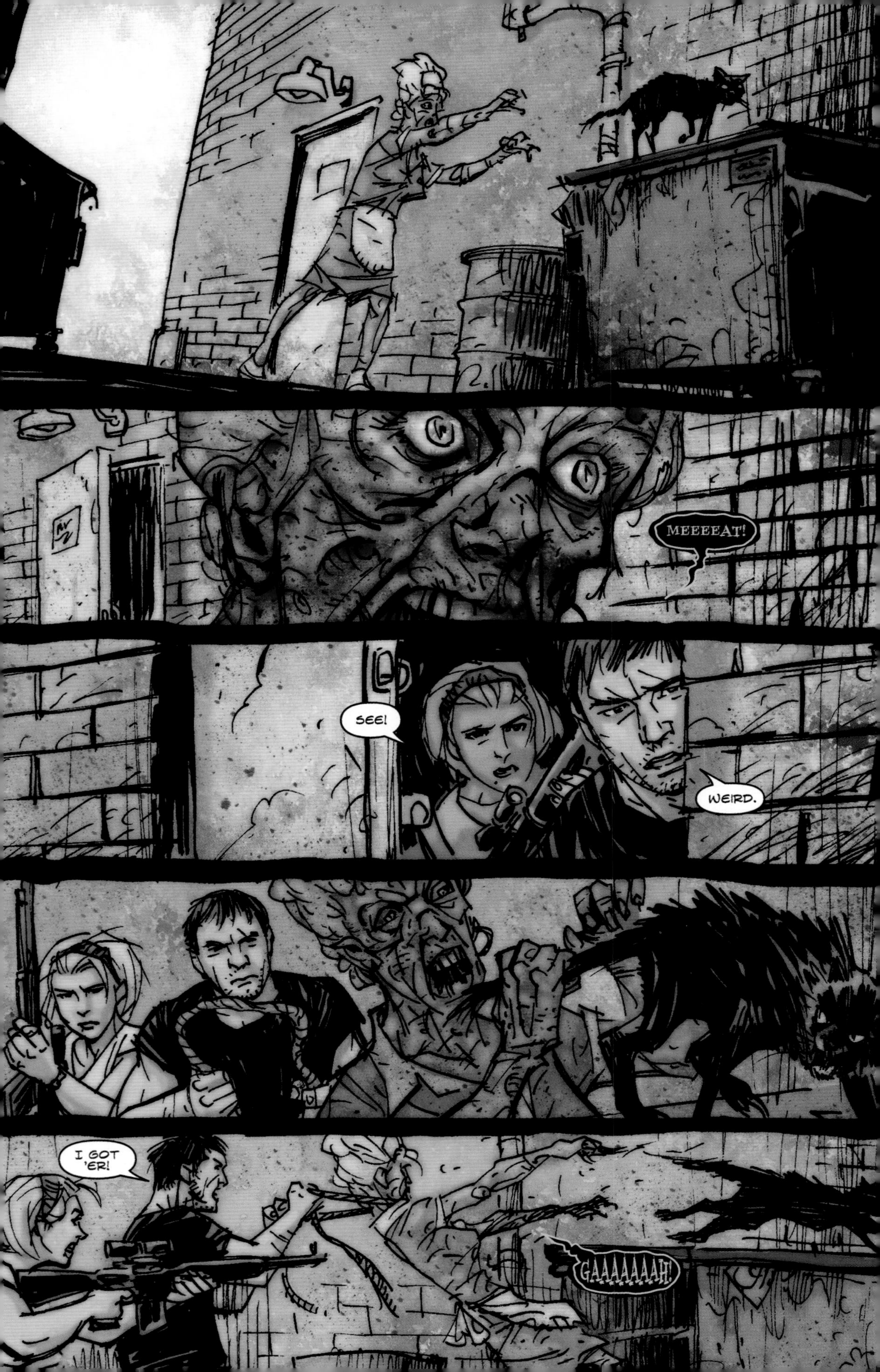
MEEEEAT!
SEE!
WEIRD.
I GOT 'ER!
GAAAAAAAH!

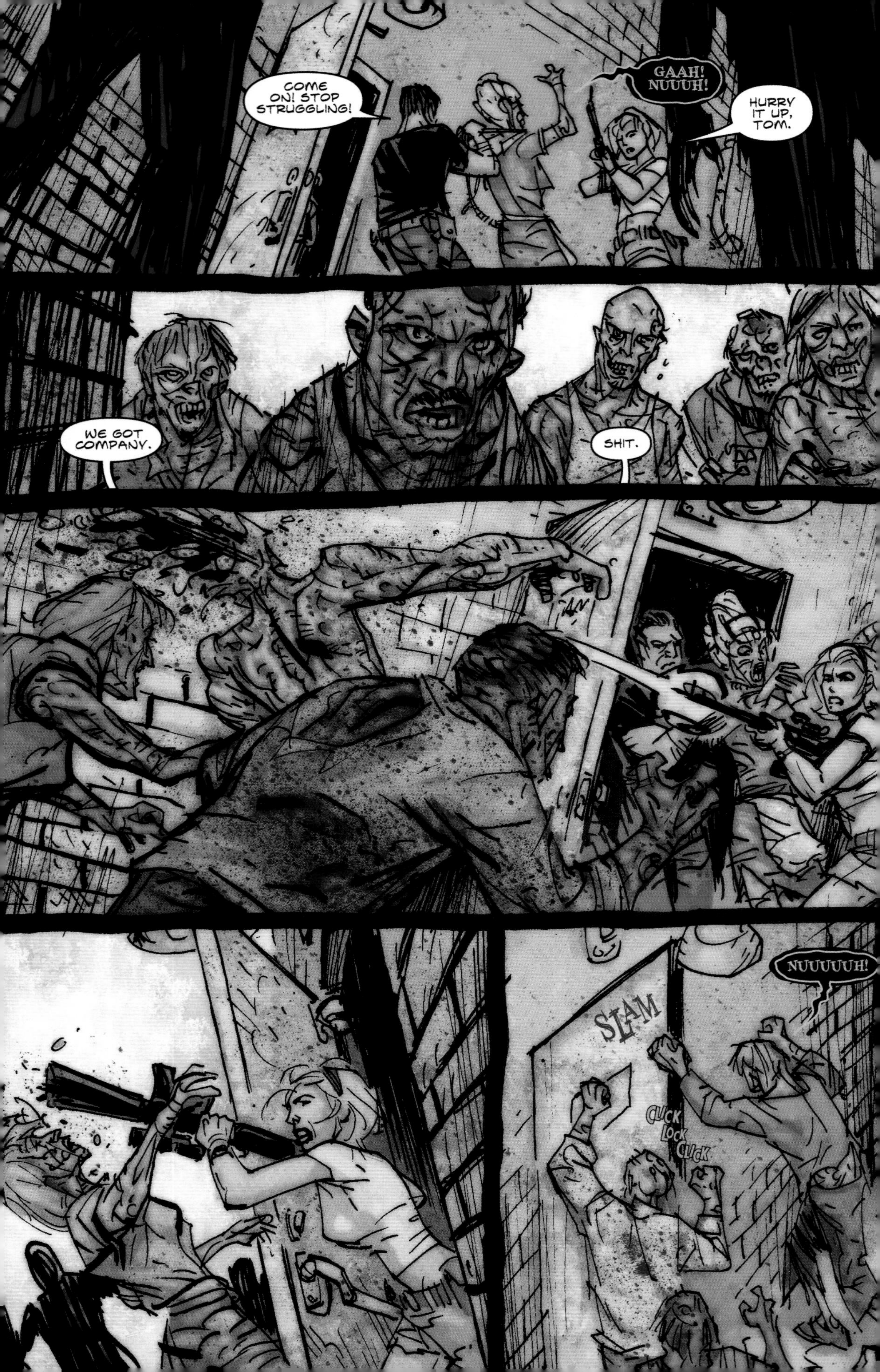
COME ON! STOP STRUGGLING!
GAAH! NUUUH!
HURRY IT UP, TOM.
WE GOT COMPANY.
SHIT.
NUUUUUH!
SLAM
CLICK
LOCK
CLICK

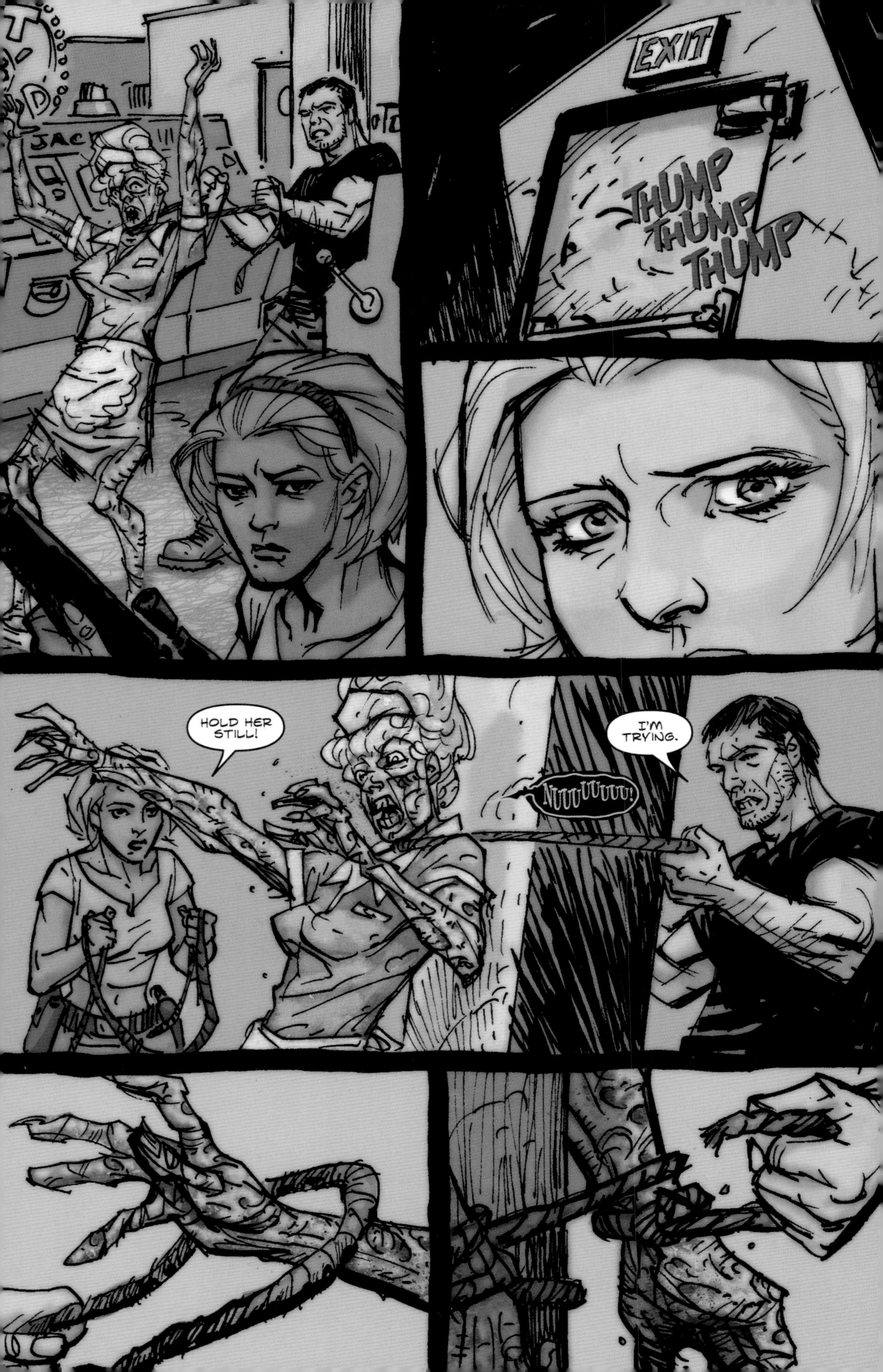
THUMP
THUMP
THUMP
HOLD HER STILL!
I'M TRYING.
NUUUUUUU!

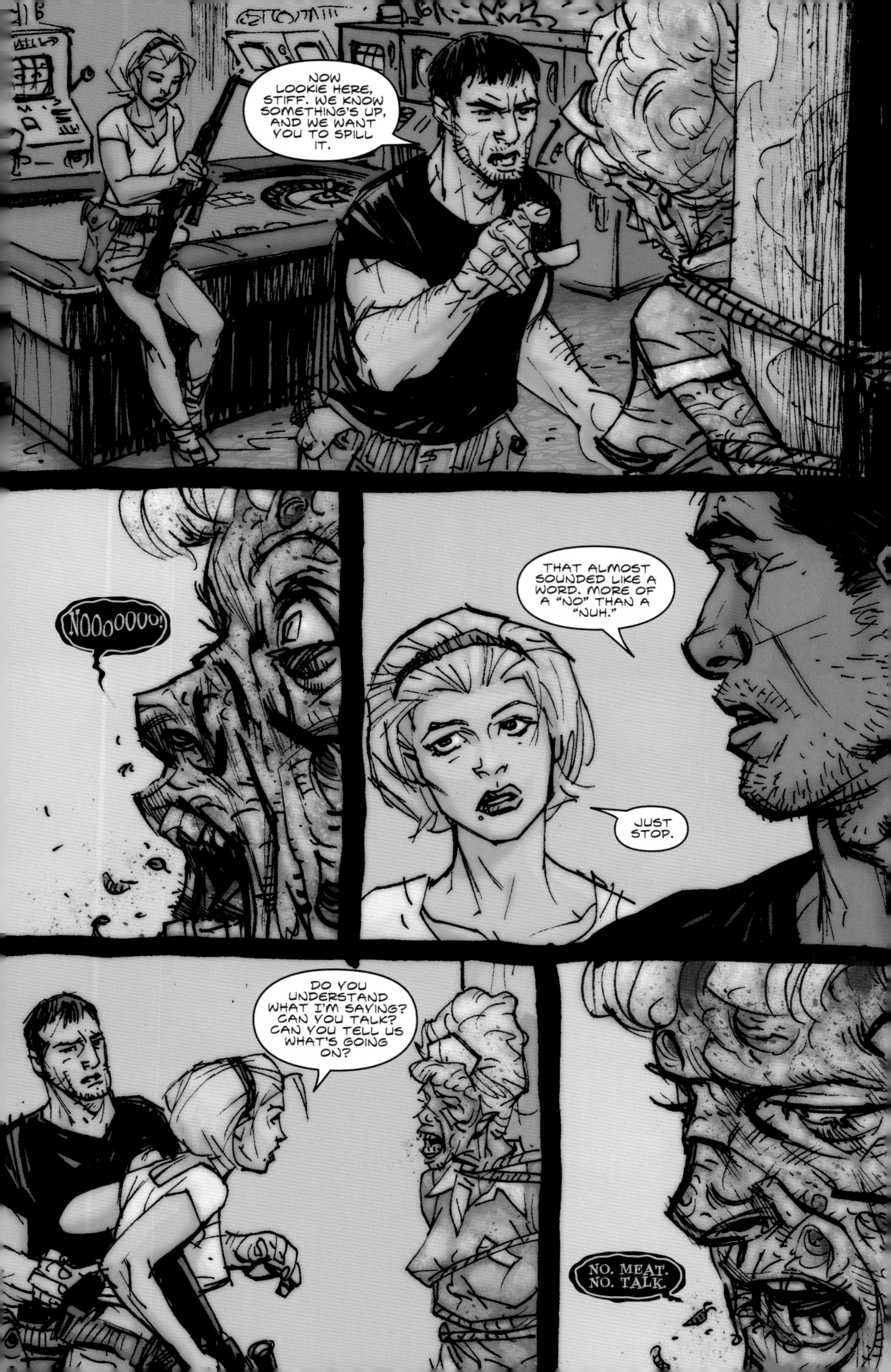
NOW LOOKIE HERE, STIFF. WE KNOW SOMETHING'S UP, AND WE WANT YOU TO SPILL IT.
NOOoOOVVO!
THAT ALMOST SOUNDED LIKE A WORD. MORE OF A "NO" THAN A "NUH."
JUST STOP.
DO YOU UNDERSTAND WHAT I'M SAYING? CAN YOU TALK? CAN YOU TELL US WHAT'S GOING ON?
NO. MEAT. NO. TALK.

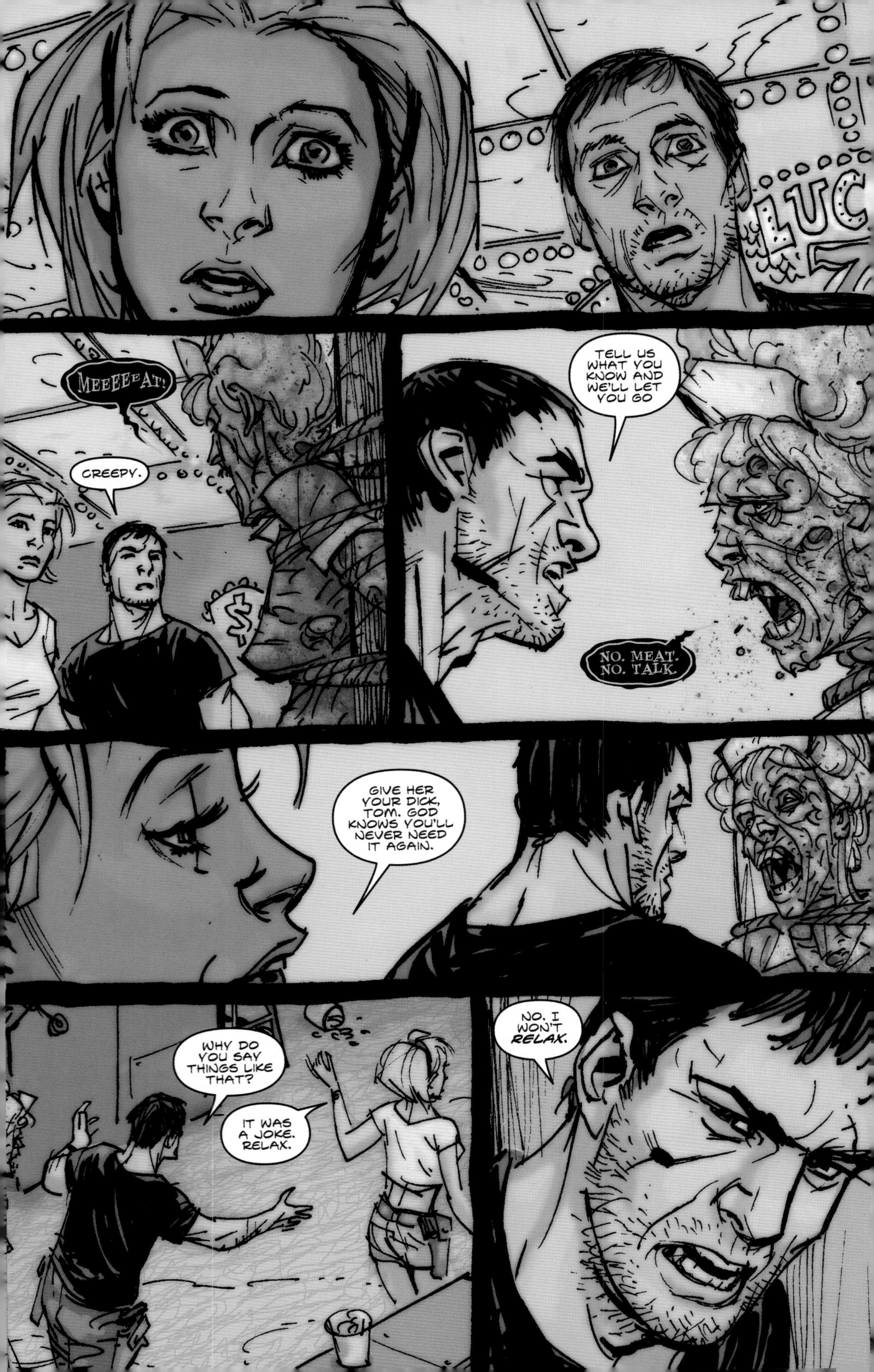
MEEEEEAT!
CREEPY.
TELL US WHAT YOU KNOW AND WE'LL LET YOU GO
NO. MEAT. NO. TALK.
GIVE HER YOUR DICK, TOM. GOD KNOWS YOU'LL NEVER NEED IT AGAIN.
WHY DO YOU SAY THINGS LIKE THAT?
IT WAS A JOKE. RELAX.
NO. I WON'T *RELAX*.

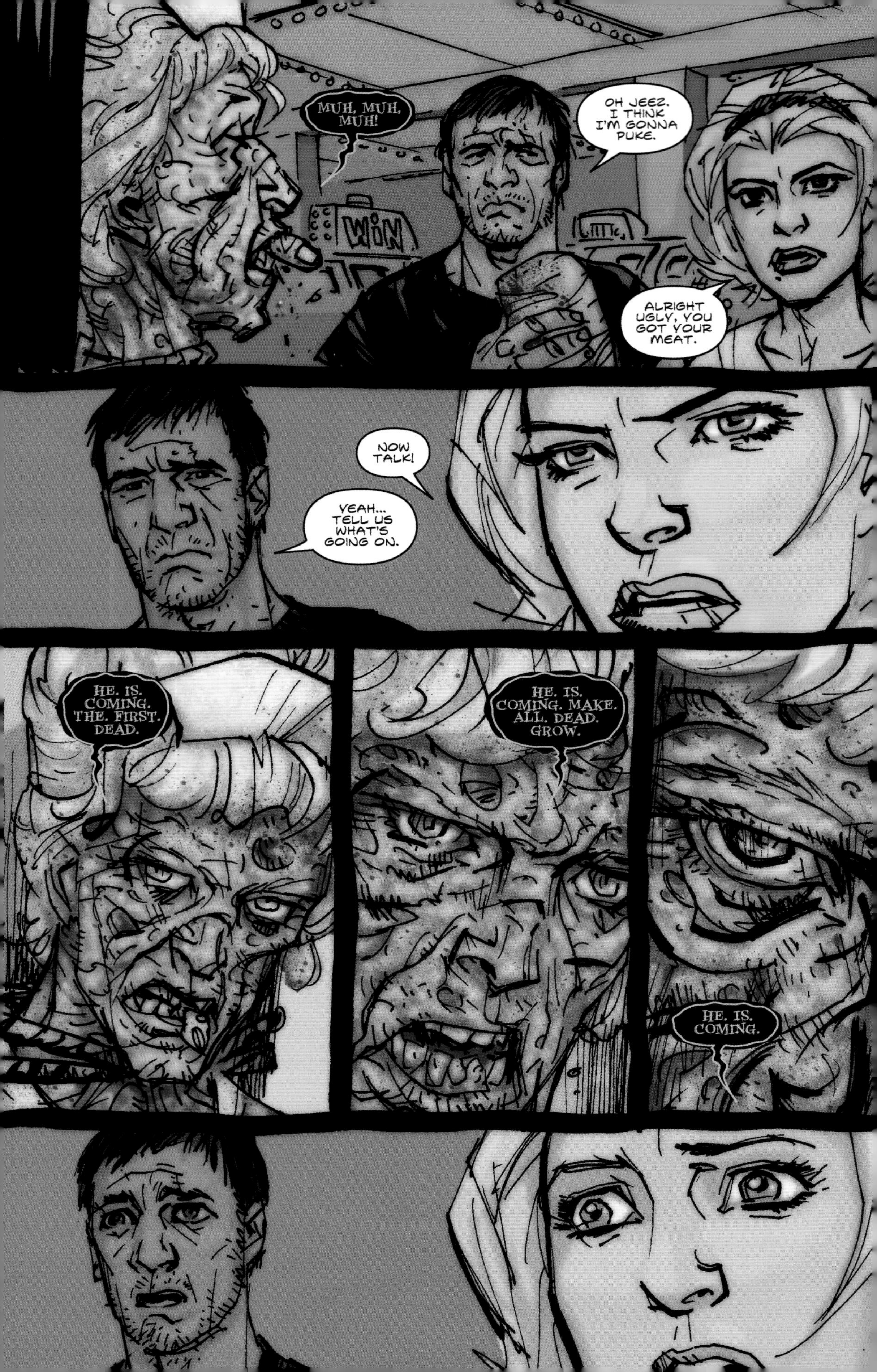
MUH, MUH, MUH!
OH JEEZ. I THINK I'M GONNA PUKE.
WIN
ALRIGHT UGLY, YOU GOT YOUR MEAT.
NOW TALK!
YEAH... TELL US WHAT'S GOING ON.
HE. IS. COMING. THE. FIRST. DEAD.
HE. IS. COMING. MAKE. ALL. DEAD. GROW.
HE. IS. COMING.

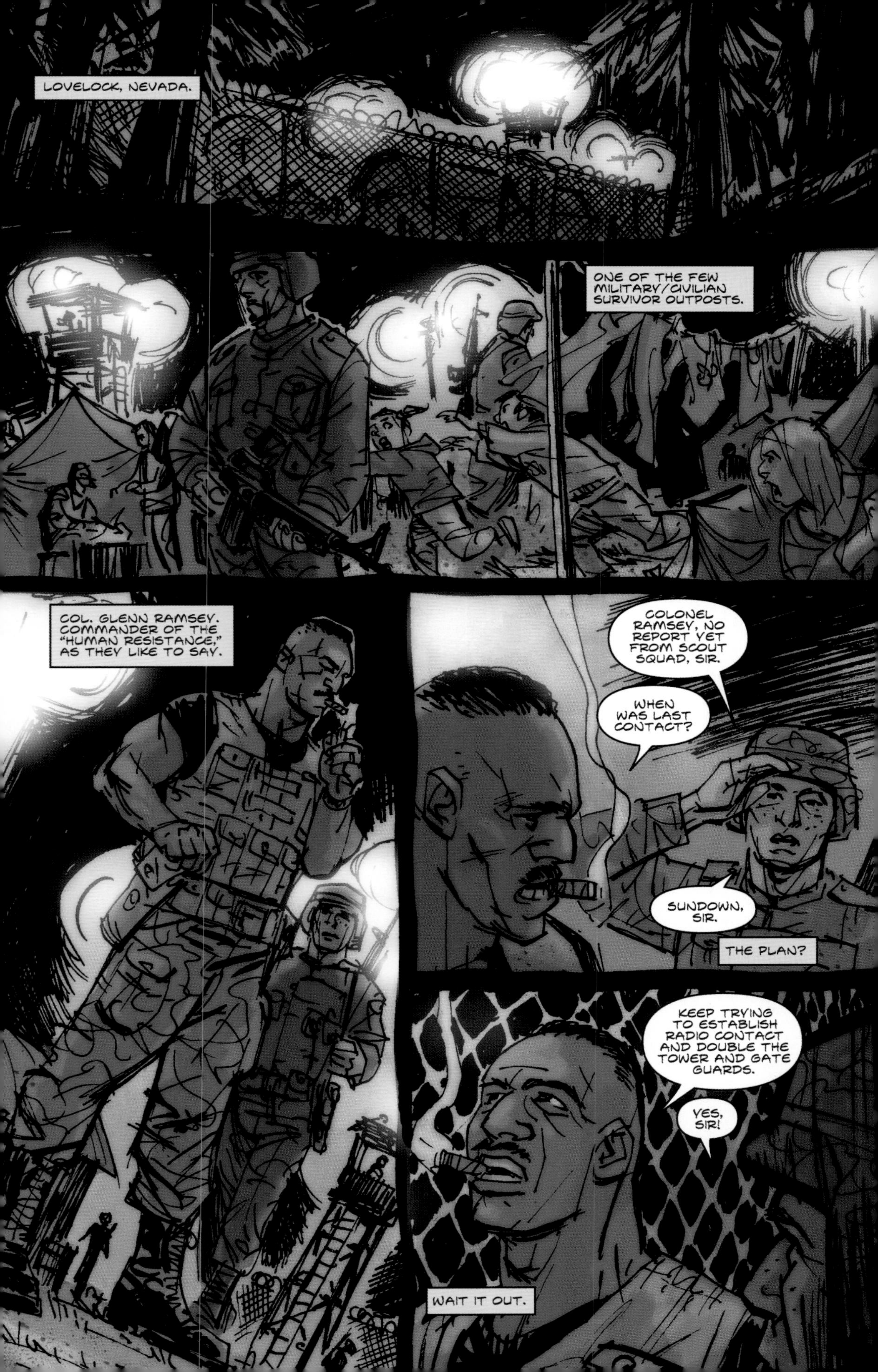
LOVELOCK, NEVADA.
ONE OF THE FEW MILITARY/CIVILIAN SURVIVOR OUTPOSTS.
COL. GLENN RAMSEY. COMMANDER OF THE "HUMAN RESISTANCE," AS THEY LIKE TO SAY.
COLONEL RAMSEY, NO REPORT YET FROM SCOUT SQUAD, SIR.
WHEN WAS LAST CONTACT?
SUNDOWN, SIR.
THE PLAN?
KEEP TRYING TO ESTABLISH RADIO CONTACT AND DOUBLE THE TOWER AND GATE GUARDS.
YES, SIR!
WAIT IT OUT.

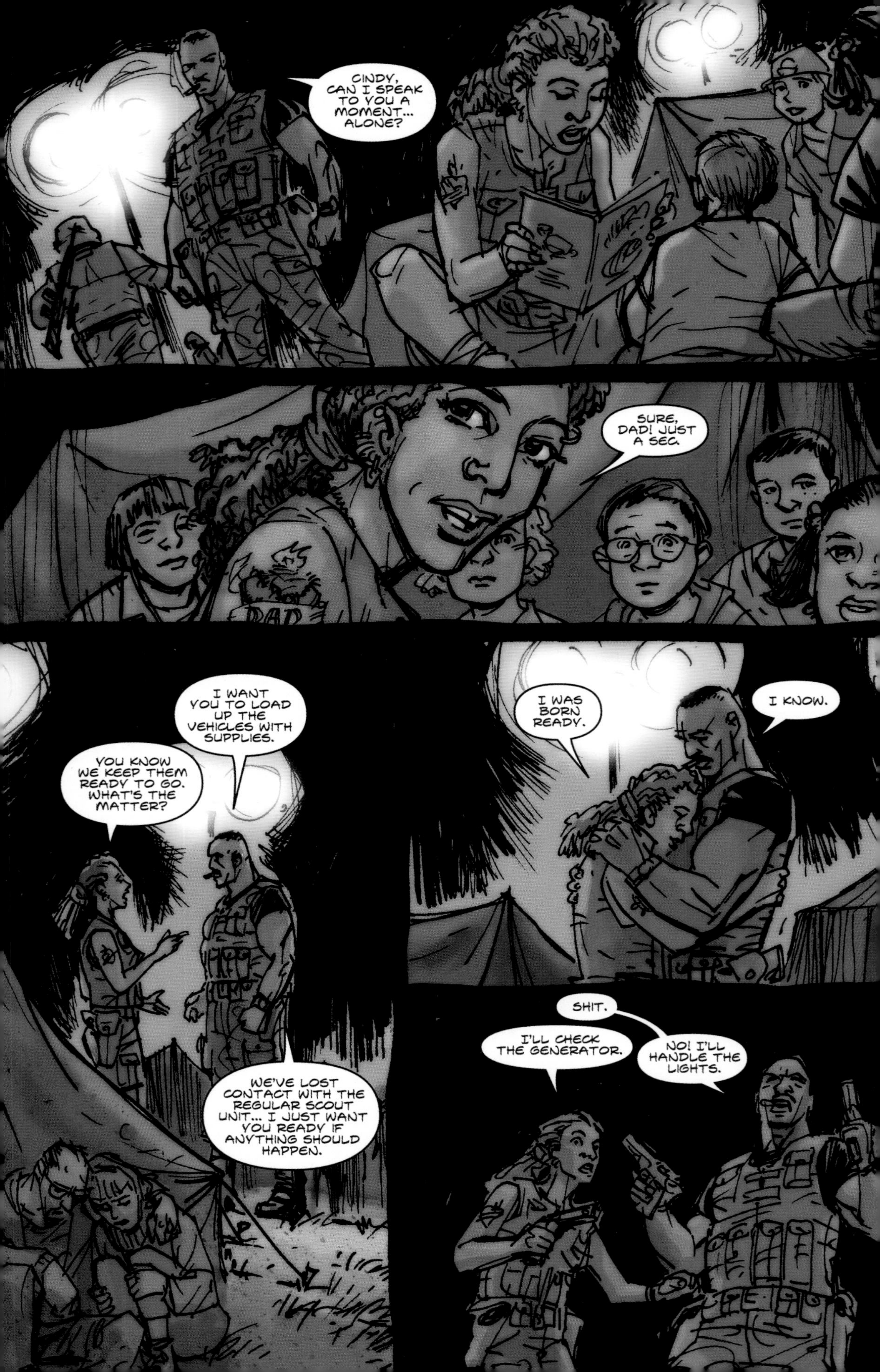
CINDY, CAN I SPEAK TO YOU A MOMENT... ALONE?
SURE, DAD! JUST A SEC.
YOU KNOW WE KEEP THEM READY TO GO. WHAT'S THE MATTER?
I WANT YOU TO LOAD UP THE VEHICLES WITH SUPPLIES.
WE'VE LOST CONTACT WITH THE REGULAR SCOUT UNIT... I JUST WANT YOU READY IF ANYTHING SHOULD HAPPEN.
I WAS BORN READY.
I KNOW.
SHIT.
I'LL CHECK THE GENERATOR.
NO! I'LL HANDLE THE LIGHTS.

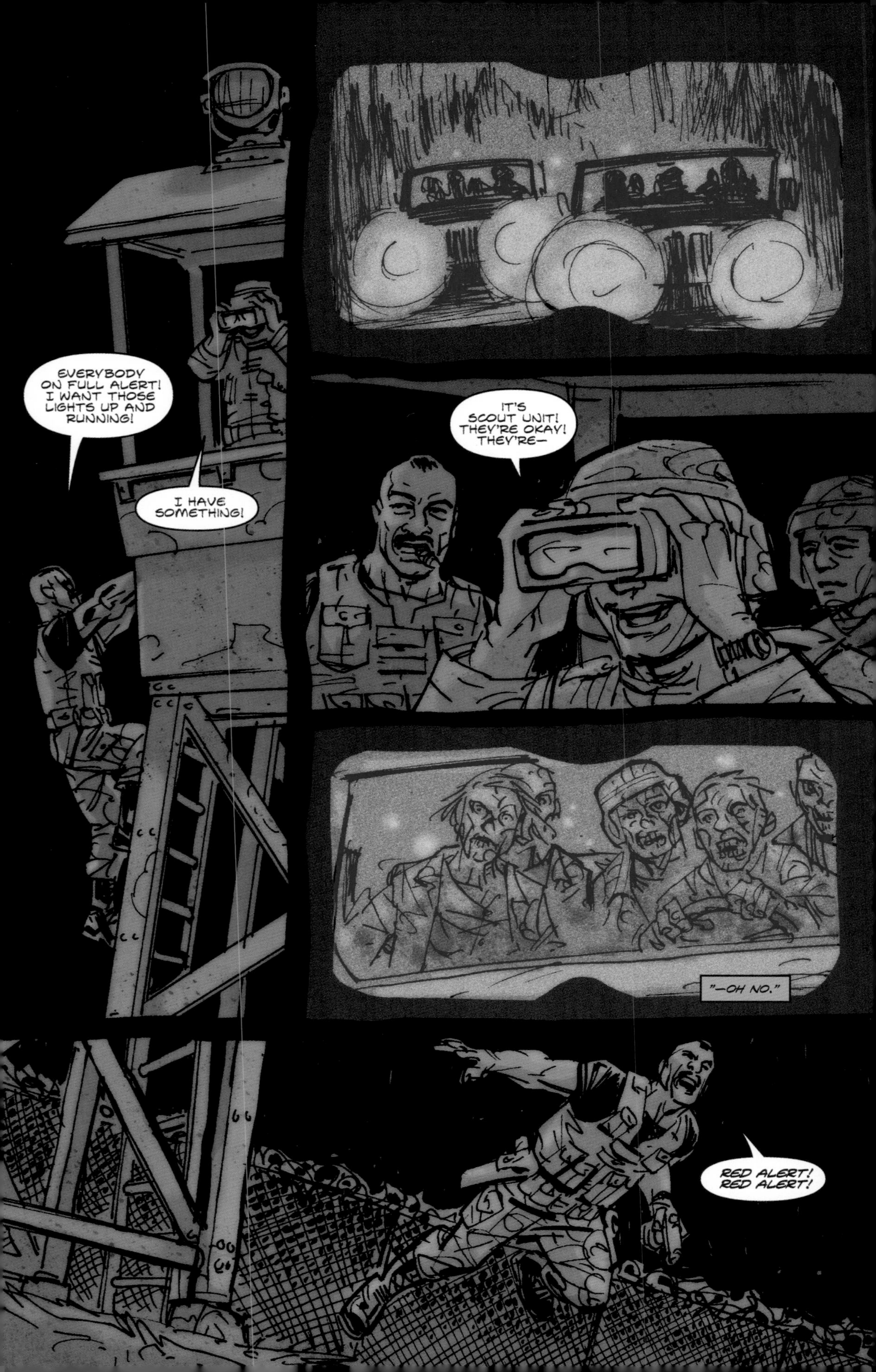
EVERYBODY ON FULL ALERT! I WANT THOSE LIGHTS UP AND RUNNING!
I HAVE SOMETHING!
IT'S SCOUT UNIT! THEY'RE OKAY! THEY'RE—
"—OH NO."
RED ALERT! RED ALERT!

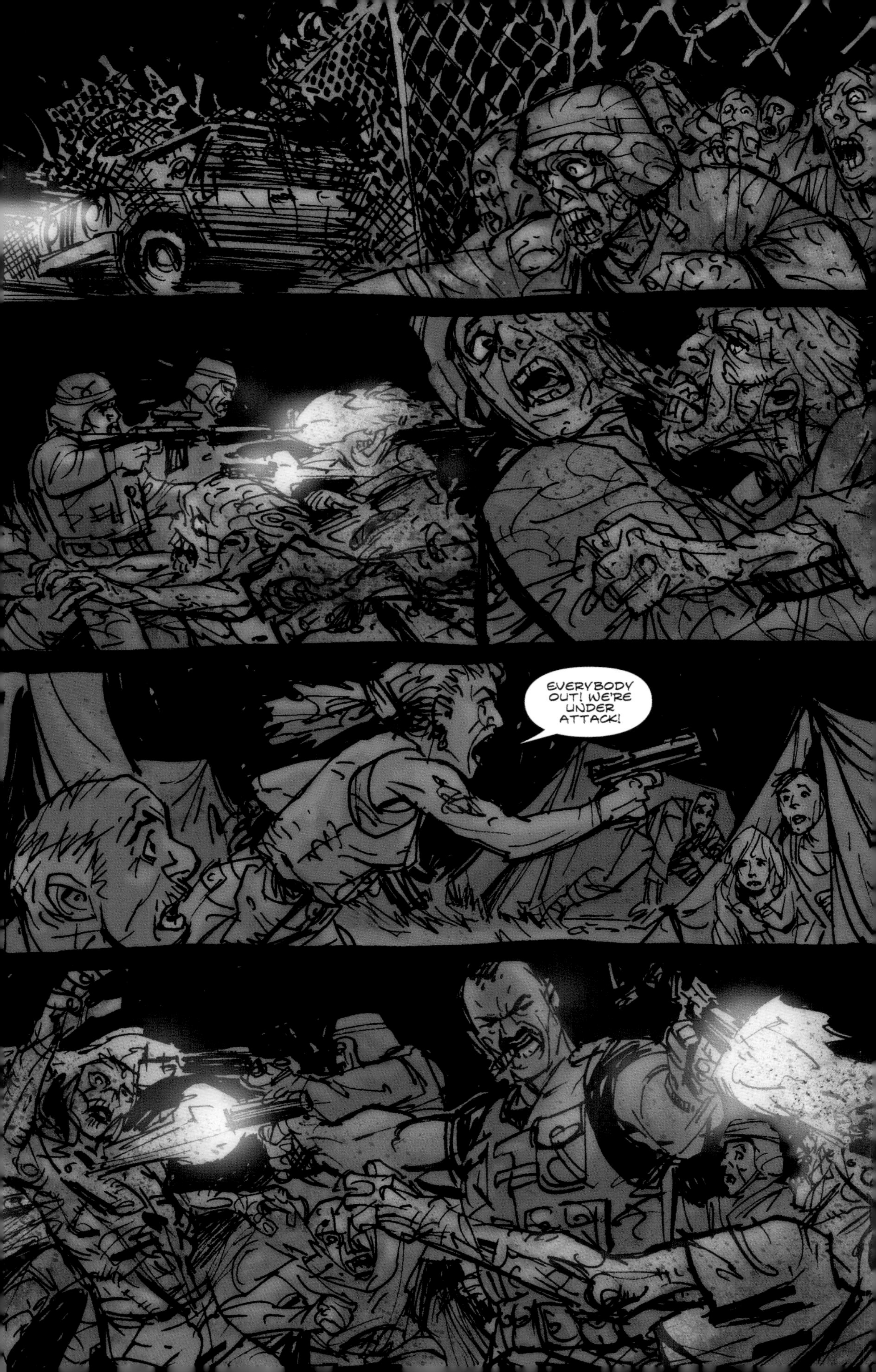
EVERYBODY OUT! WE'RE UNDER ATTACK!

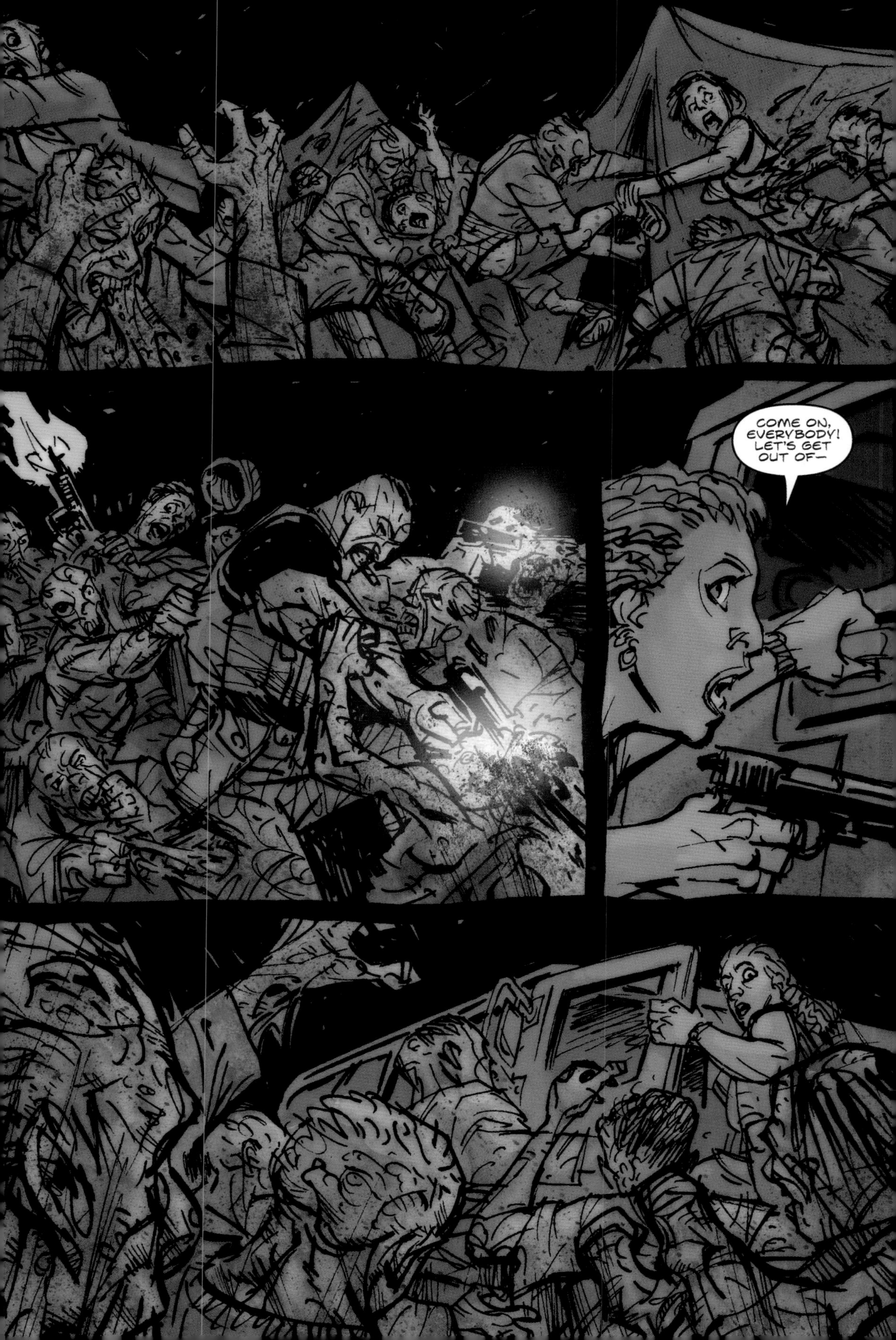
COME ON, EVERYBODY! LET'S GET OUT OF—

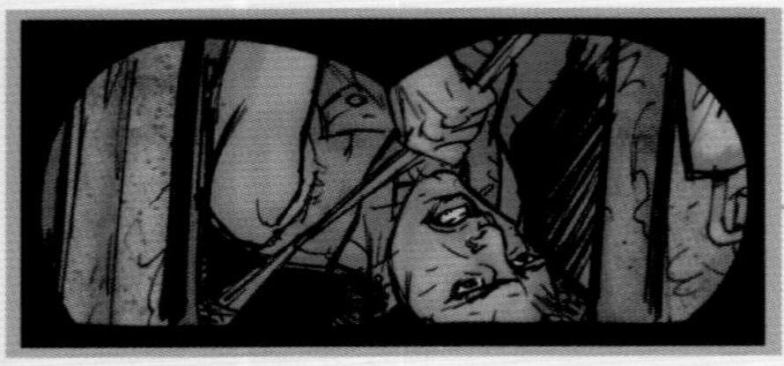

4 chapter

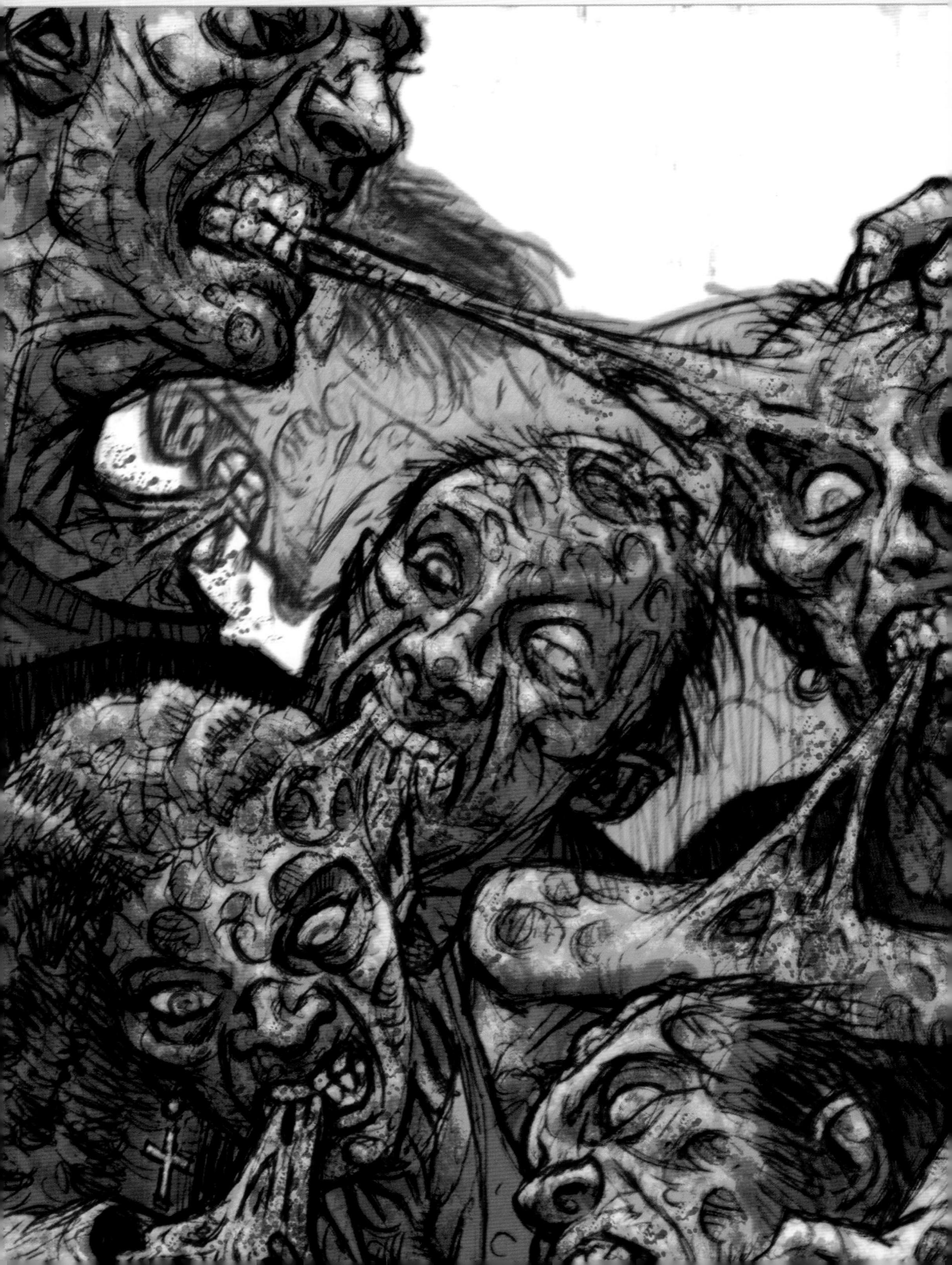

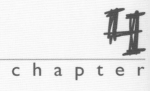

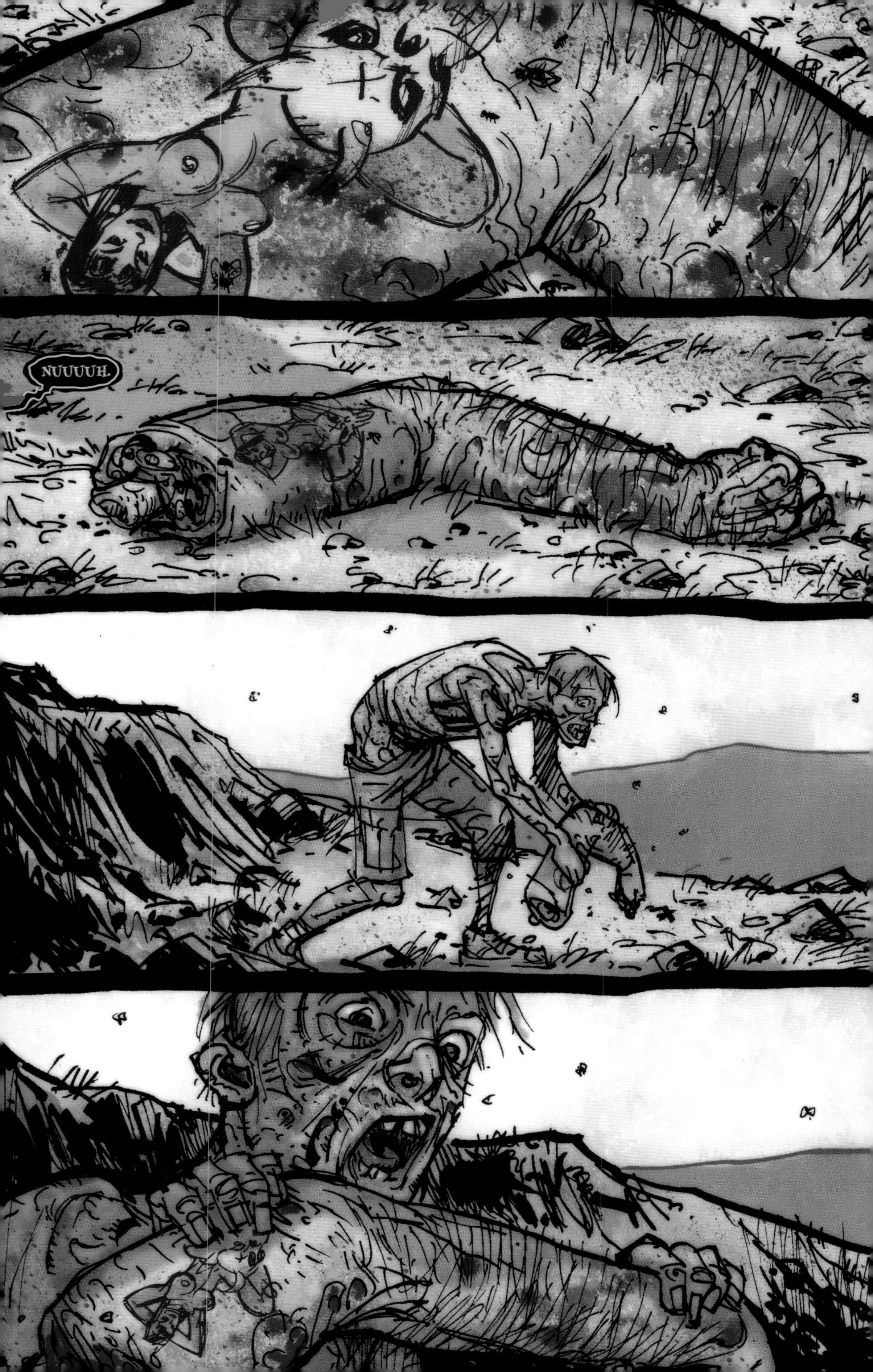
NUUUUH.

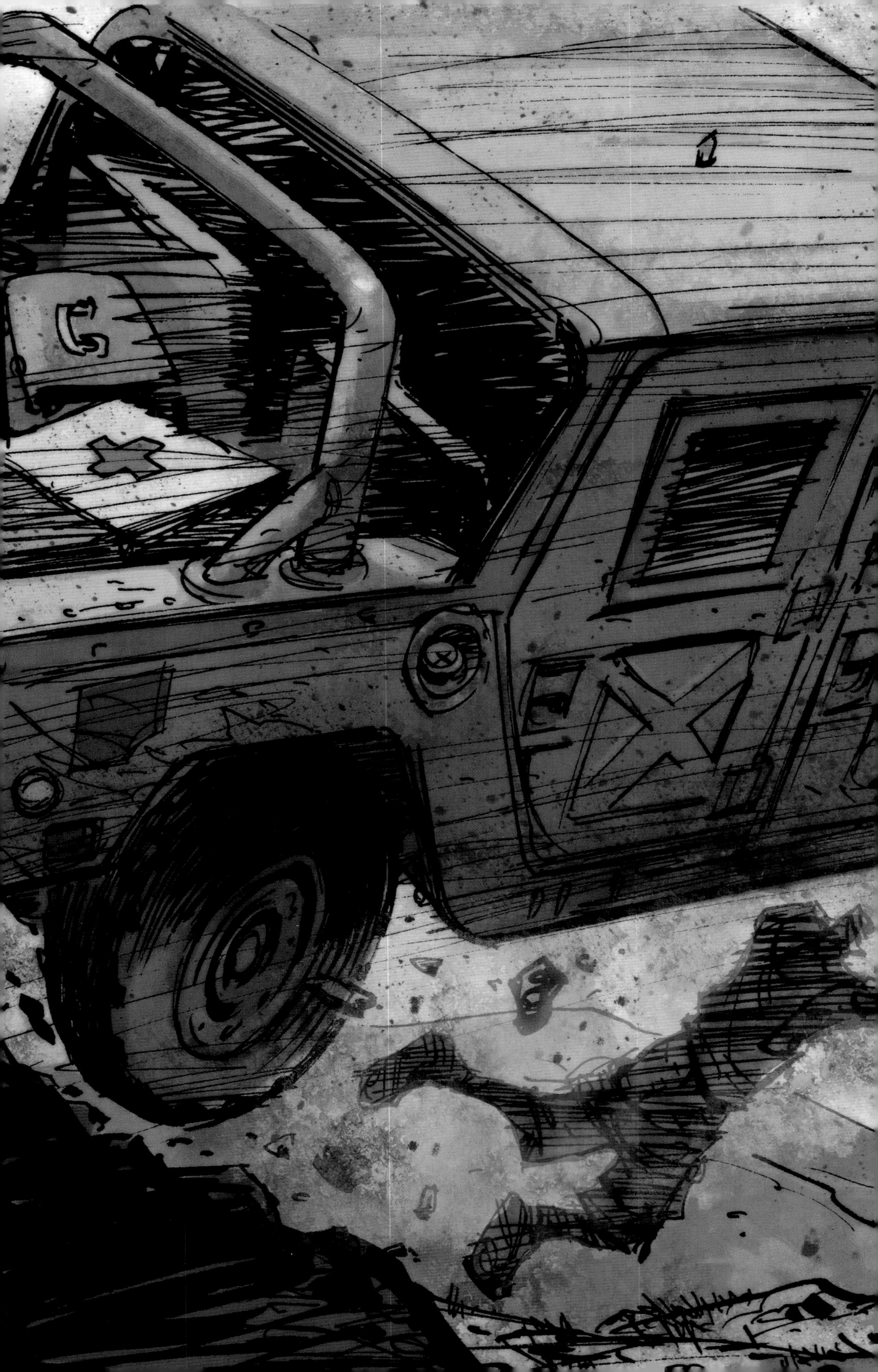

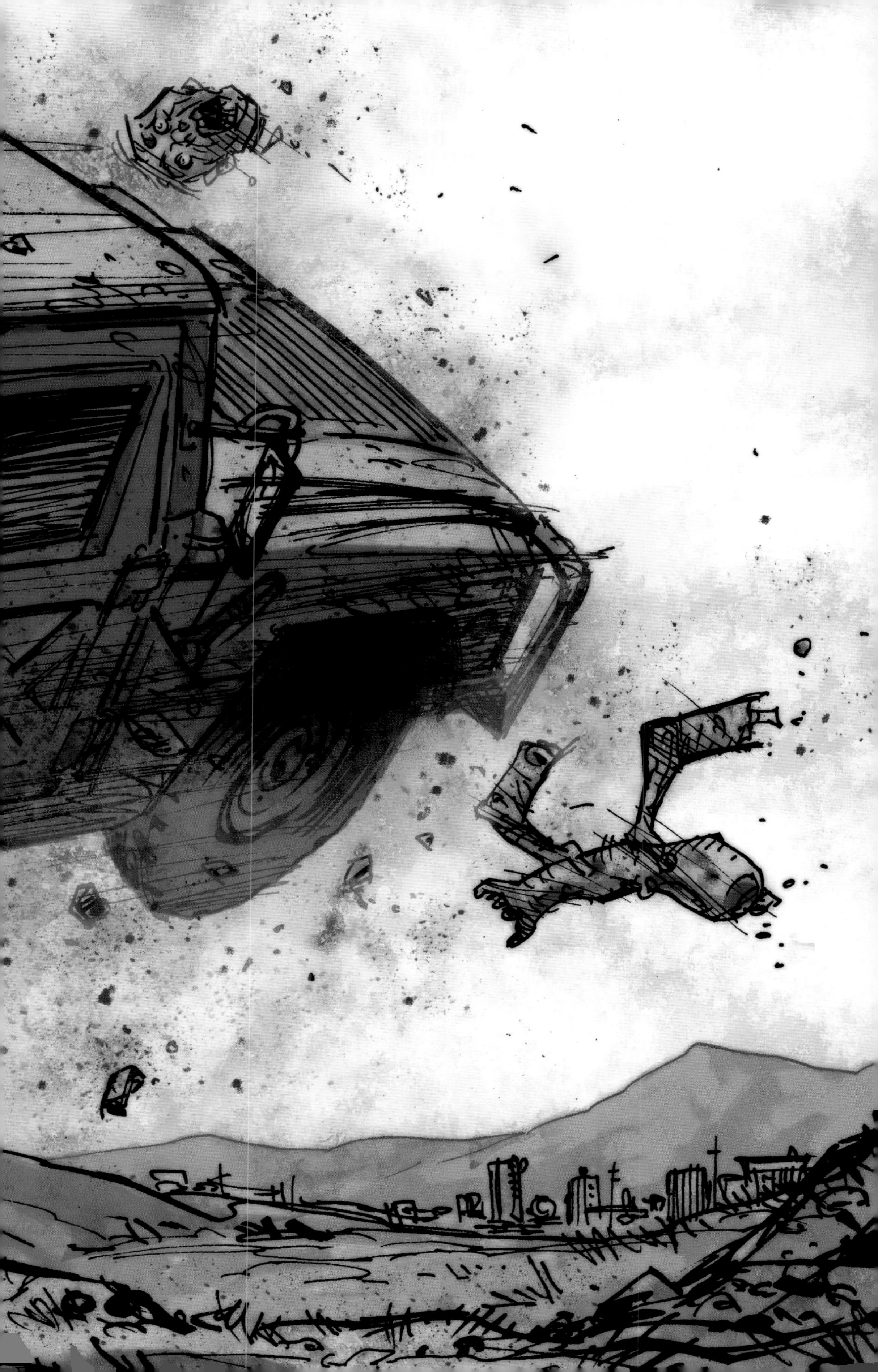

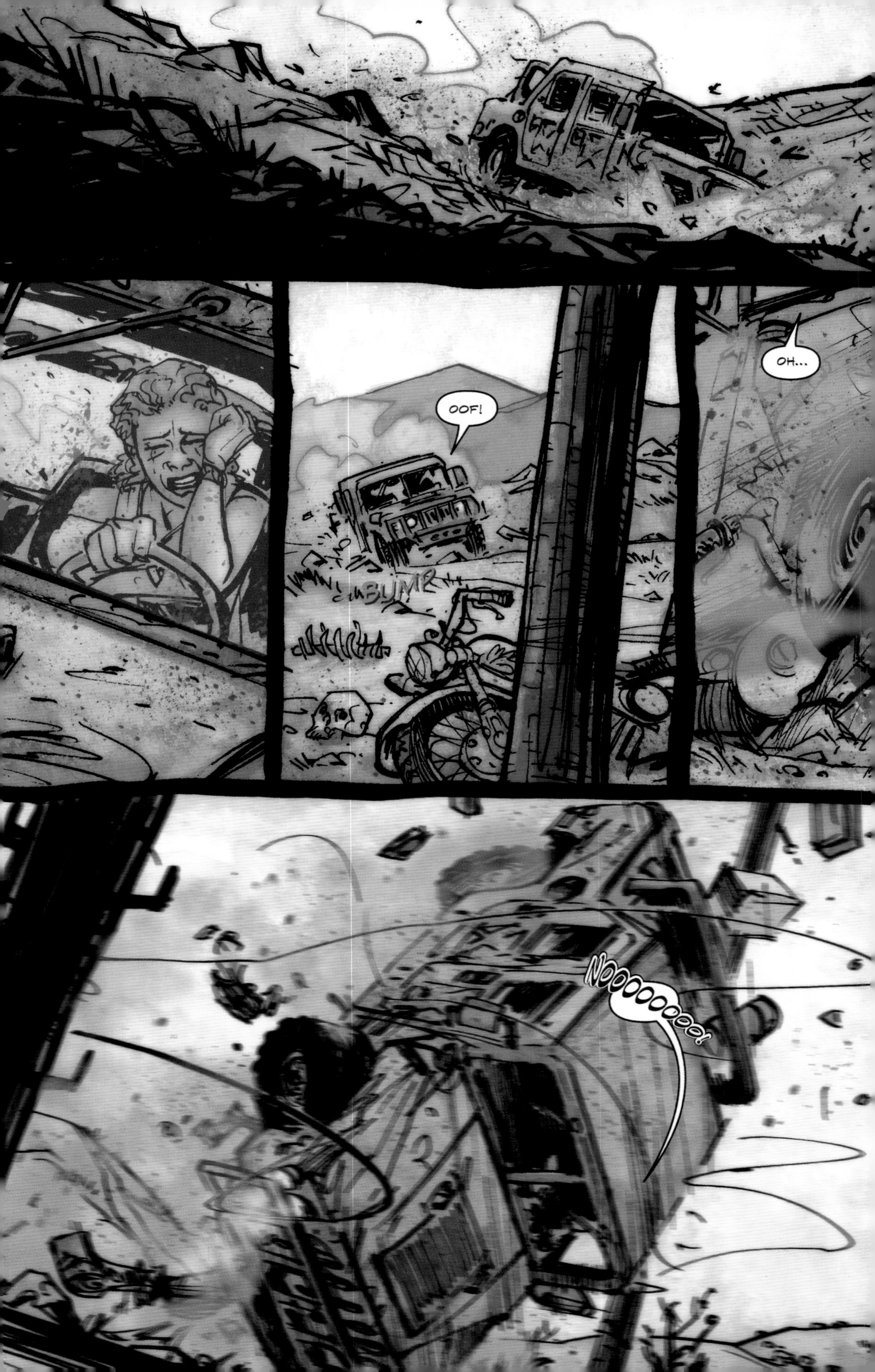
OOF!
BUMP
OH...
NOOOOOOOOE!

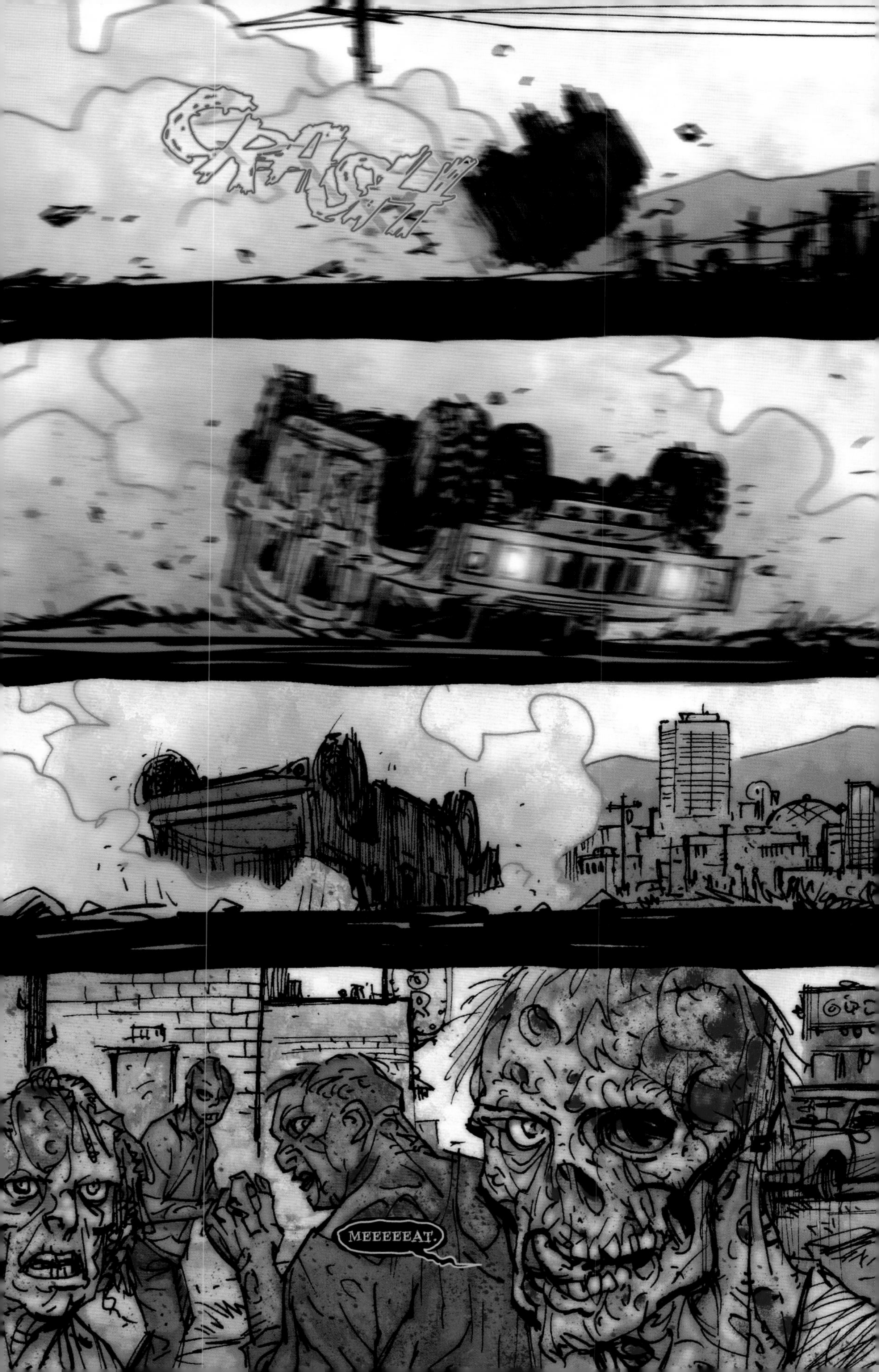
CRASH
MEEEEEAT.

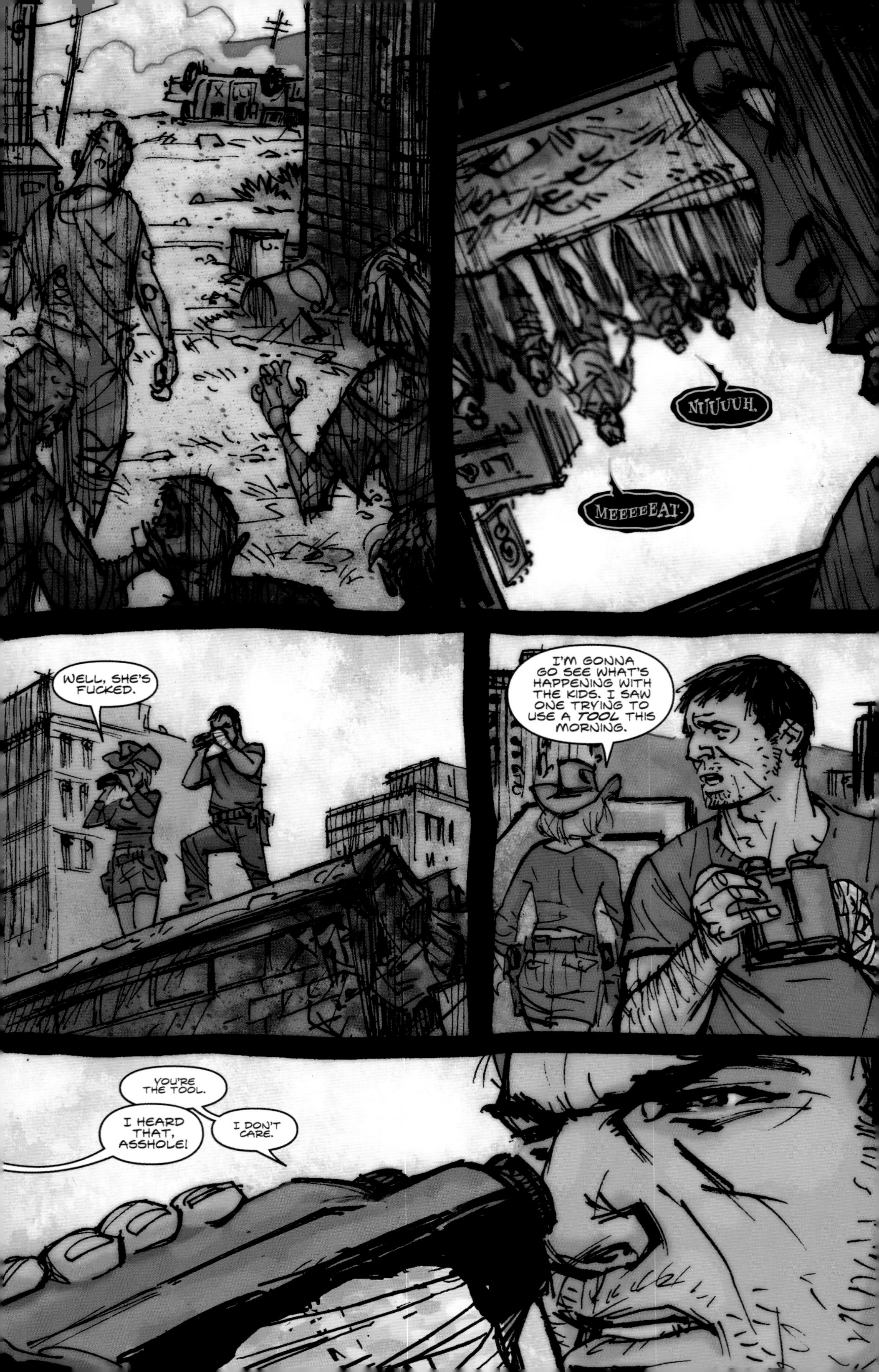
NUUUUH.
MEEEEEAT.
WELL, SHE'S FUCKED.
I'M GONNA GO SEE WHAT'S HAPPENING WITH THE KIDS. I SAW ONE TRYING TO USE A *TOOL* THIS MORNING.
YOU'RE THE TOOL.
I HEARD THAT, ASSHOLE!
I DON'T CARE.

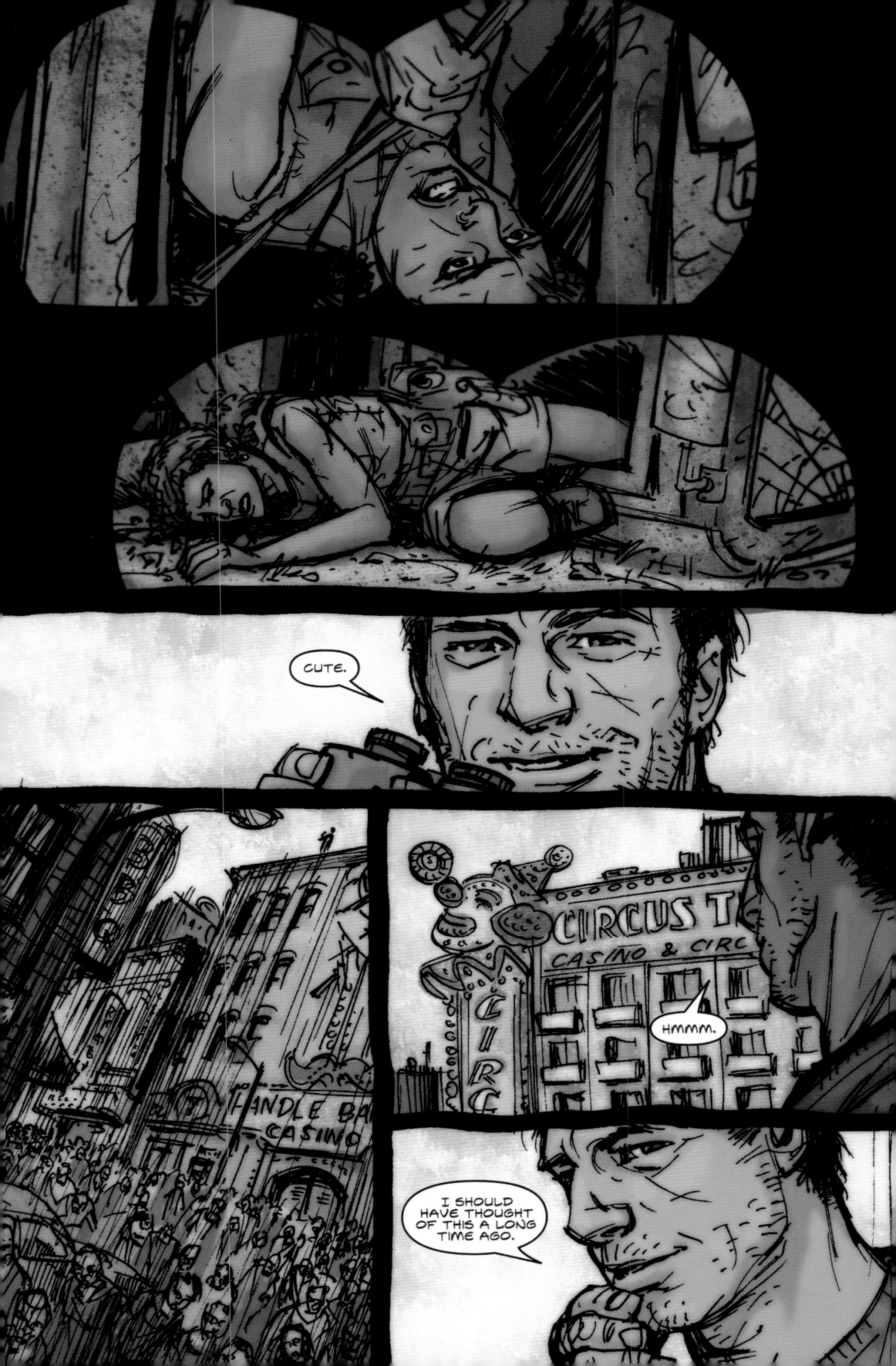
CUTE.
CIRCUS C
CASINO & CIRC
HMMM.
HANDLE BA
CASINO
I SHOULD HAVE THOUGHT OF THIS A LONG TIME AGO.

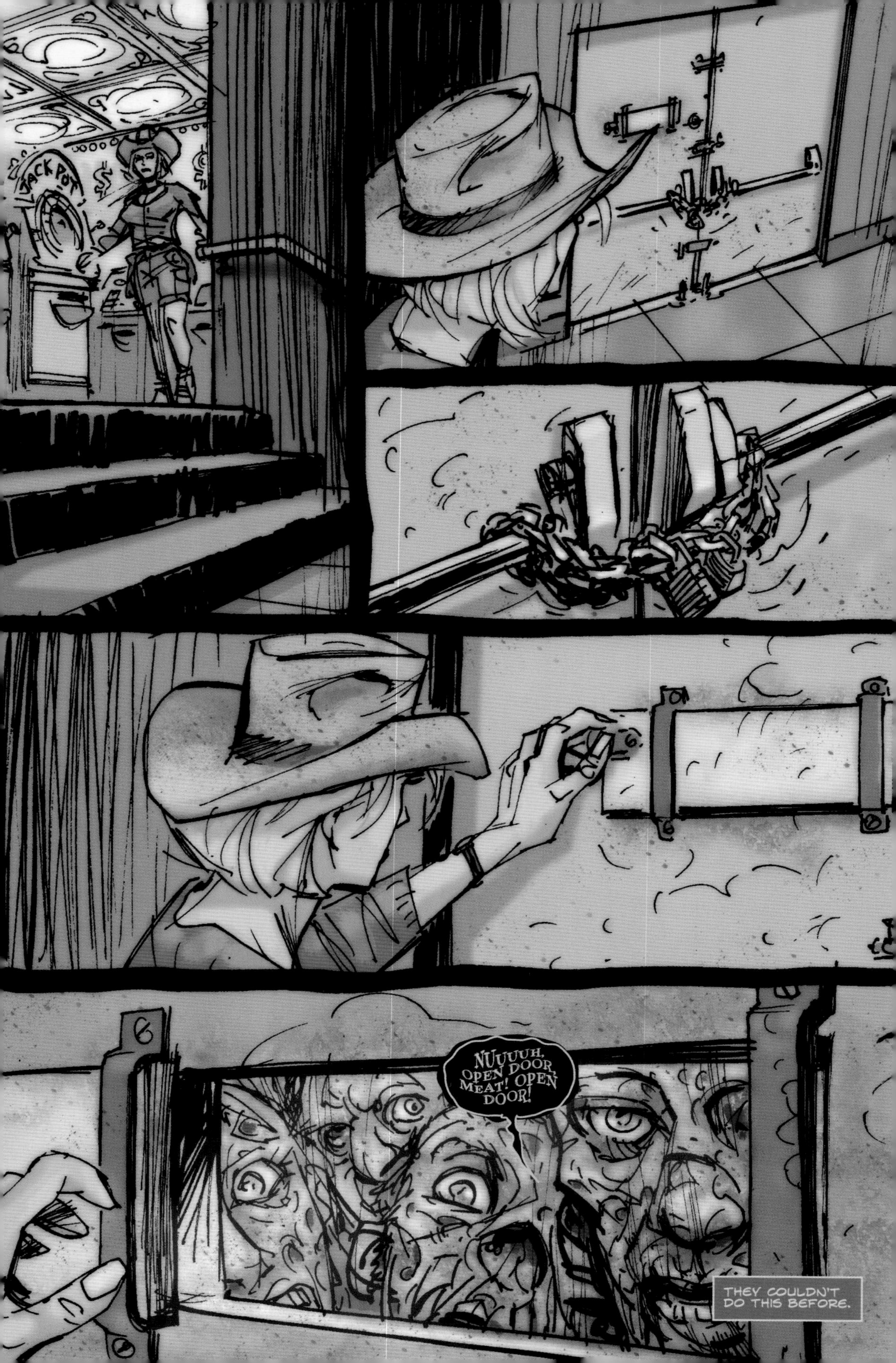

JACKPOT
NUUUUH, OPEN DOOR, MEAT! OPEN DOOR!
THEY COULDN'T DO THIS BEFORE.

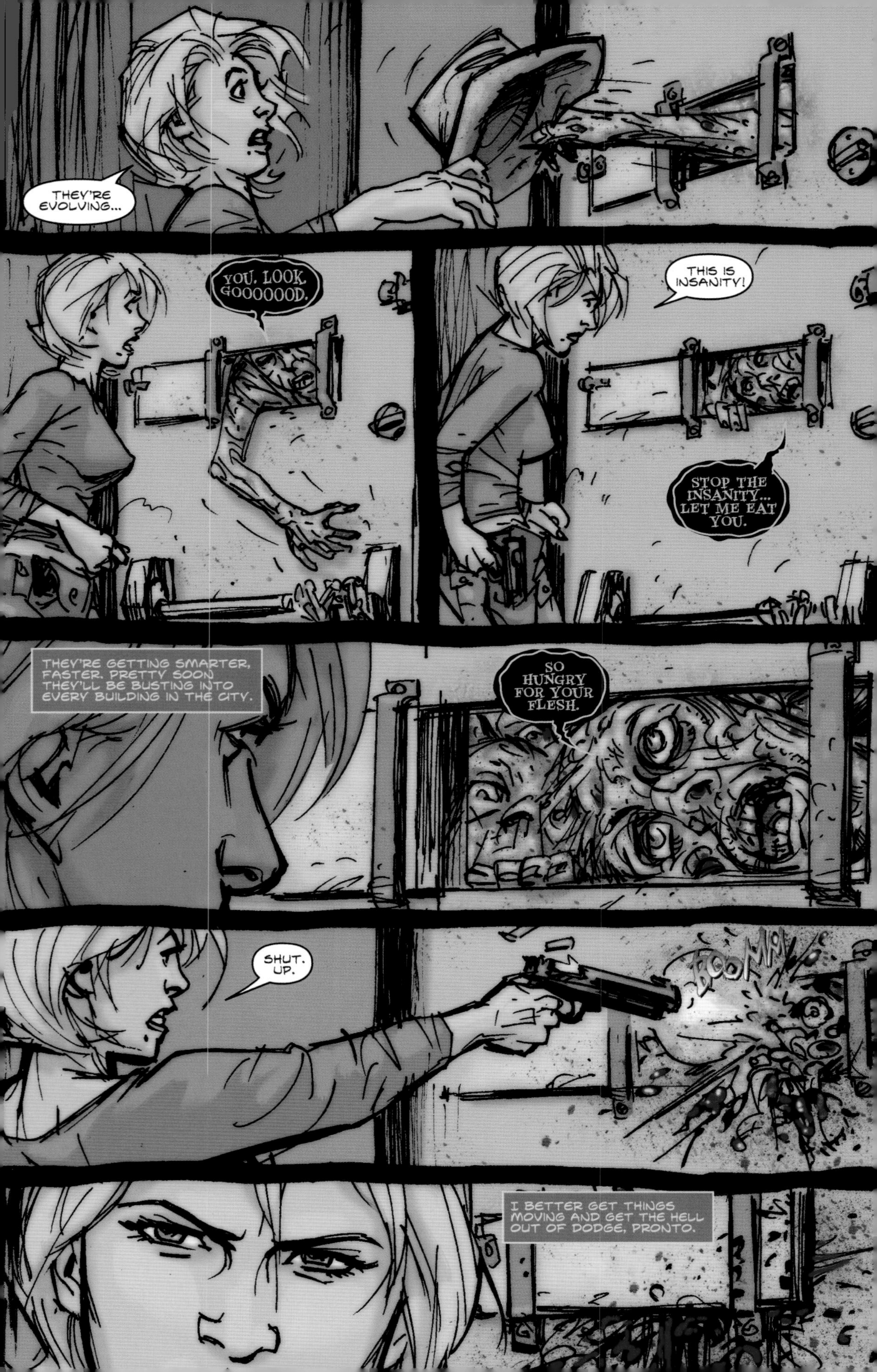
THEY'RE EVOLVING...
YOU. LOOK. GOOOOOOD.
THIS IS INSANITY!
STOP THE INSANITY... LET ME EAT YOU.
THEY'RE GETTING SMARTER, FASTER. PRETTY SOON THEY'LL BE BUSTING INTO EVERY BUILDING IN THE CITY.
SO HUNGRY FOR YOUR FLESH.
SHUT. UP.
I BETTER GET THINGS MOVING AND GET THE HELL OUT OF DODGE, PRONTO.

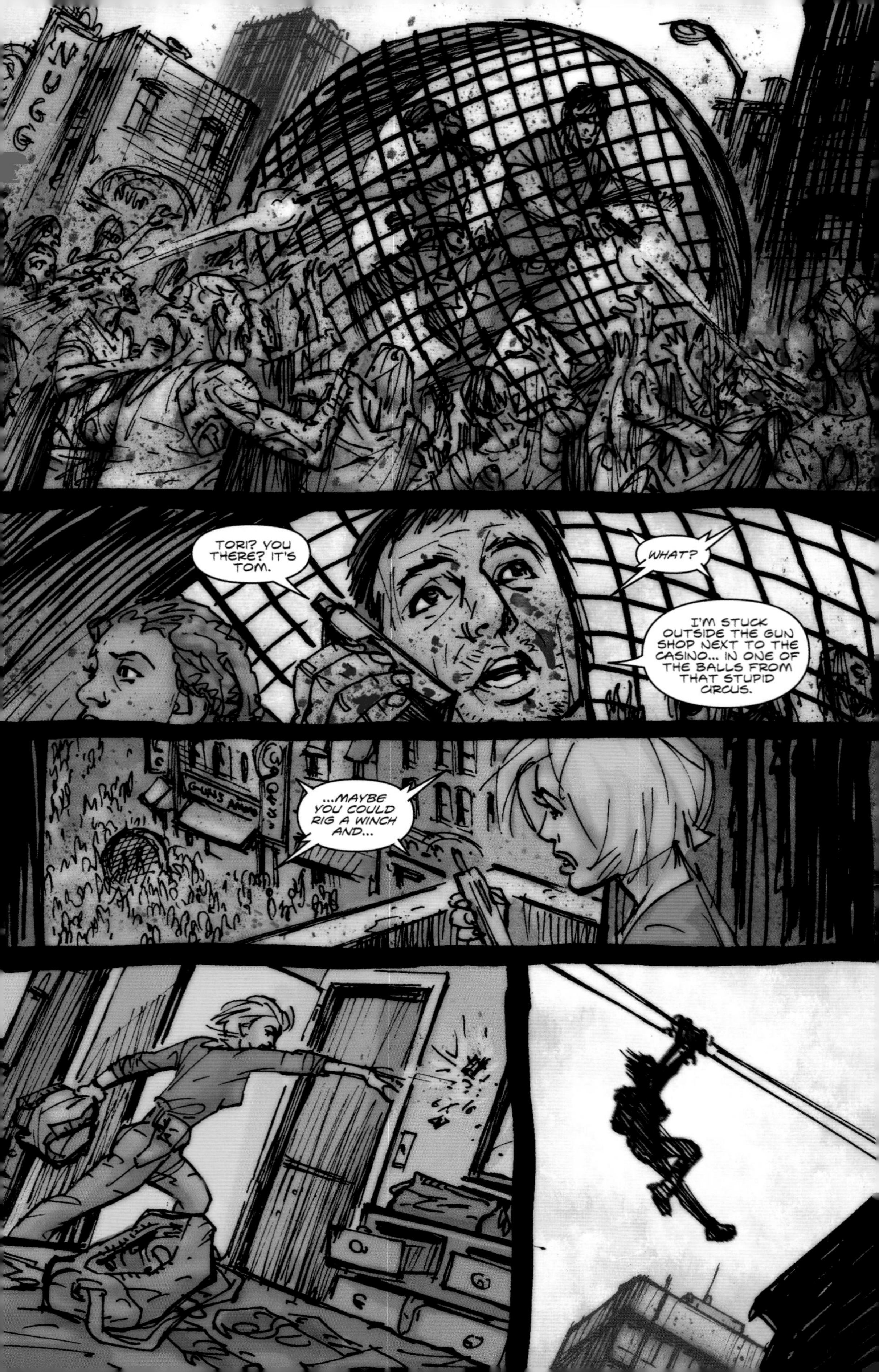
TORI? YOU THERE? IT'S TOM.
WHAT?
I'M STUCK OUTSIDE THE GUN SHOP NEXT TO THE CASINO... IN ONE OF THE BALLS FROM THAT STUPID CIRCUS.
...MAYBE YOU COULD RIG A WINCH AND...

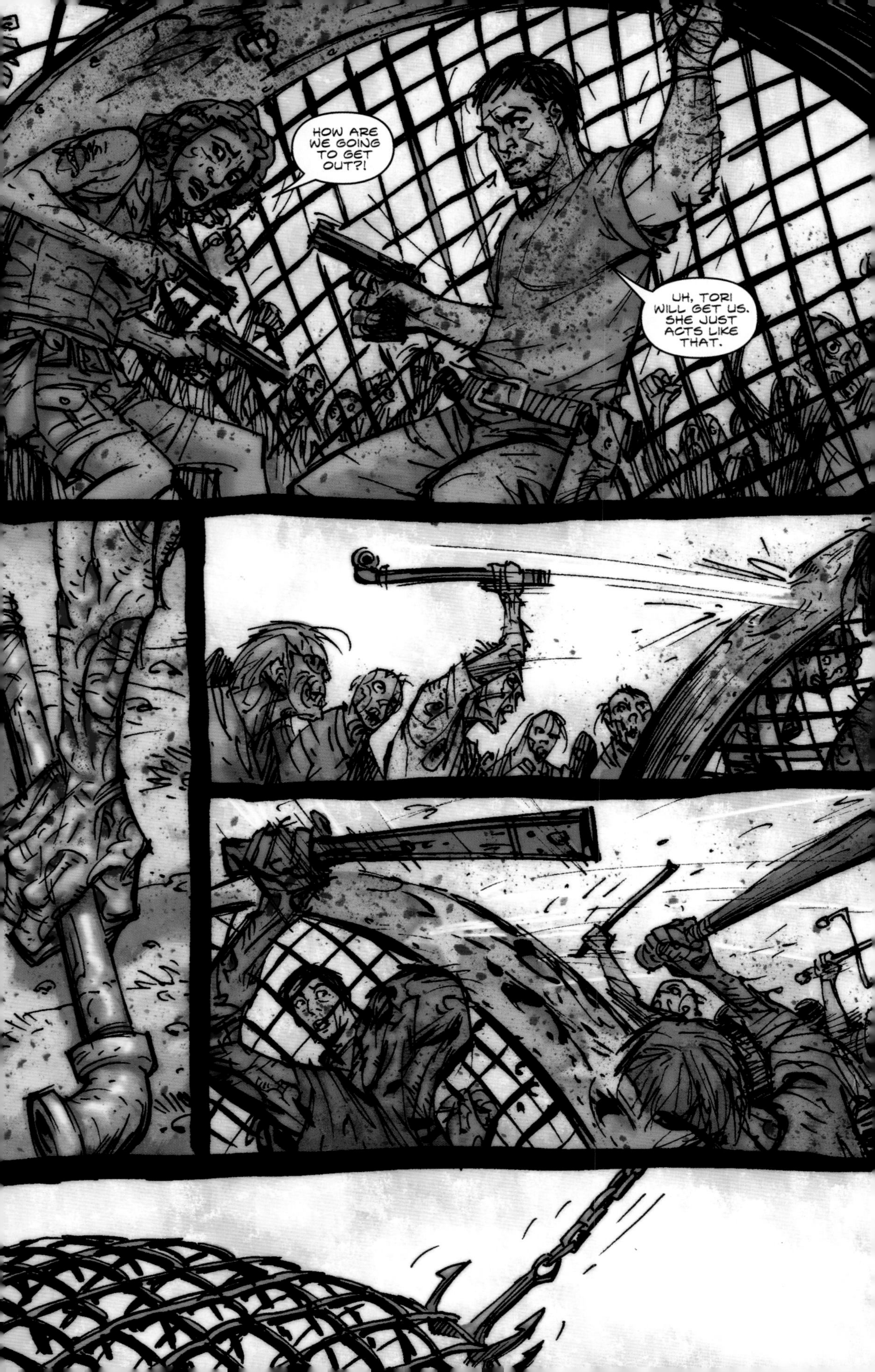
HOW ARE WE GOING TO GET OUT?!
UH, TORI WILL GET US. SHE JUST ACTS LIKE THAT.

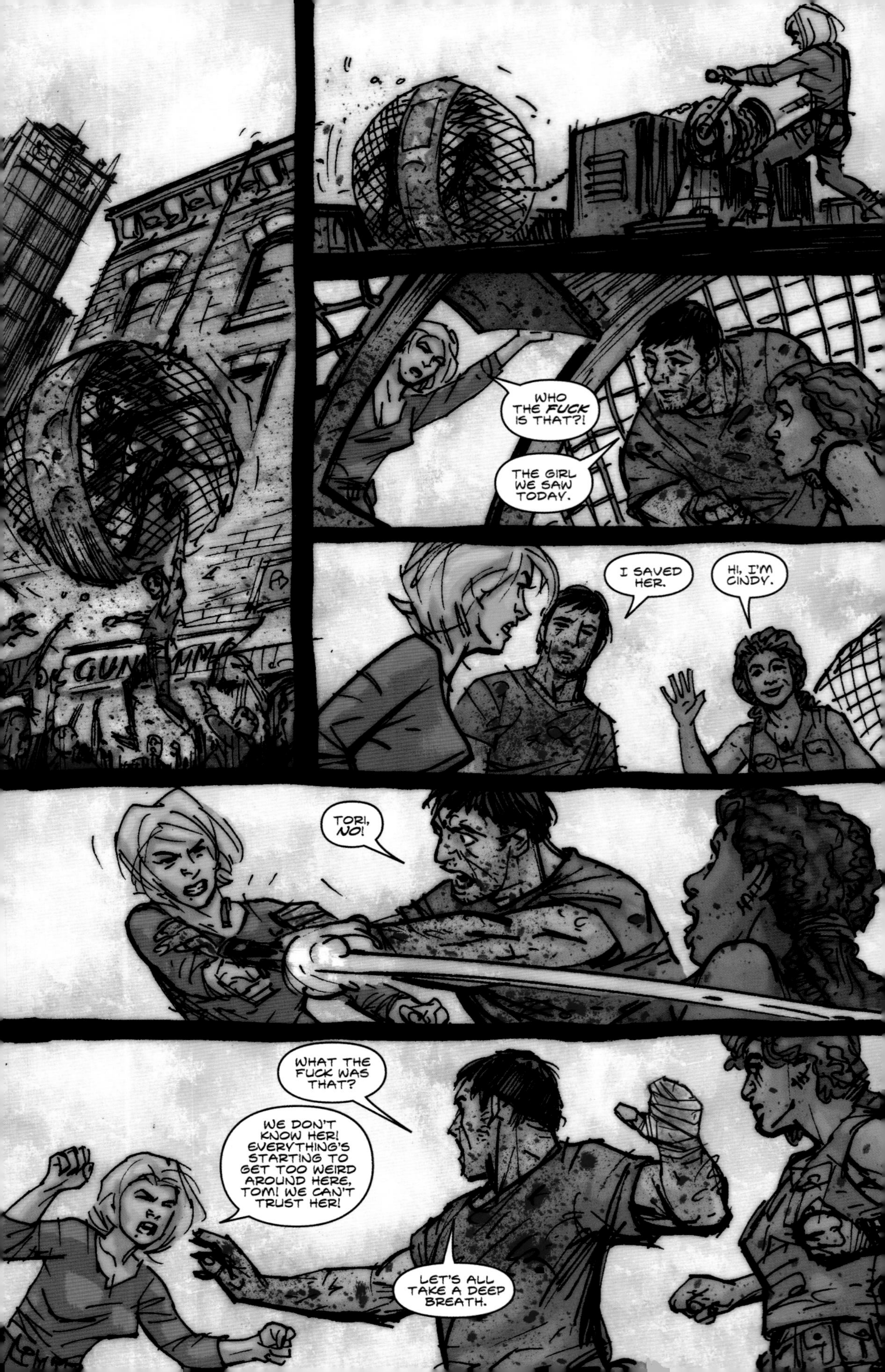
GUN
WHO THE FUCK IS THAT?!
THE GIRL WE SAW TODAY.
I SAVED HER.
HI, I'M CINDY.
TORI, NO!
WHAT THE FUCK WAS THAT?
WE DON'T KNOW HER! EVERYTHING'S STARTING TO GET TOO WEIRD AROUND HERE, TOM! WE CAN'T TRUST HER!
LET'S ALL TAKE A DEEP BREATH.

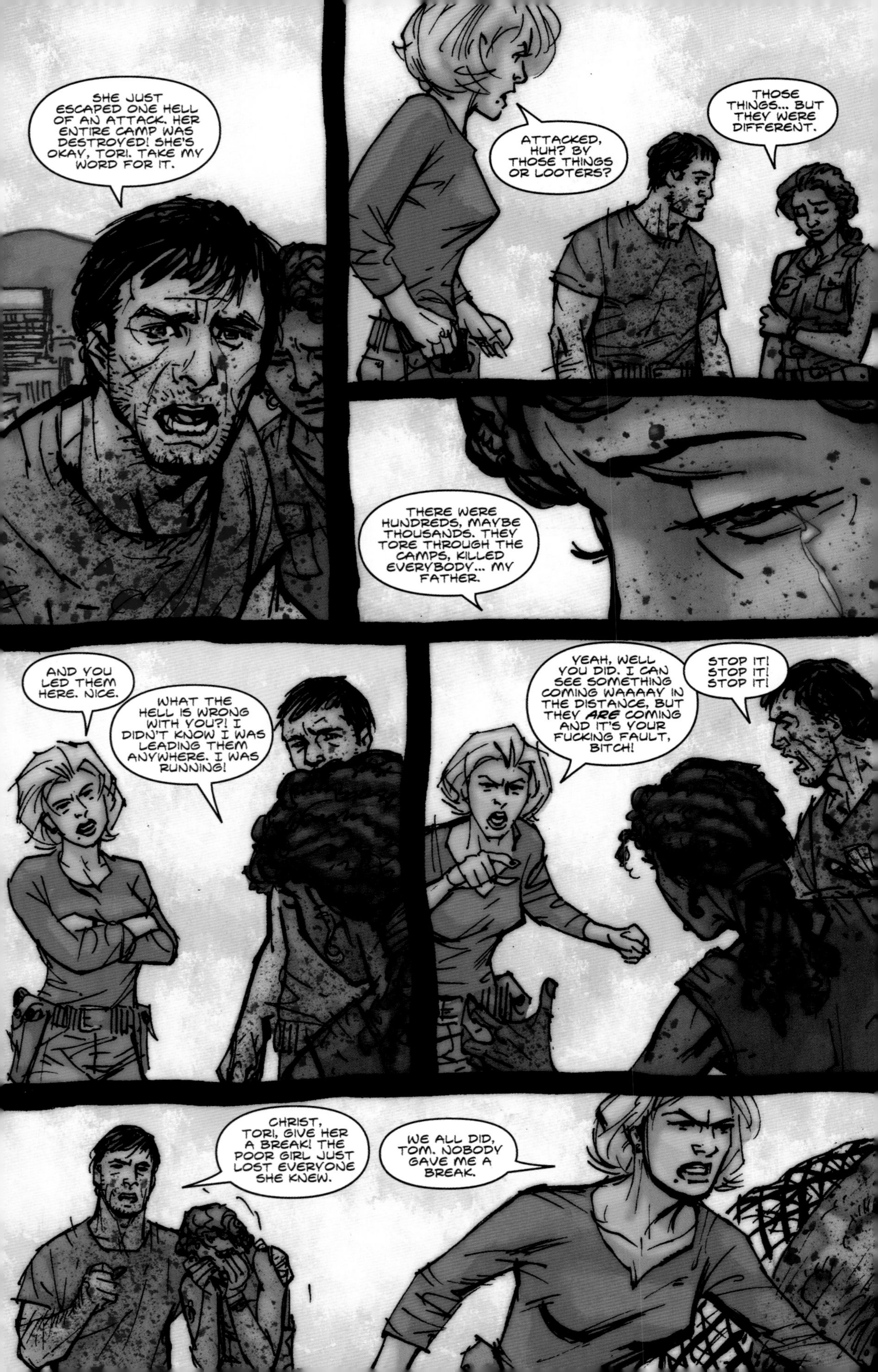
SHE JUST ESCAPED ONE HELL OF AN ATTACK. HER ENTIRE CAMP WAS DESTROYED! SHE'S OKAY, TORI. TAKE MY WORD FOR IT.
ATTACKED, HUH? BY THOSE THINGS OR LOOTERS?
THOSE THINGS... BUT THEY WERE DIFFERENT.
THERE WERE HUNDREDS, MAYBE THOUSANDS. THEY TORE THROUGH THE CAMPS, KILLED EVERYBODY... MY FATHER.
AND YOU LED THEM HERE. NICE.
WHAT THE HELL IS WRONG WITH YOU?! I DIDN'T KNOW I WAS LEADING THEM ANYWHERE. I WAS RUNNING!
YEAH, WELL YOU DID. I CAN SEE SOMETHING COMING WAAAAY IN THE DISTANCE, BUT THEY *ARE* COMING AND IT'S YOUR FUCKING FAULT, BITCH!
STOP IT! STOP IT! STOP IT!
CHRIST, TORI, GIVE HER A BREAK! THE POOR GIRL JUST LOST EVERYONE SHE KNEW.
WE ALL DID, TOM. NOBODY GAVE ME A BREAK.

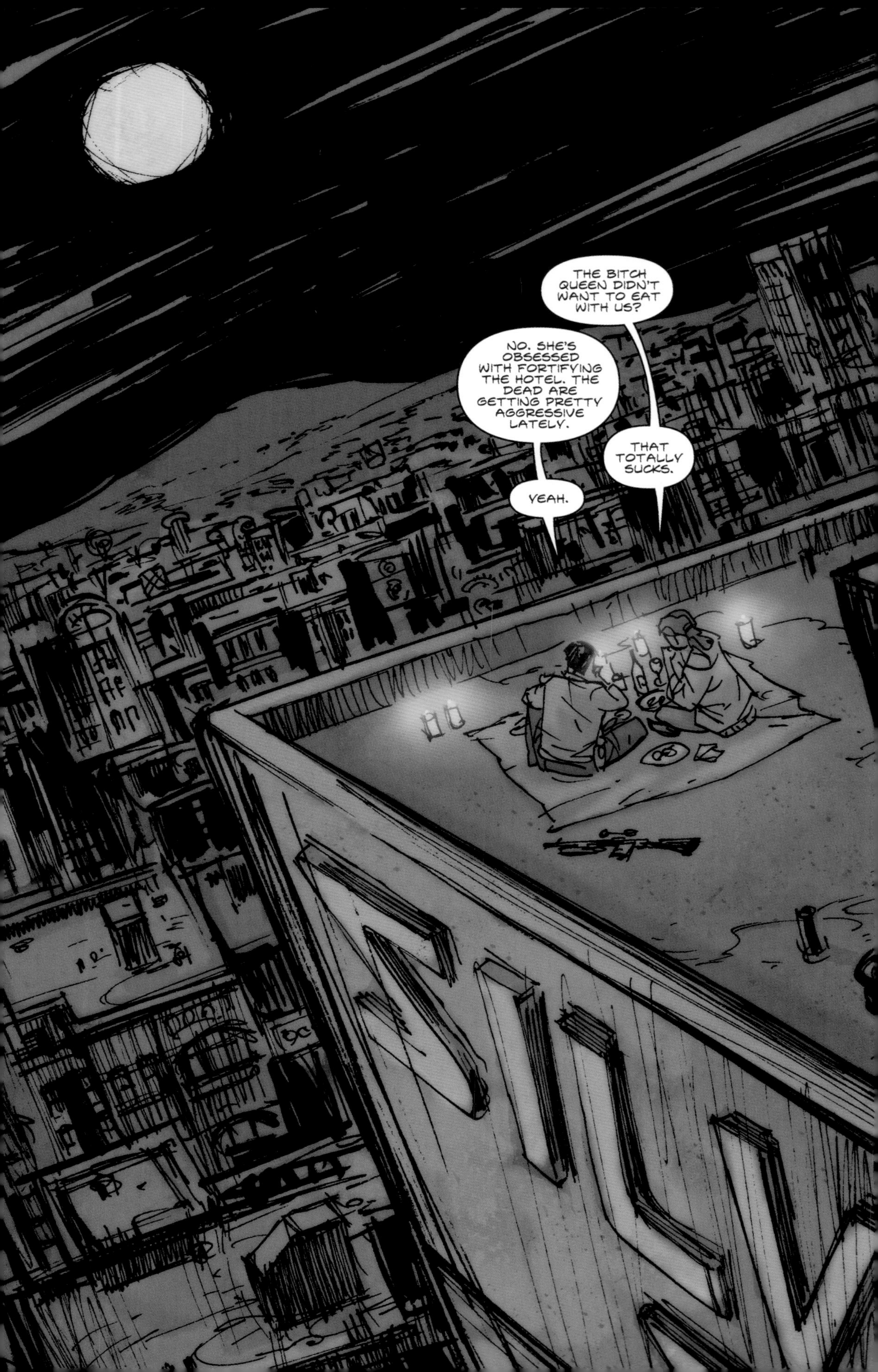
THE BITCH QUEEN DIDN'T WANT TO EAT WITH US?
NO. SHE'S OBSESSED WITH FORTIFYING THE HOTEL. THE DEAD ARE GETTING PRETTY AGGRESSIVE LATELY.
THAT TOTALLY SUCKS.
YEAH.

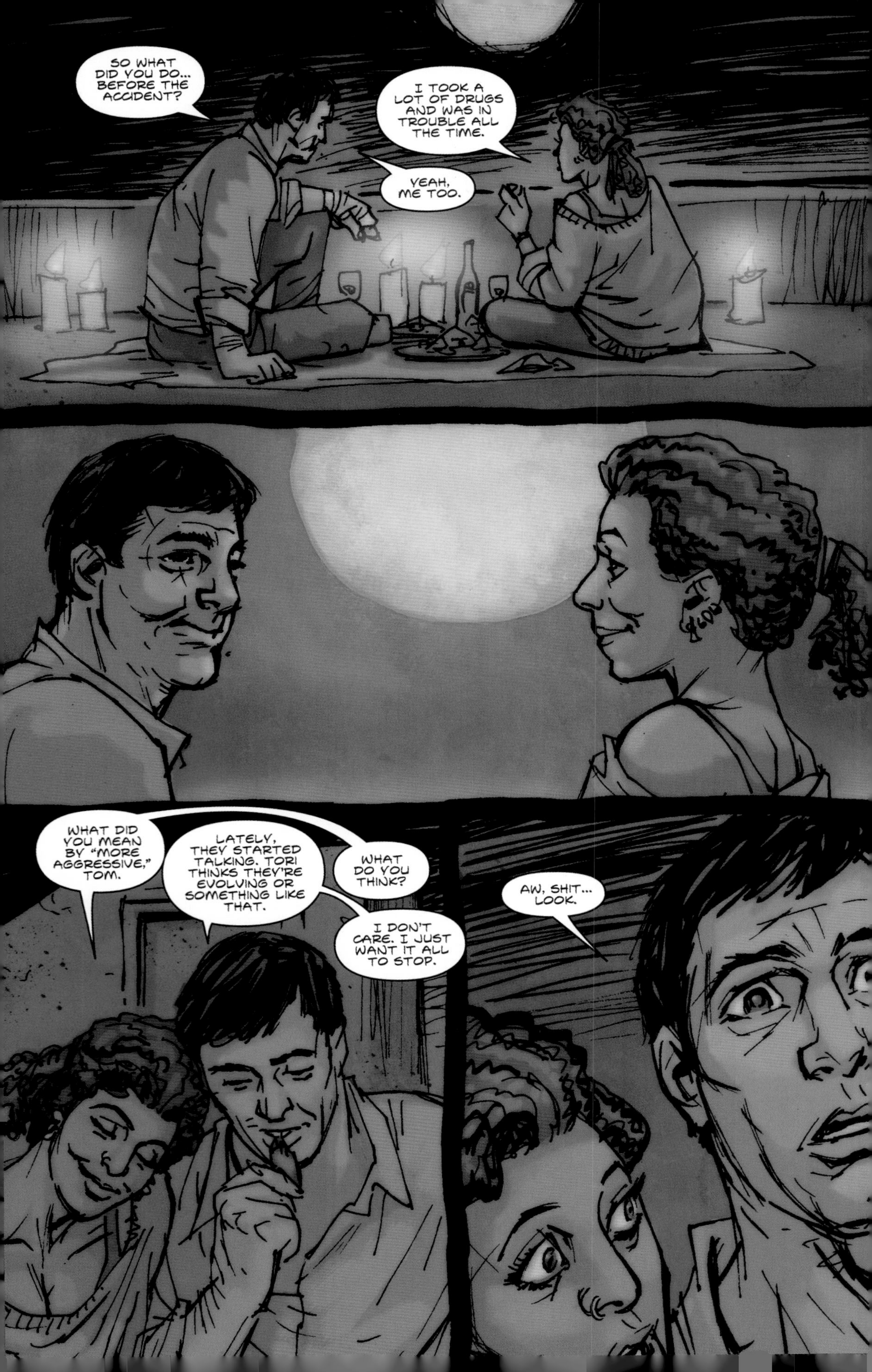
SO WHAT DID YOU DO... BEFORE THE ACCIDENT?
I TOOK A LOT OF DRUGS AND WAS IN TROUBLE ALL THE TIME.
YEAH, ME TOO.
WHAT DID YOU MEAN BY "MORE AGGRESSIVE," TOM.
LATELY, THEY STARTED TALKING. TORI THINKS THEY'RE EVOLVING OR SOMETHING LIKE THAT.
WHAT DO YOU THINK?
I DON'T CARE. I JUST WANT IT ALL TO STOP.
AW, SHIT... LOOK.

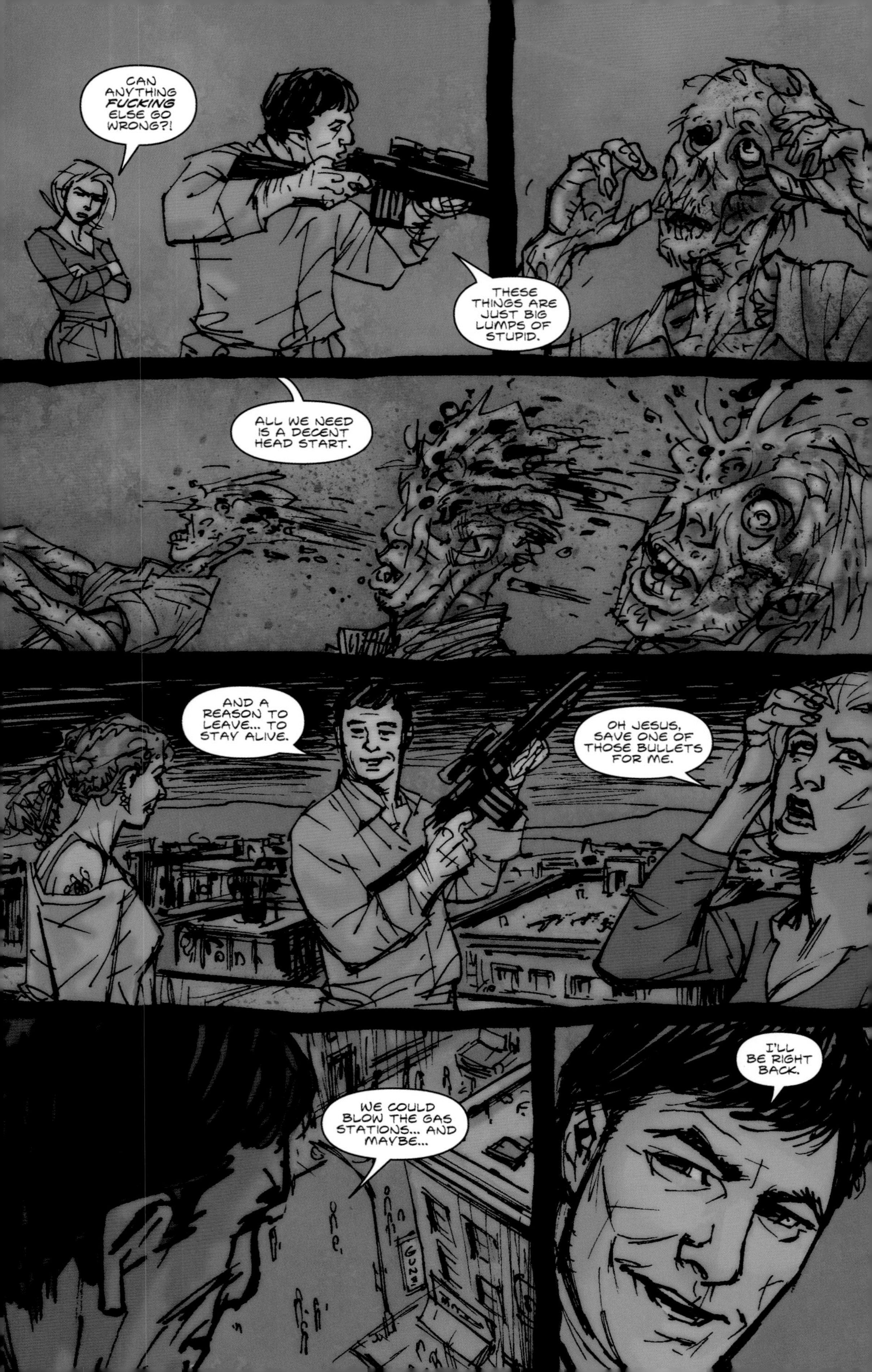
CAN ANYTHING *FUCKING* ELSE GO WRONG?!
THESE THINGS ARE JUST BIG LUMPS OF STUPID.
ALL WE NEED IS A DECENT HEAD START.
AND A REASON TO LEAVE... TO STAY ALIVE.
OH JESUS, SAVE ONE OF THOSE BULLETS FOR ME.
WE COULD BLOW THE GAS STATIONS... AND MAYBE...
I'LL BE RIGHT BACK.

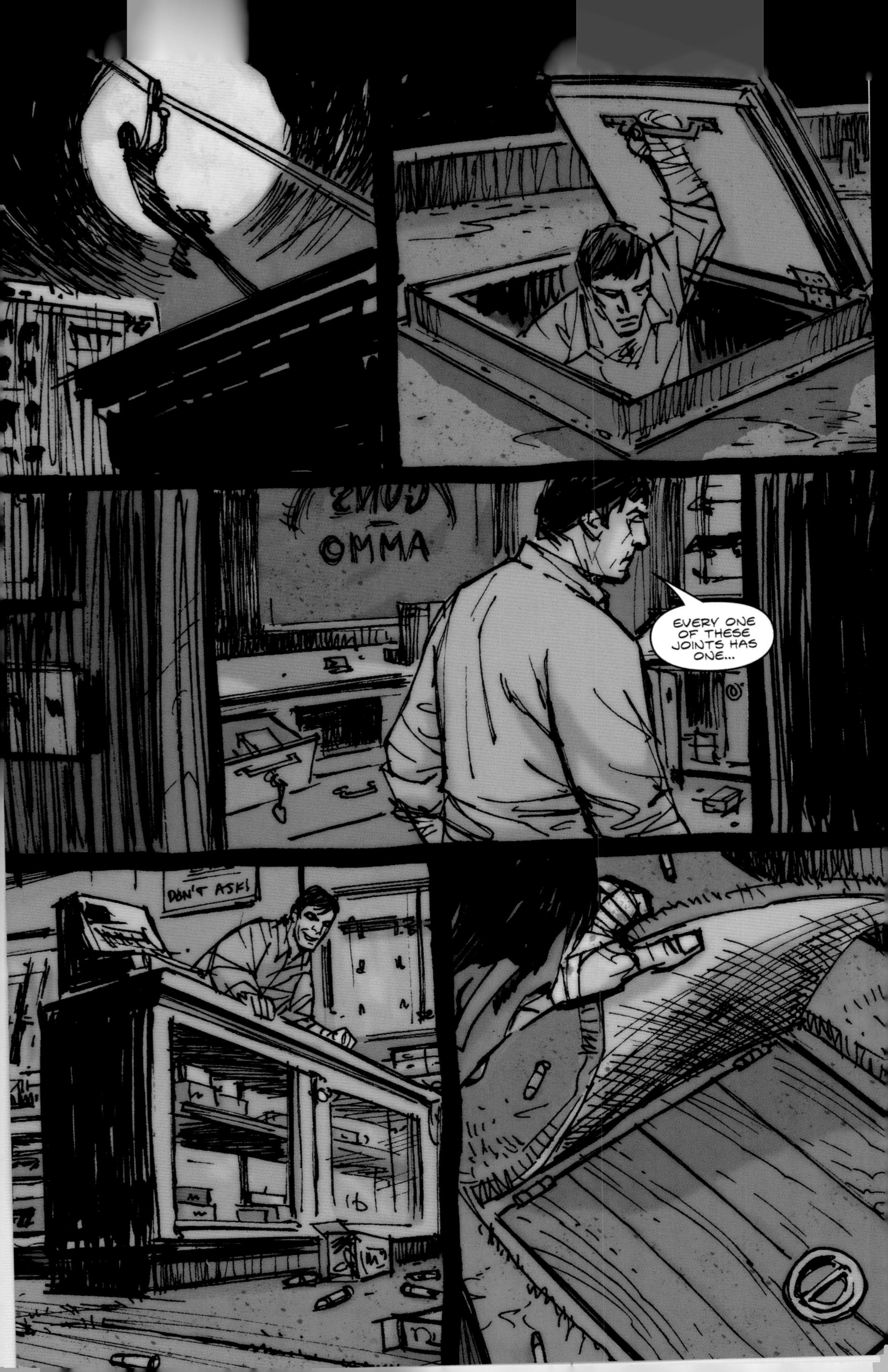
OMMA
EVERY ONE OF THESE JOINTS HAS ONE...
DON'T ASK!

5
chapte

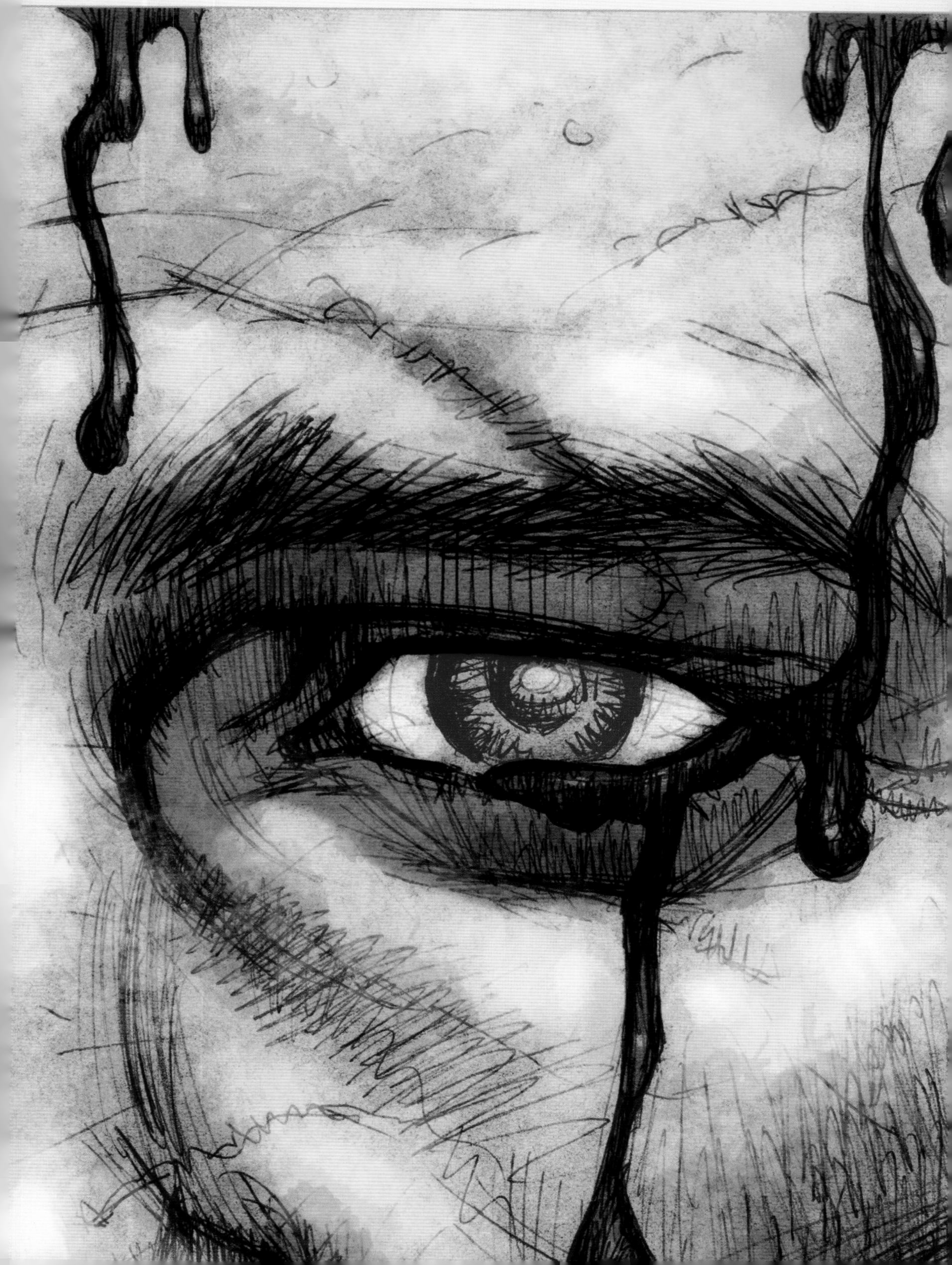

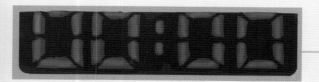

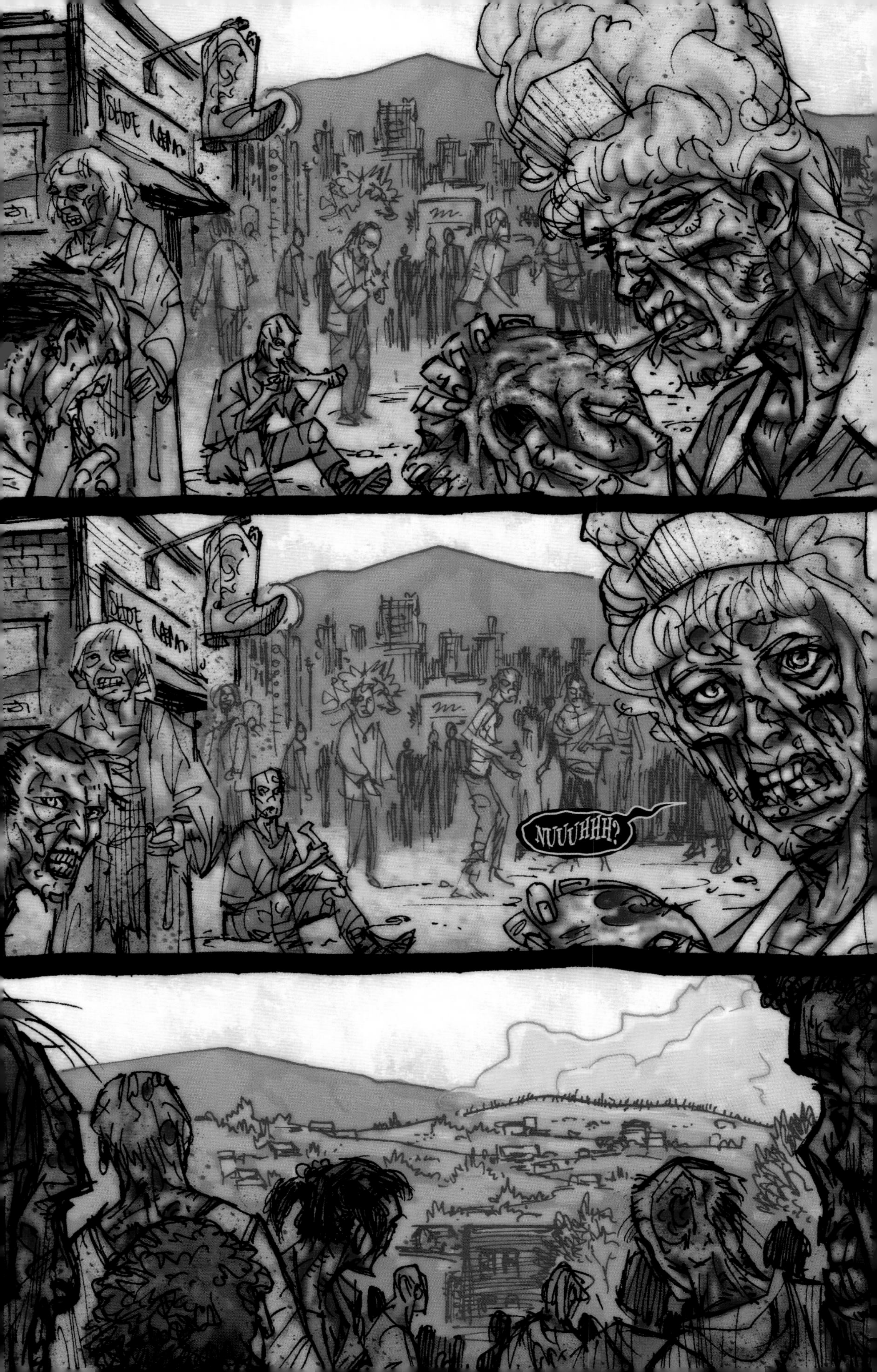
NUUUHHH?

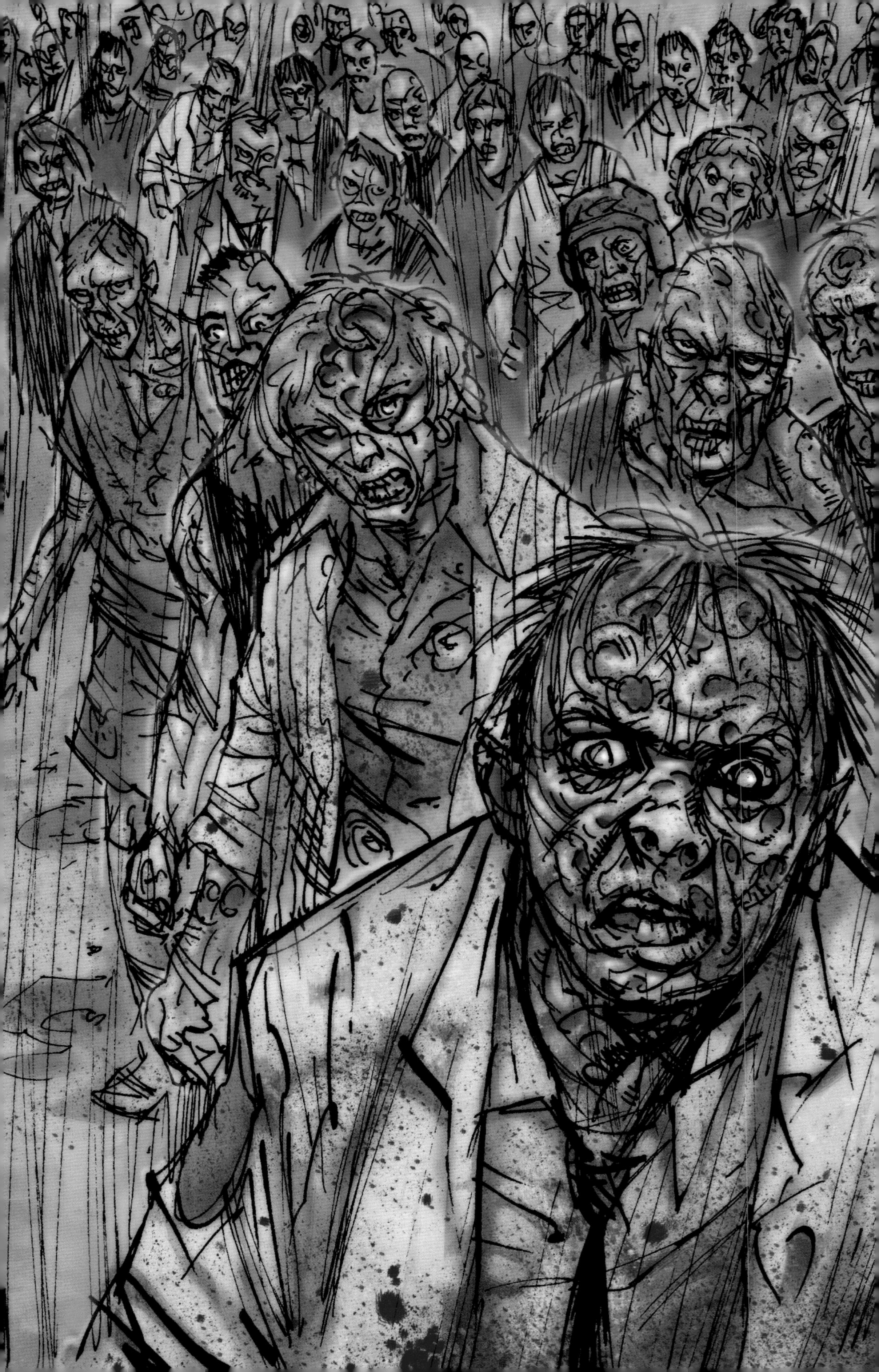

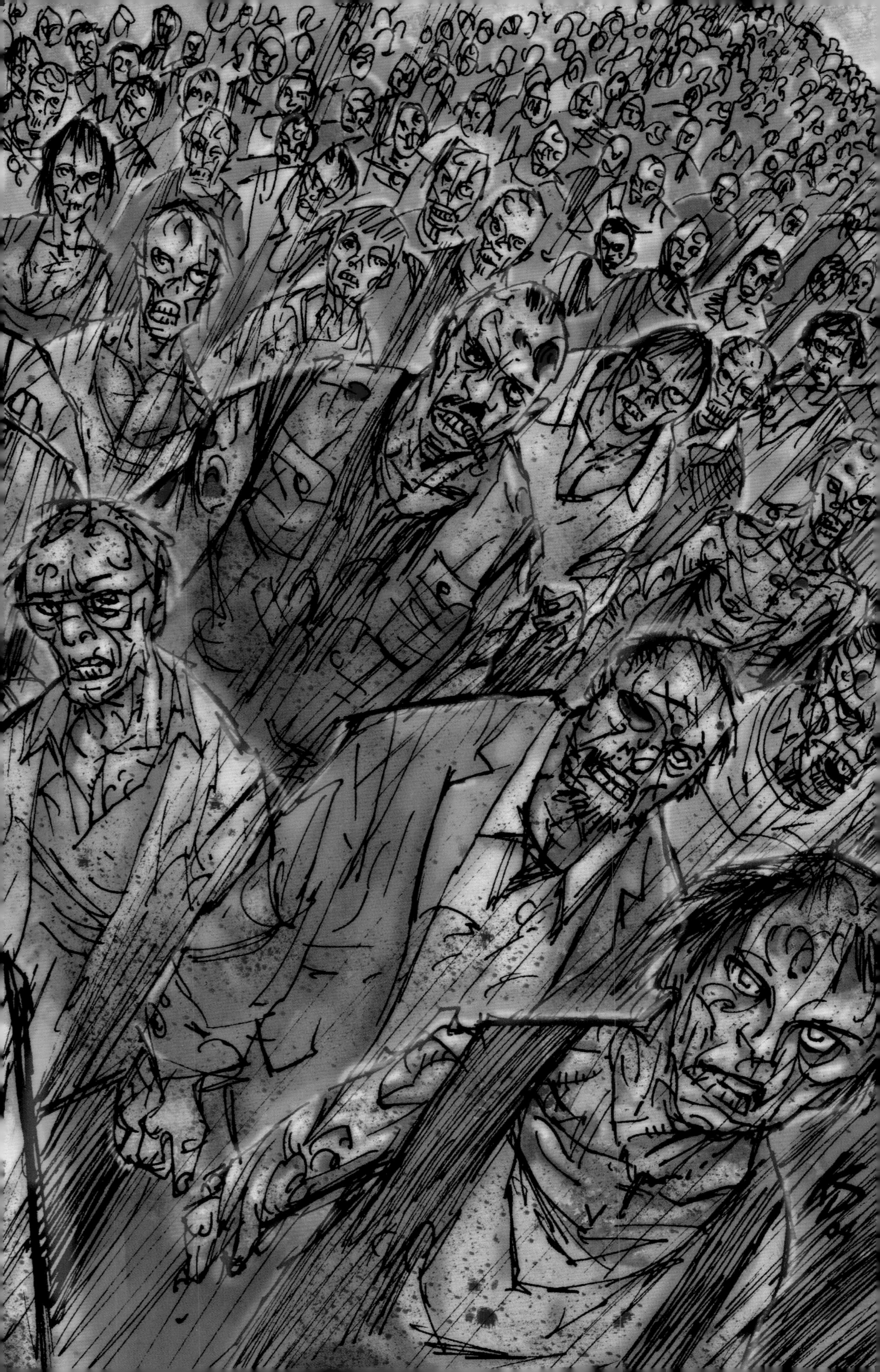

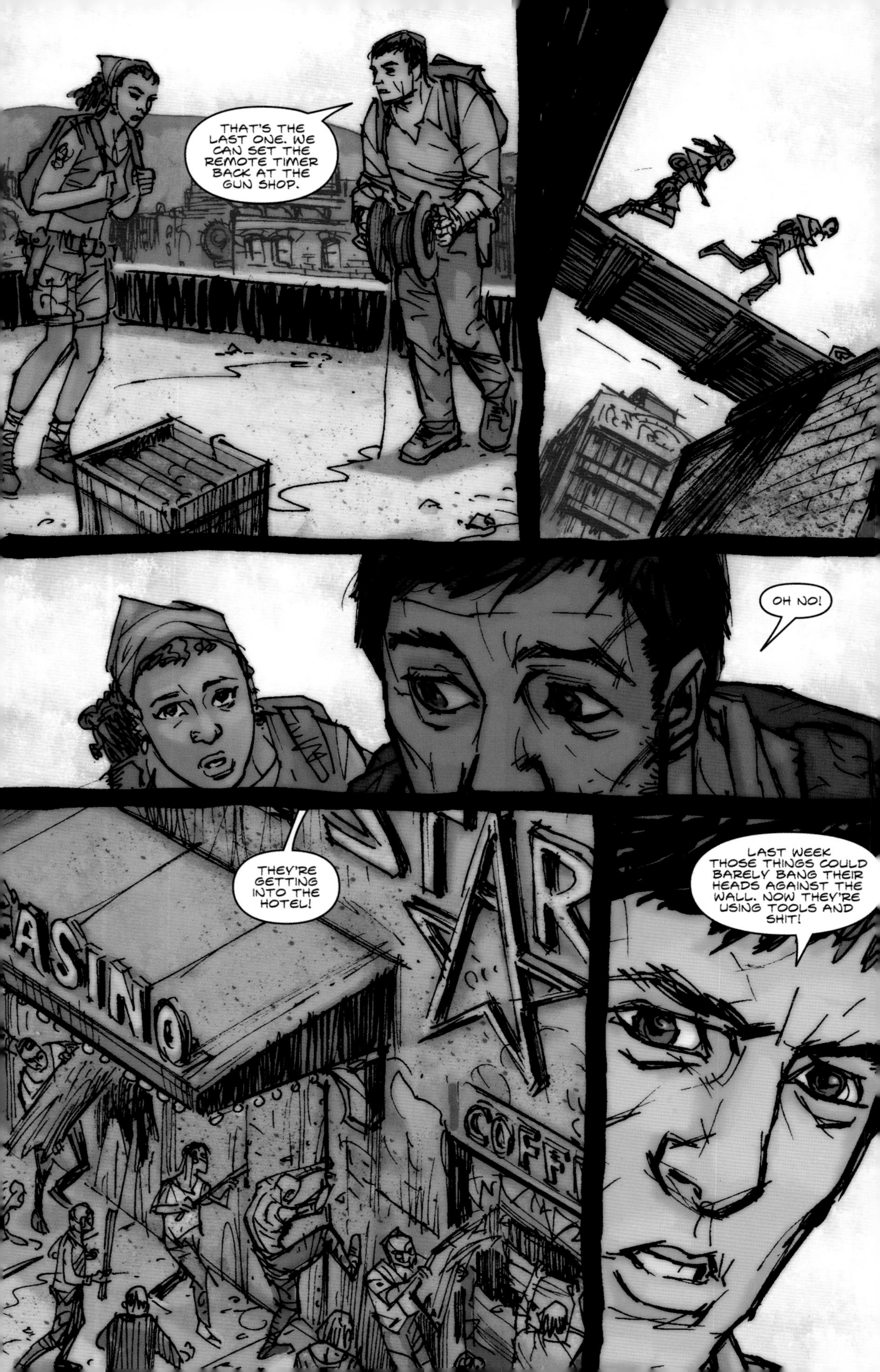
THAT'S THE LAST ONE. WE CAN SET THE REMOTE TIMER BACK AT THE GUN SHOP.
OH NO!
THEY'RE GETTING INTO THE HOTEL!
LAST WEEK THOSE THINGS COULD BARELY BANG THEIR HEADS AGAINST THE WALL. NOW THEY'RE USING TOOLS AND SHIT!
ASINO
COFF

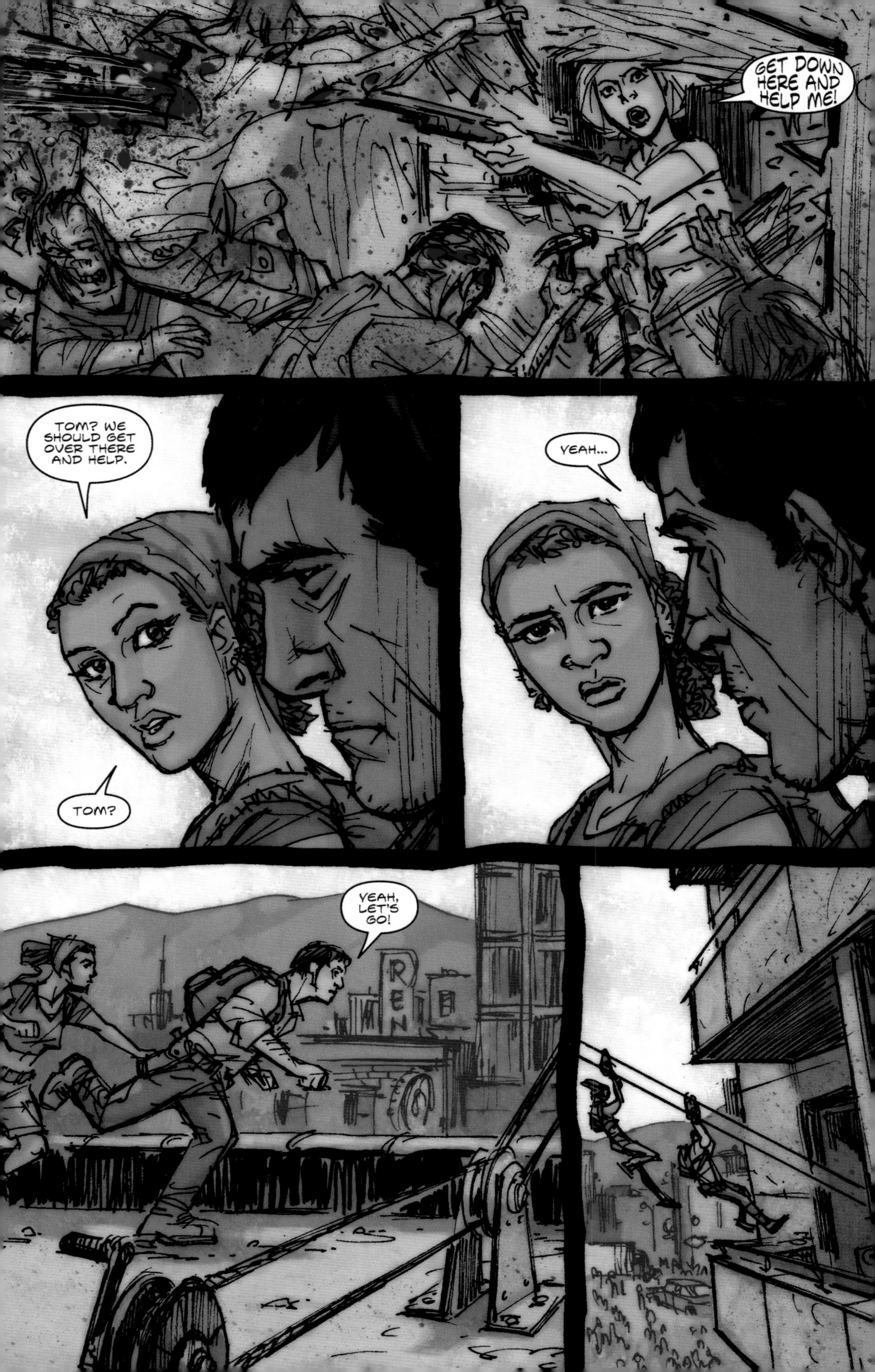
GET DOWN HERE AND HELP ME!
TOM? WE SHOULD GET OVER THERE AND HELP.
TOM?
YEAH...
YEAH, LET'S GO!
REN

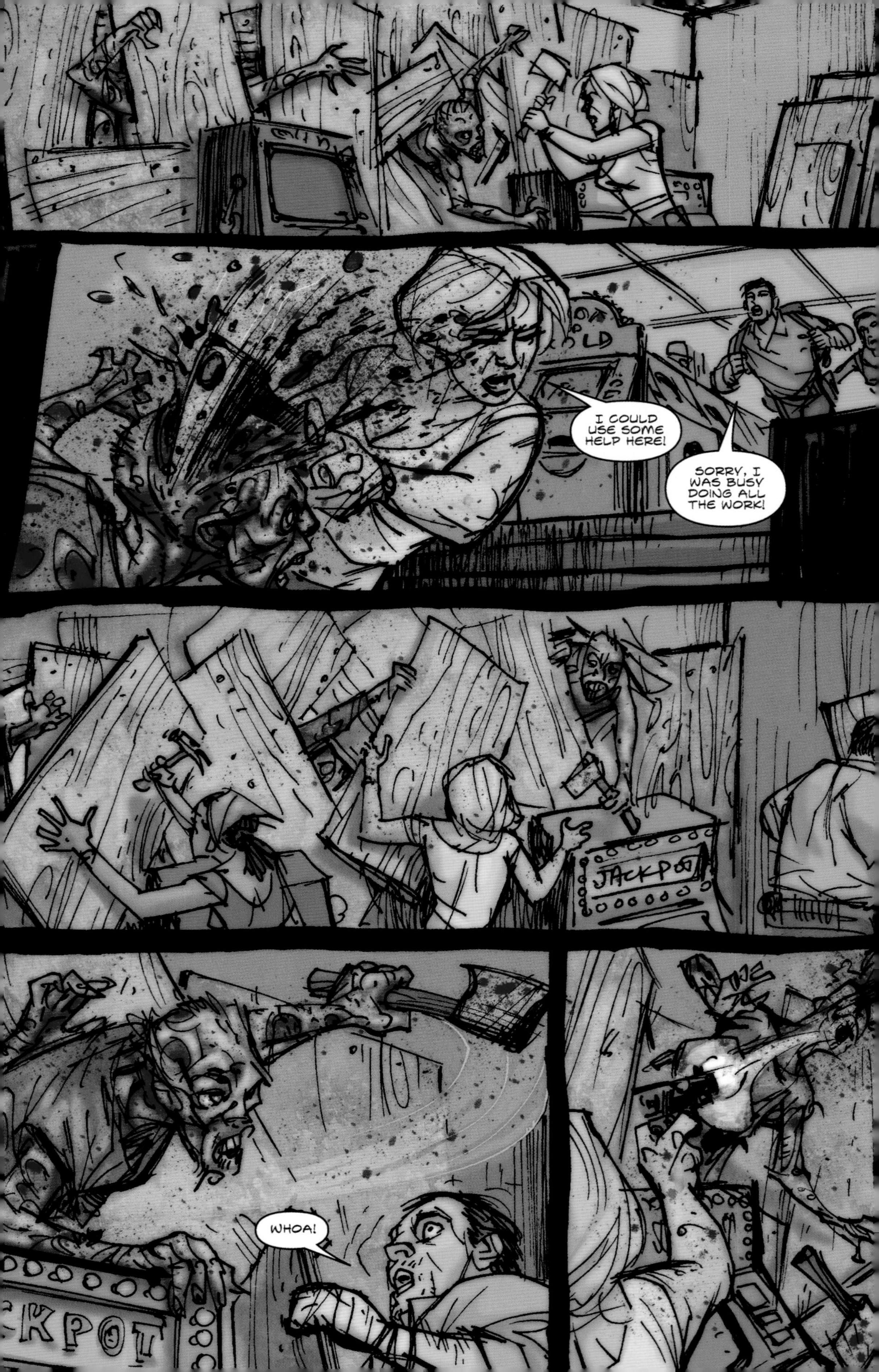
I COULD USE SOME HELP HERE!
SORRY, I WAS BUSY DOING ALL THE WORK!
JACKPOT
WHOA!
KPOT

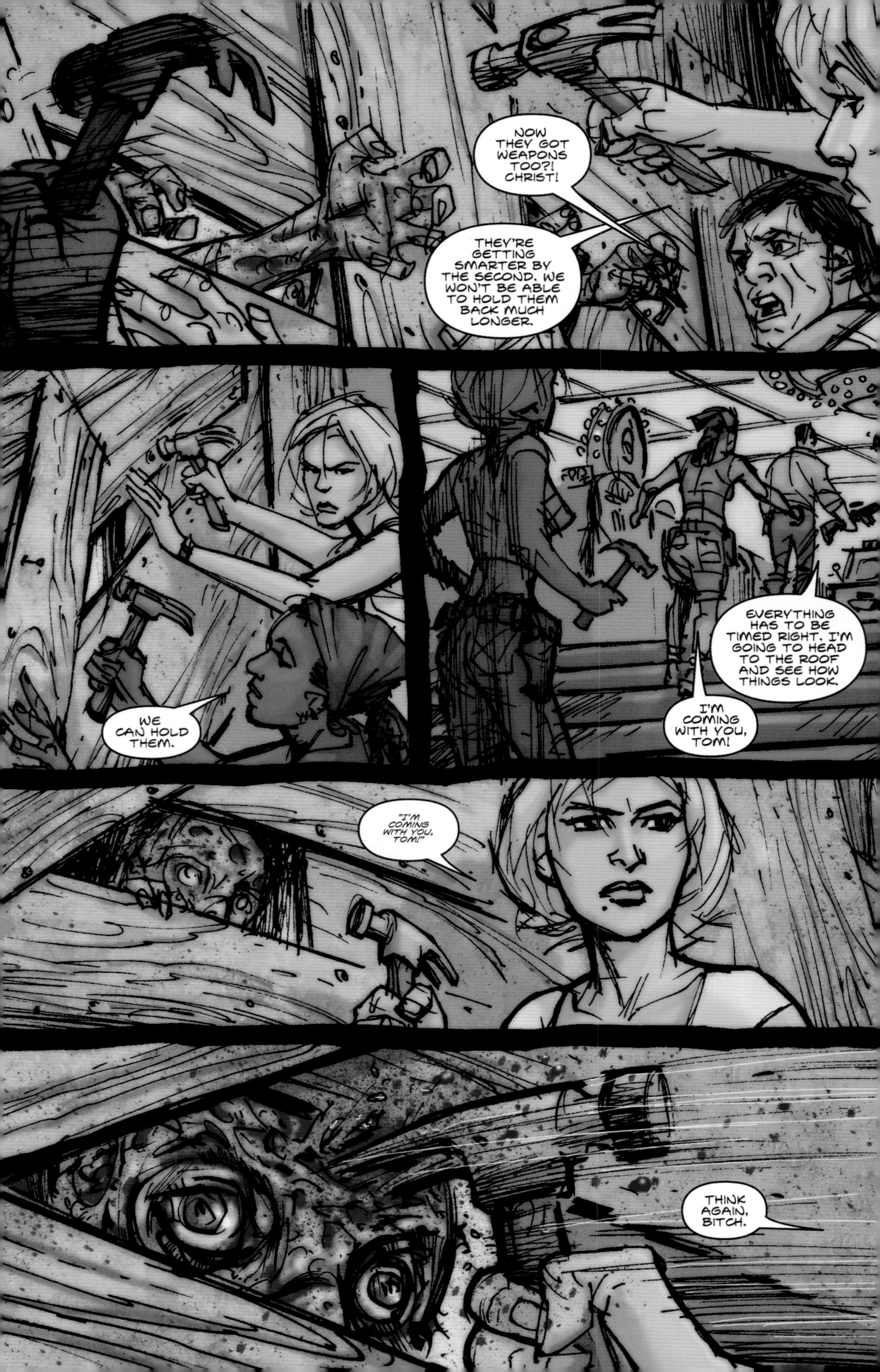
NOW THEY GOT WEAPONS TOO?! CHRIST!
THEY'RE GETTING SMARTER BY THE SECOND. WE WON'T BE ABLE TO HOLD THEM BACK MUCH LONGER.
WE CAN HOLD THEM.
EVERYTHING HAS TO BE TIMED RIGHT. I'M GOING TO HEAD TO THE ROOF AND SEE HOW THINGS LOOK.
I'M COMING WITH YOU, TOM!
"I'M COMING WITH YOU, TOM!"
THINK AGAIN, BITCH.

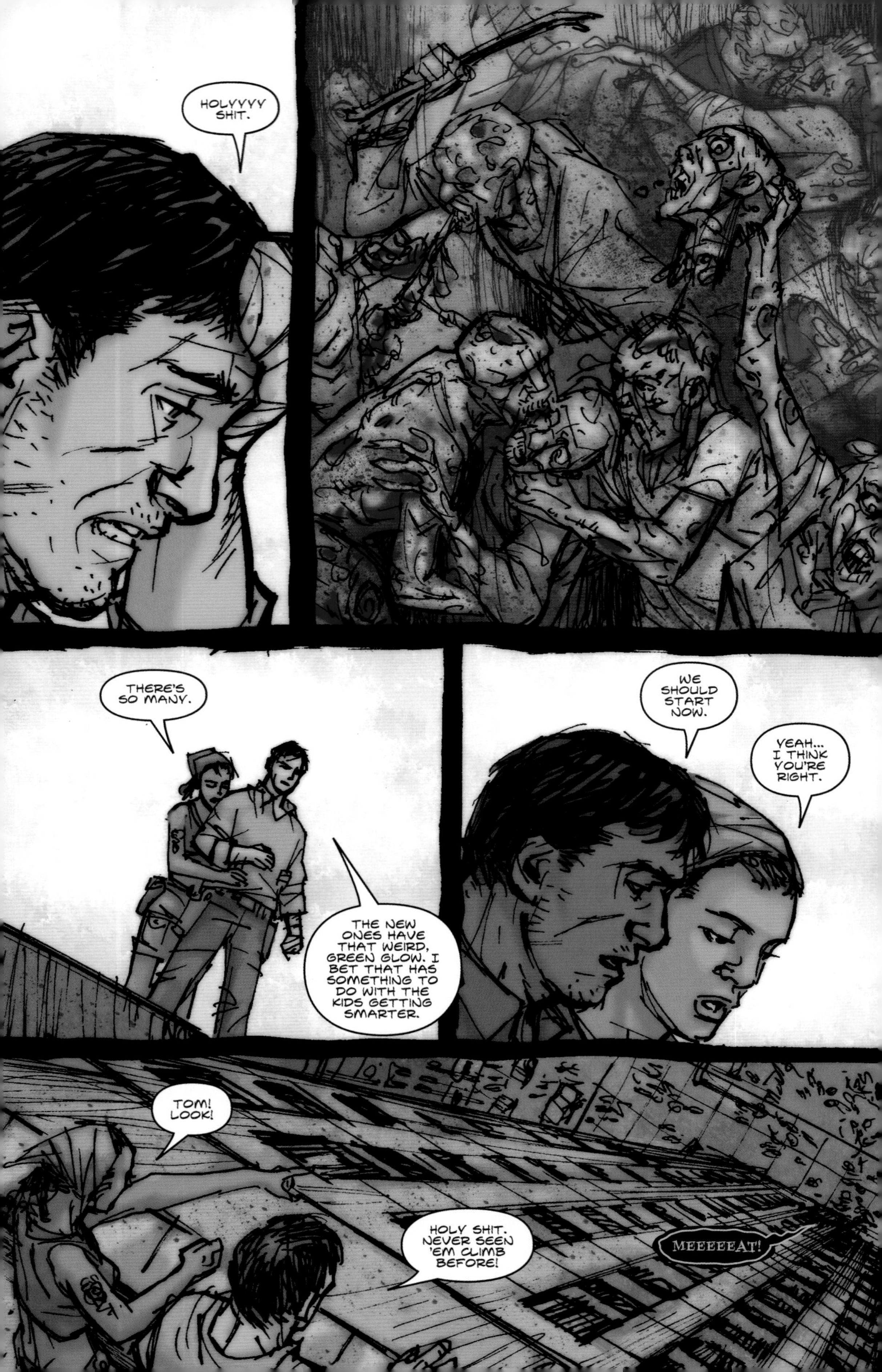
HOLYYYY SHIT.
THERE'S SO MANY.
THE NEW ONES HAVE THAT WEIRD, GREEN GLOW. I BET THAT HAS SOMETHING TO DO WITH THE KIDS GETTING SMARTER.
WE SHOULD START NOW.
YEAH... I THINK YOU'RE RIGHT.
TOM! LOOK!
HOLY SHIT. NEVER SEEN 'EM CLIMB BEFORE!
MEEEEEAT!

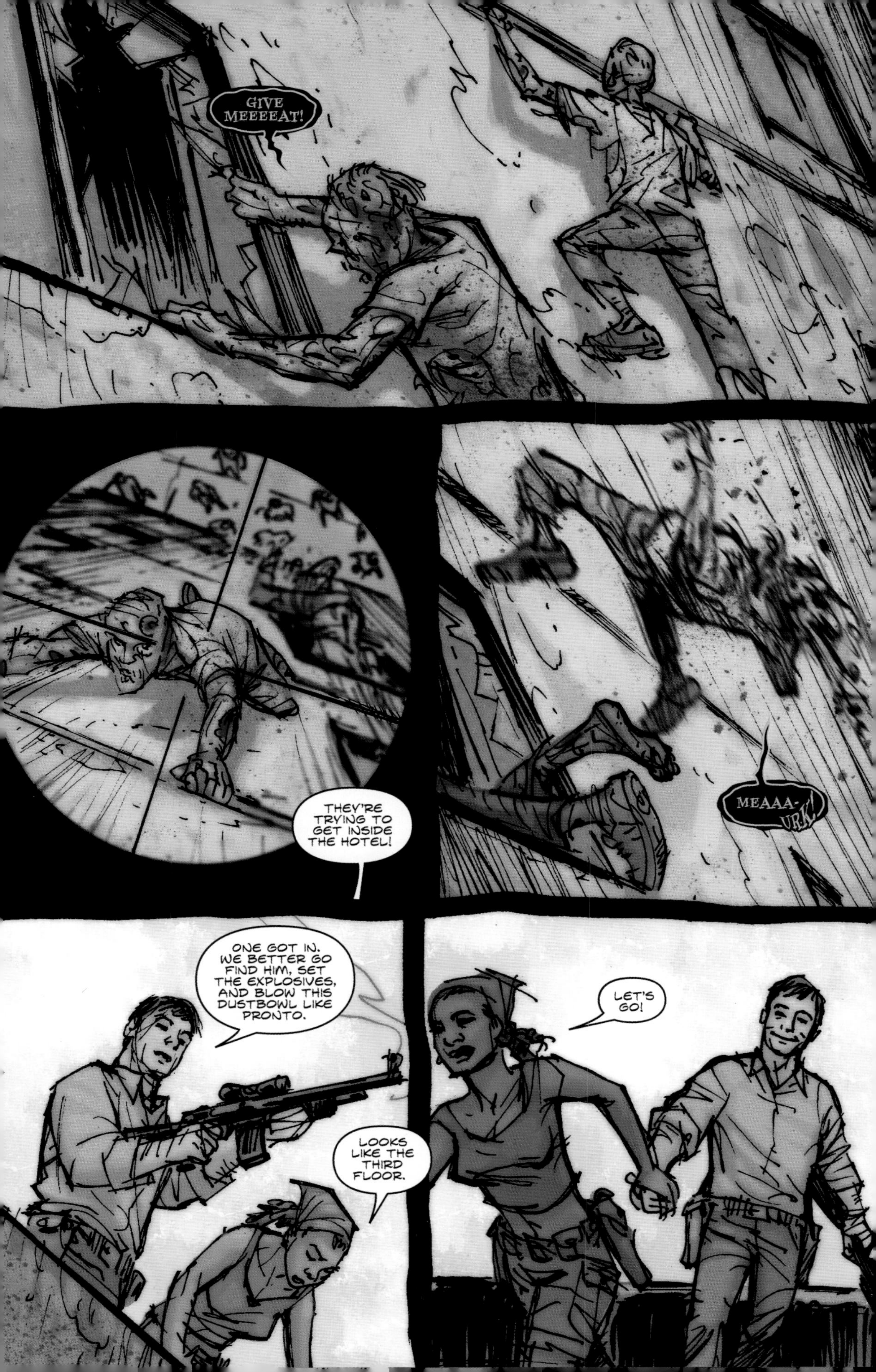
GIVE MEEEEAT!
THEY'RE TRYING TO GET INSIDE THE HOTEL!
MEAAA-URK!
ONE GOT IN. WE BETTER GO FIND HIM, SET THE EXPLOSIVES, AND BLOW THIS DUSTBOWL LIKE PRONTO.
LOOKS LIKE THE THIRD FLOOR.
LET'S GO!

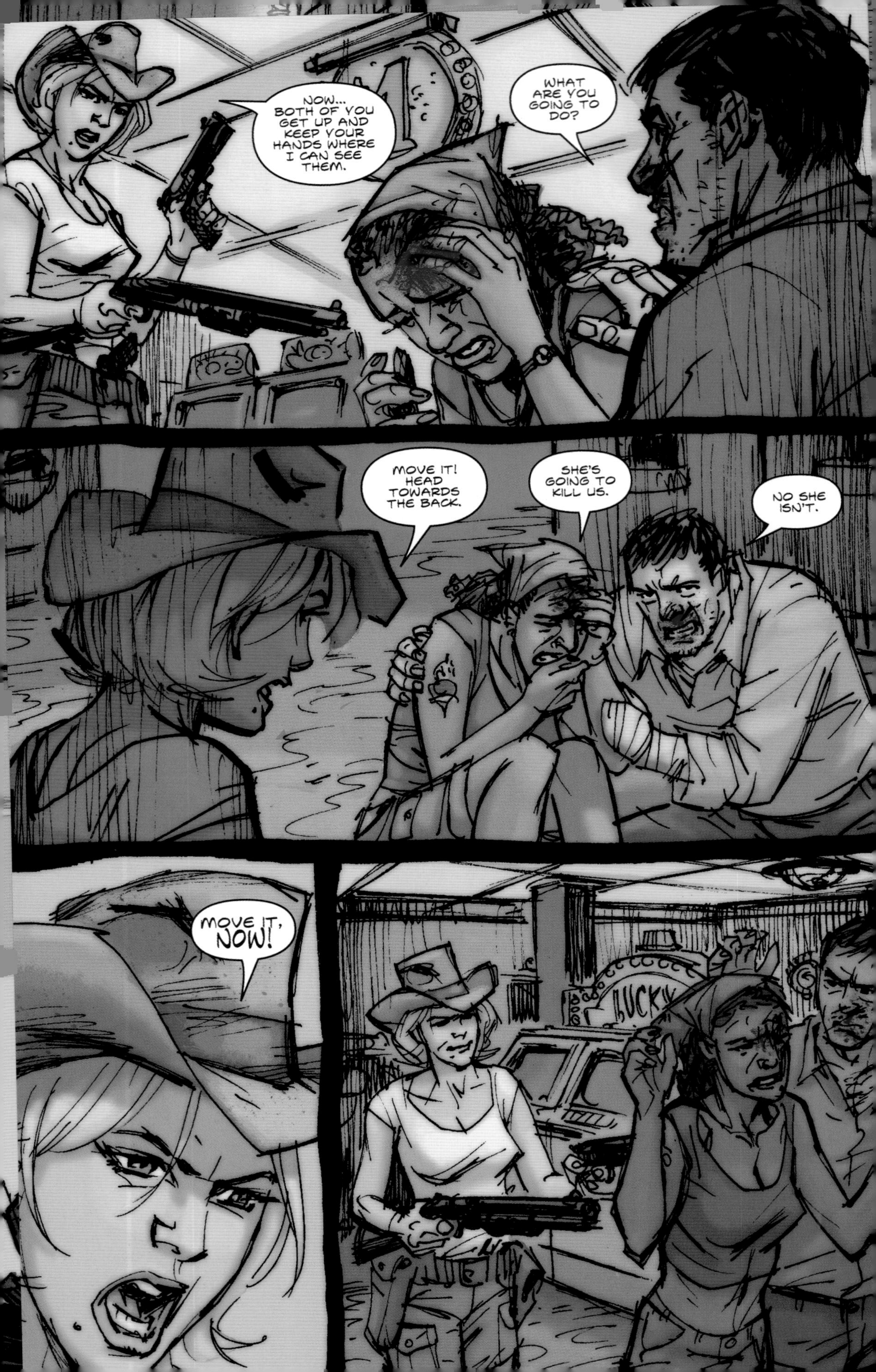
NOW... BOTH OF YOU GET UP AND KEEP YOUR HANDS WHERE I CAN SEE THEM.
WHAT ARE YOU GOING TO DO?
MOVE IT! HEAD TOWARDS THE BACK.
SHE'S GOING TO KILL US.
NO SHE ISN'T.
MOVE IT, NOW!
LUCKY

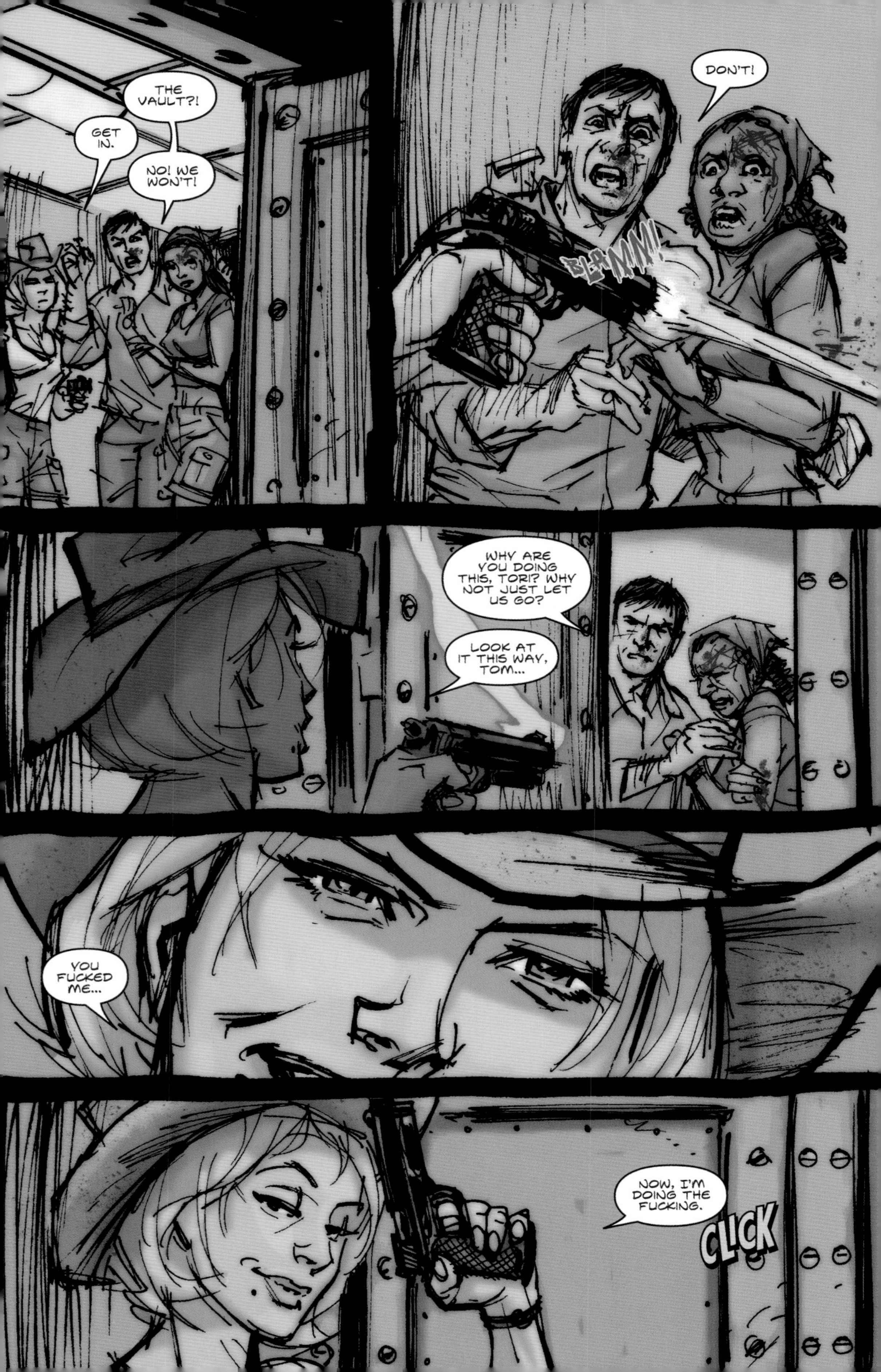
GET IN.
THE VAULT?!
NO! WE WON'T!
DON'T!
BLAMM!
WHY ARE YOU DOING THIS, TORI? WHY NOT JUST LET US GO?
LOOK AT IT THIS WAY, TOM...
YOU FUCKED ME...
NOW, I'M DOING THE FUCKING.
CLICK

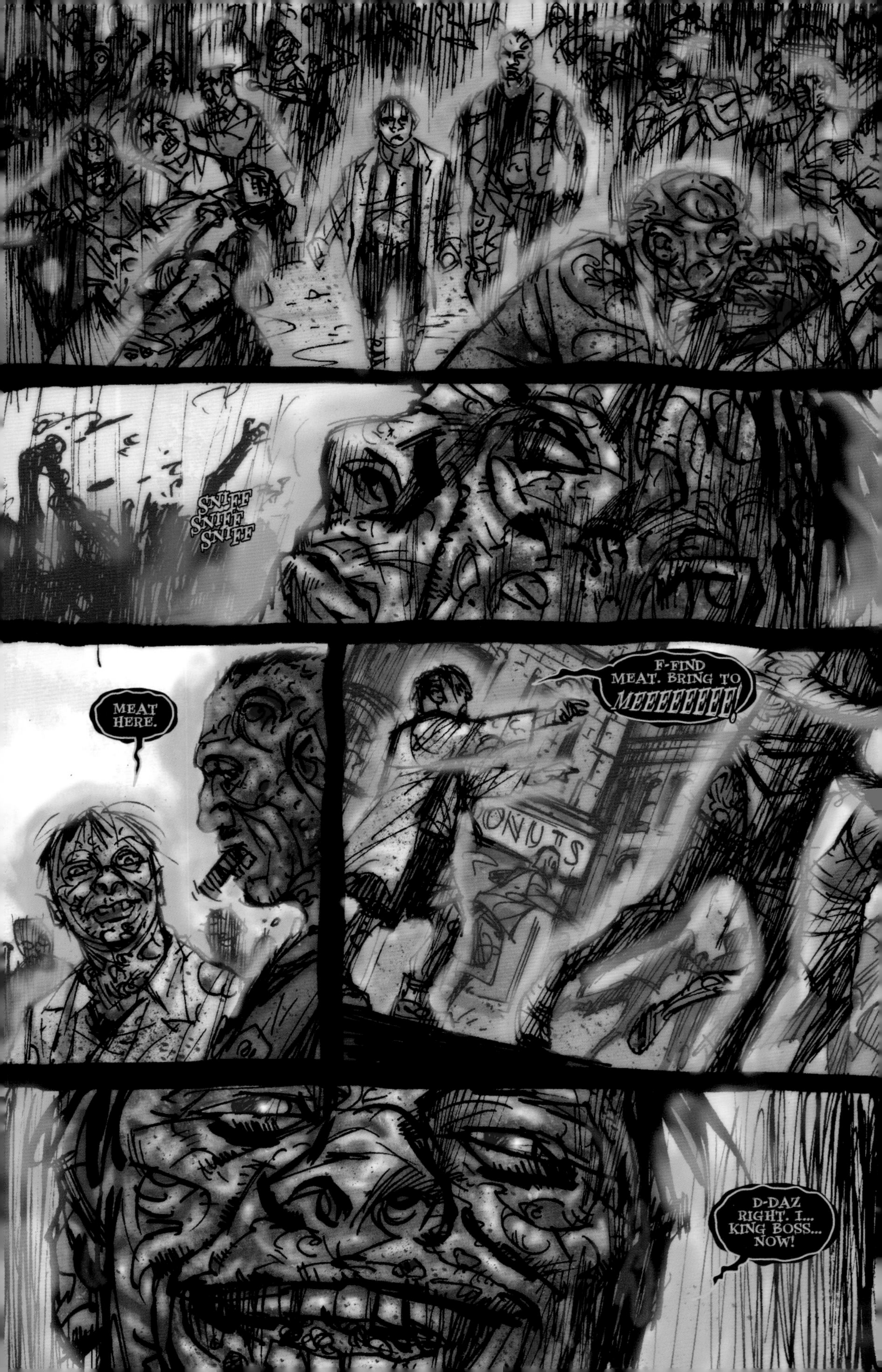
SNIFF
SNIFF
SNIFF
MEAT HERE.
F-FIND MEAT. BRING TO MEEEEEEEE!
ONUTS
D-DAZ RIGHT. I... KING BOSS... NOW!

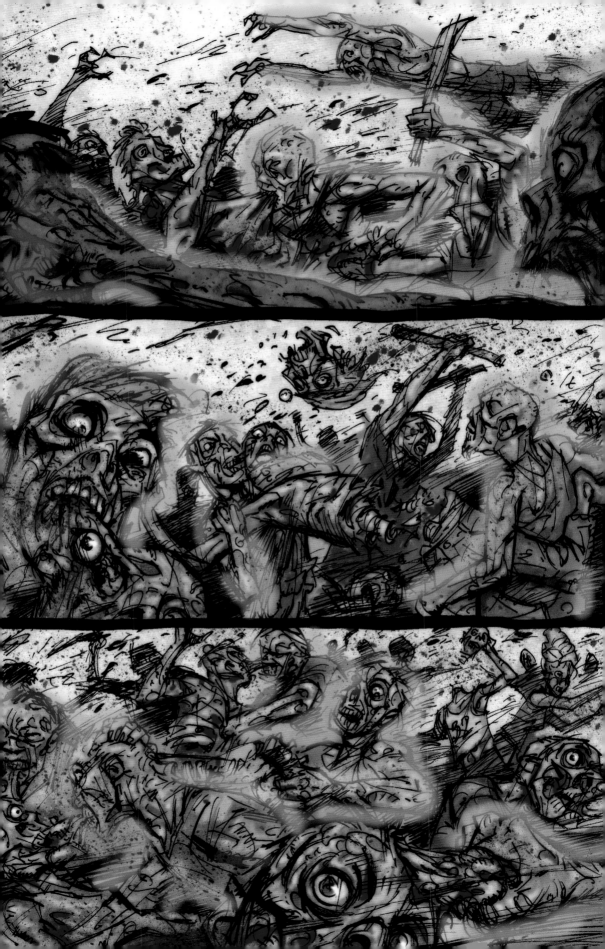

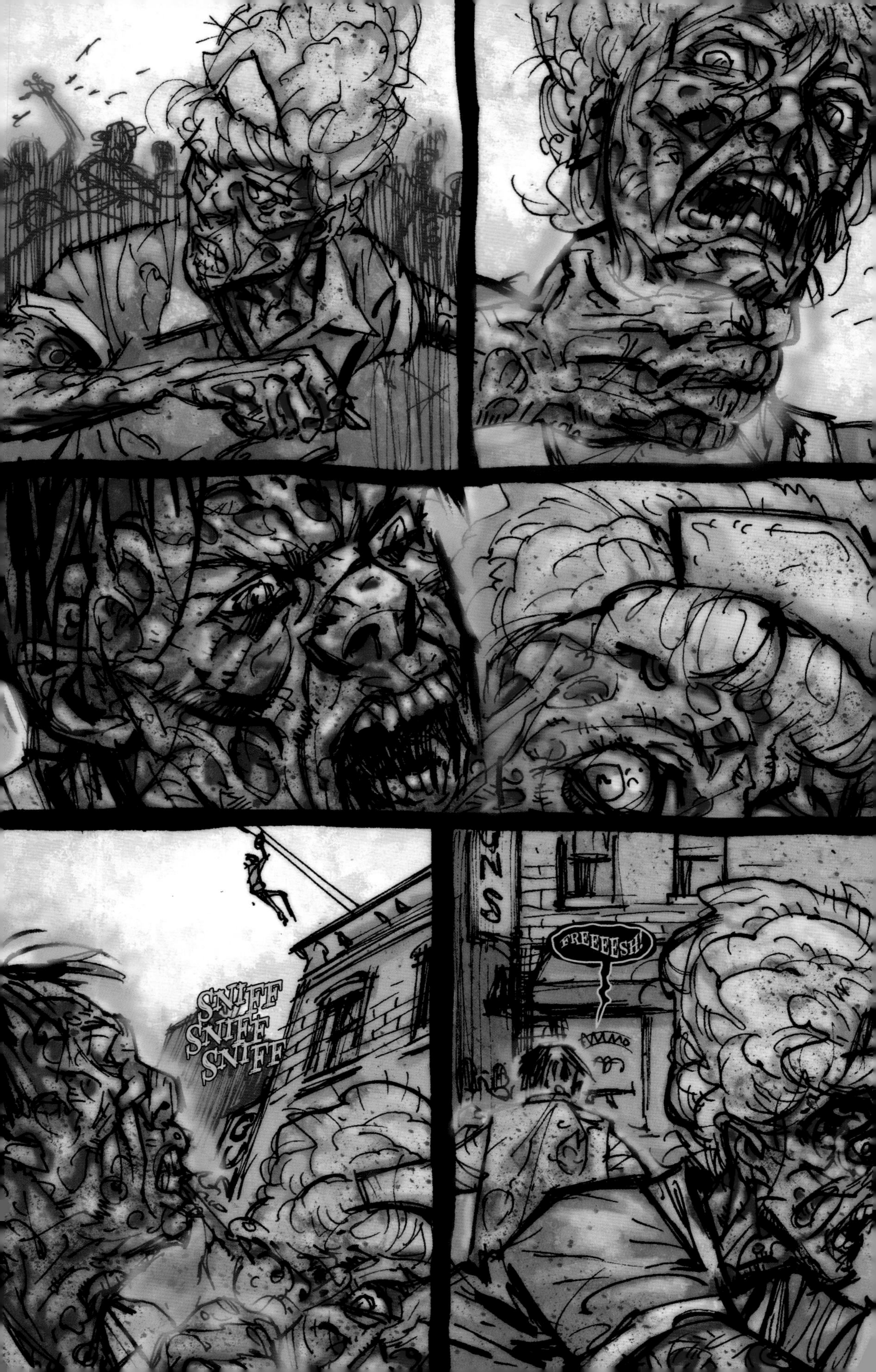
SNIFF
SNIFF
SNIFF
FREEEESH!

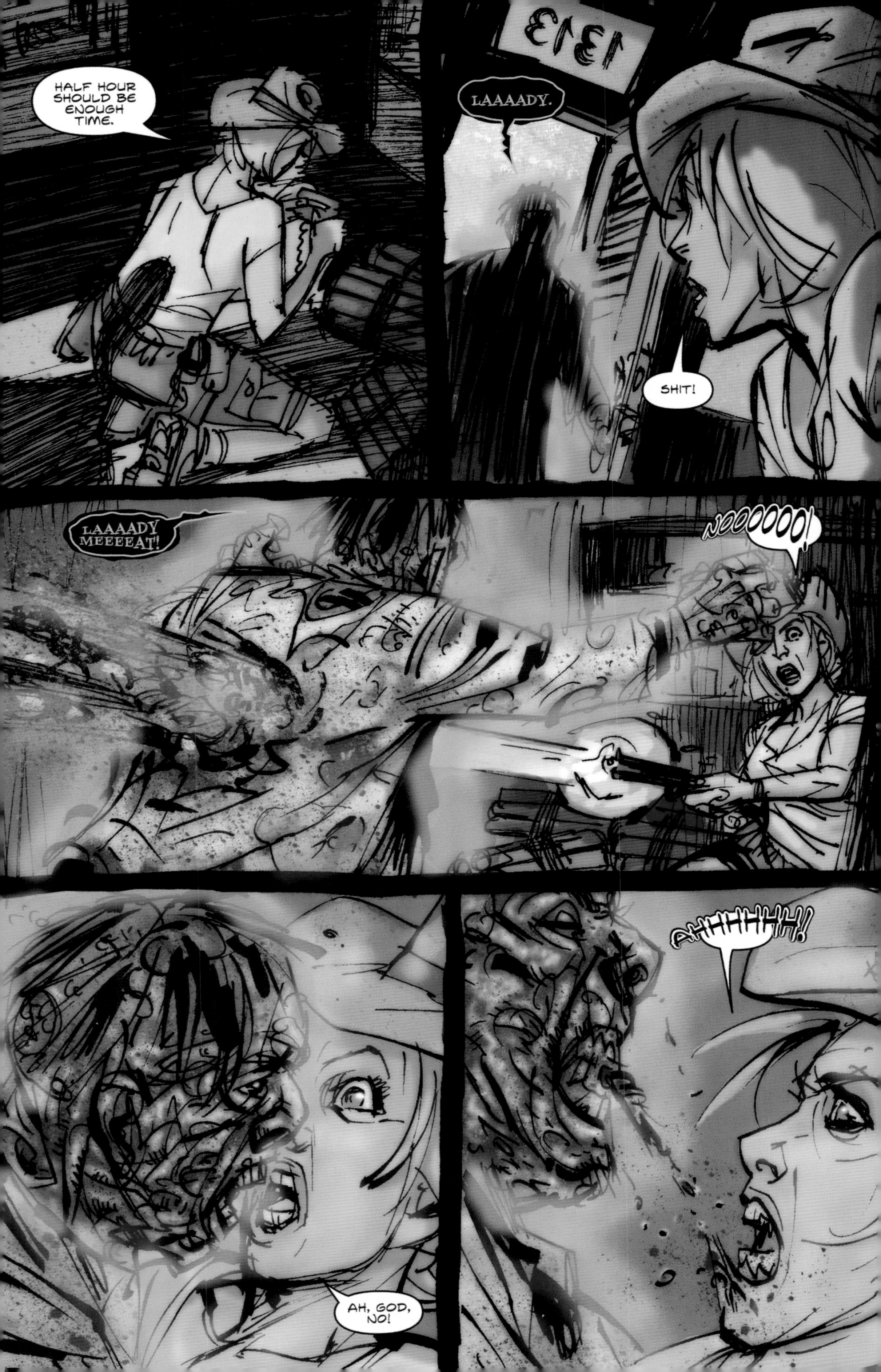
1313
HALF HOUR SHOULD BE ENOUGH TIME.
LAAAADY.
SHIT!
LAAAADY MEEEEAT!
NOOOOOO!
AH, GOD, NO!
AHHHHHH!

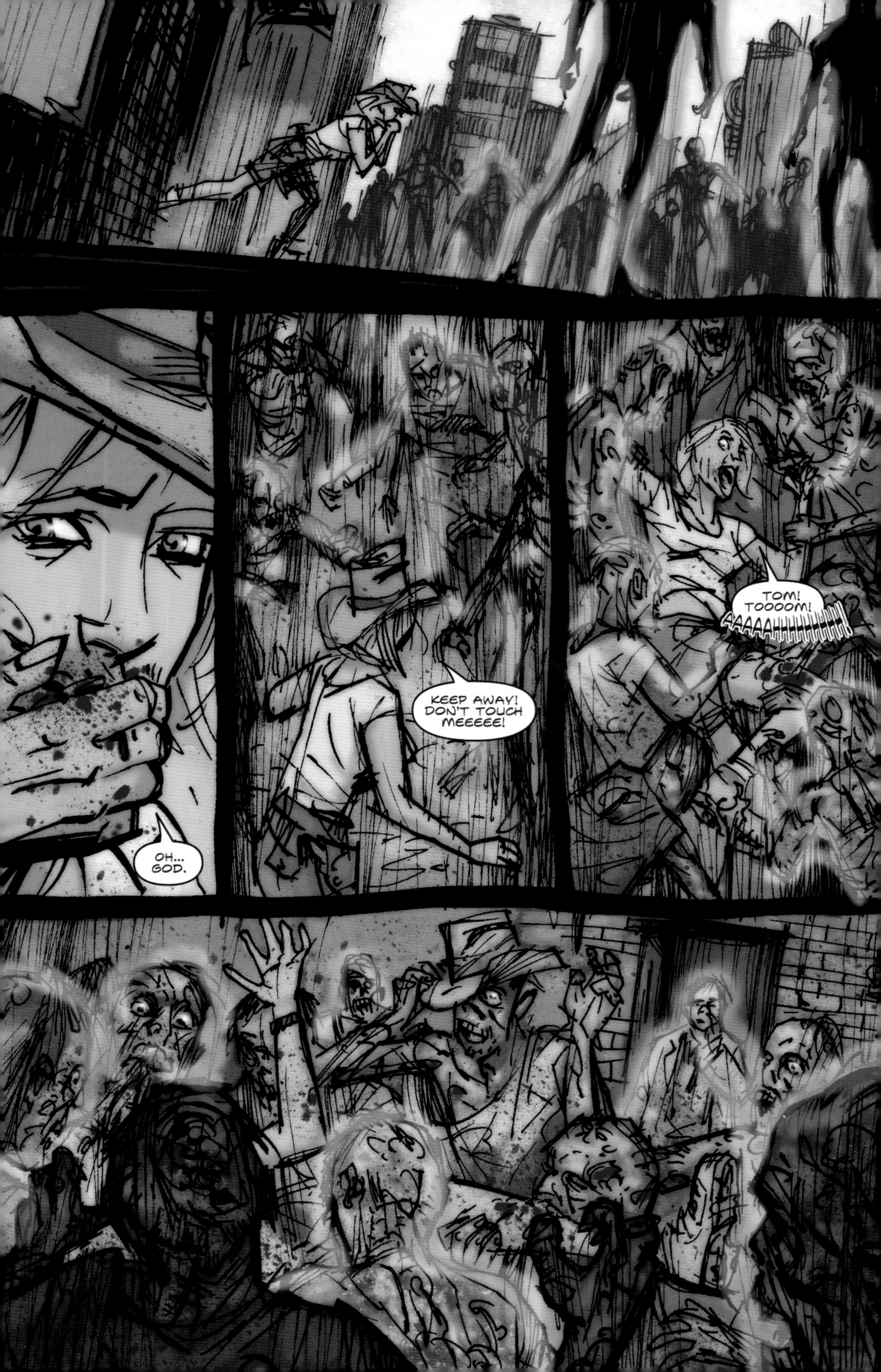
OH... GOD.
KEEP AWAY! DON'T TOUCH MEEEEE!
TOM! TOOOOM!
AAAAAHHHHHHHHH

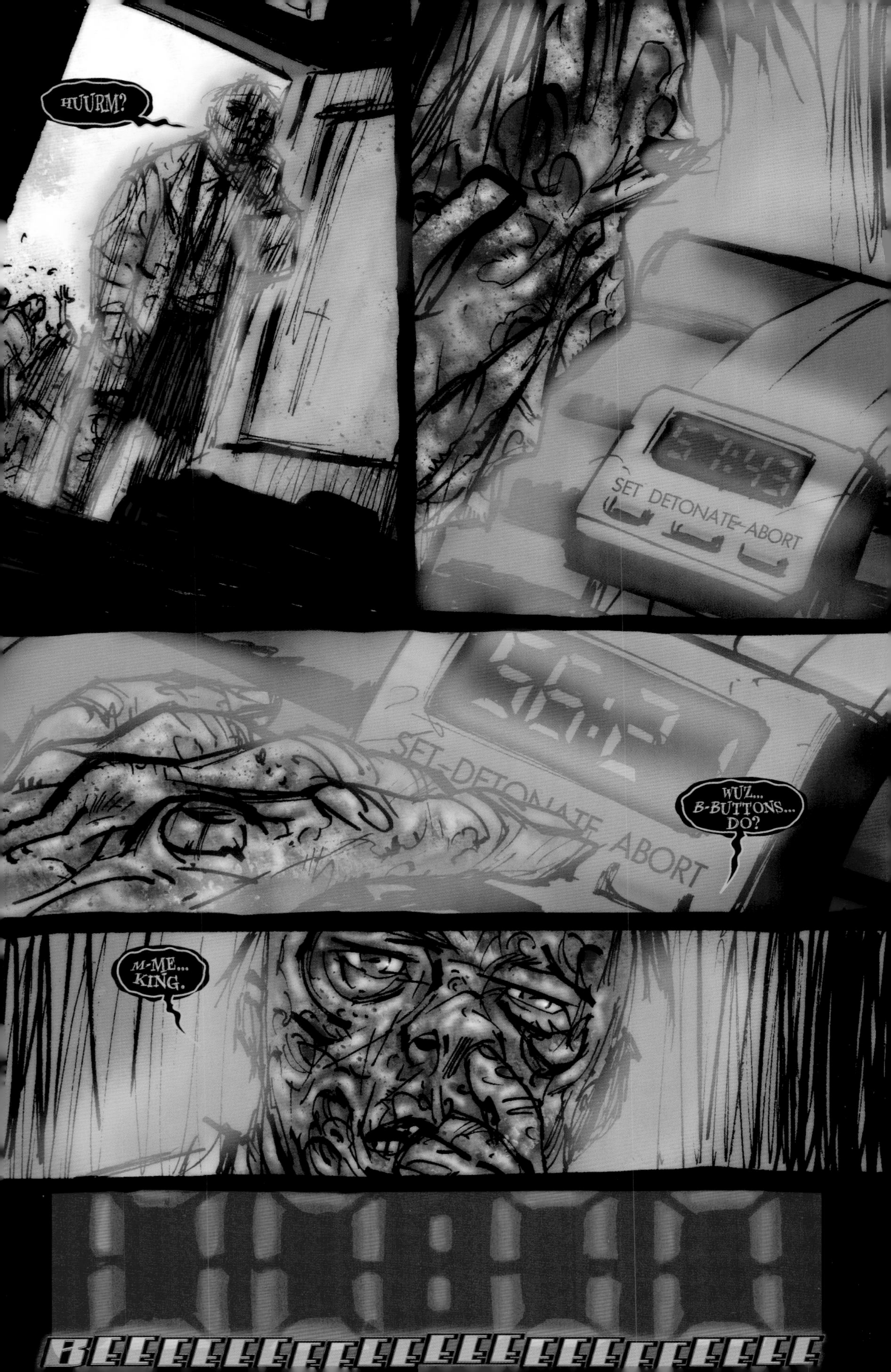

HUURM?
SET DETONATE ABORT
SET DETONATE ABORT
WUZ... B-BUTTONS... DO?
M-ME... KING.
BEEEEEEEEEEEEEEEEEEEEEEEEEEE

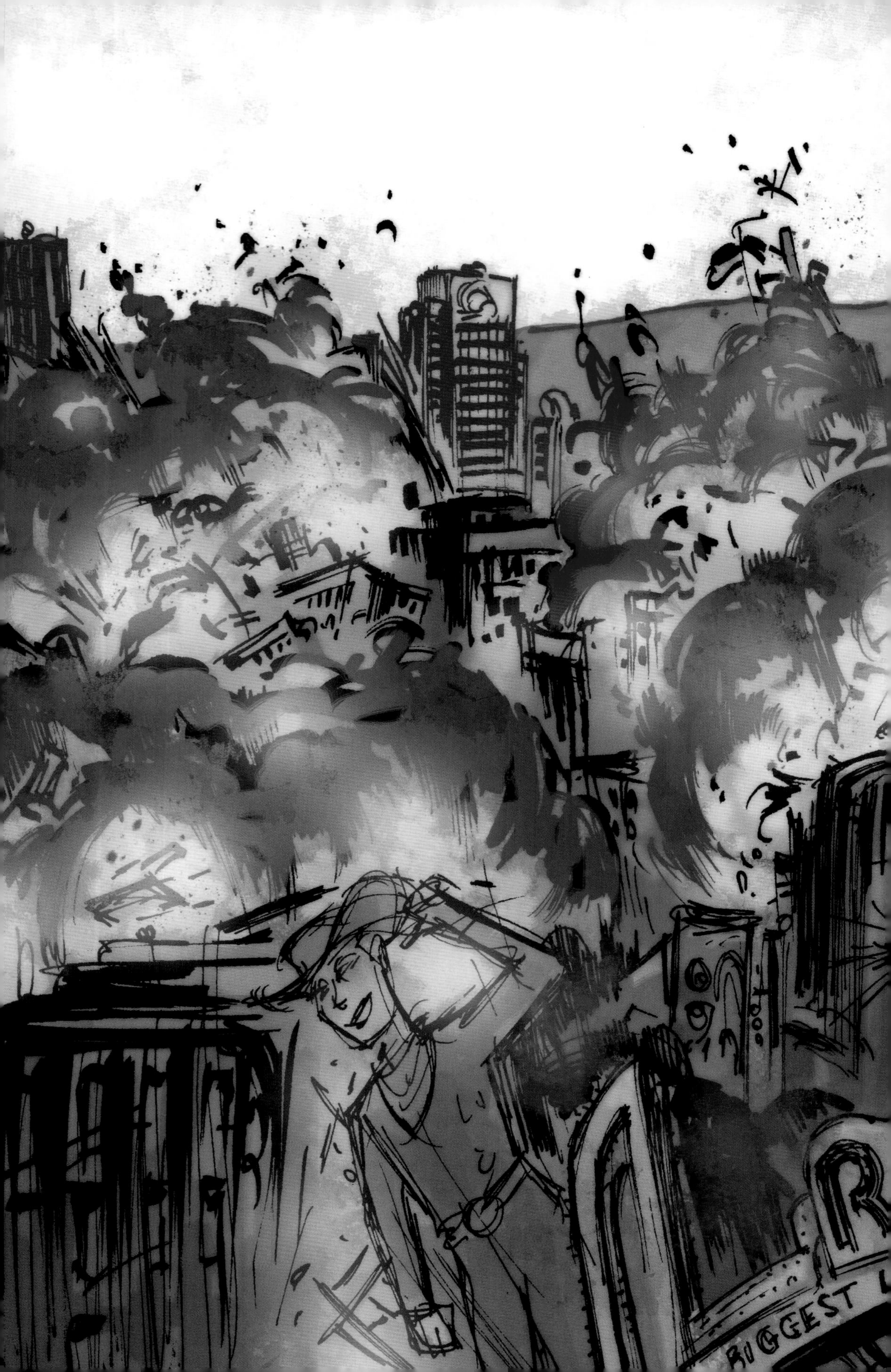
BIGGEST

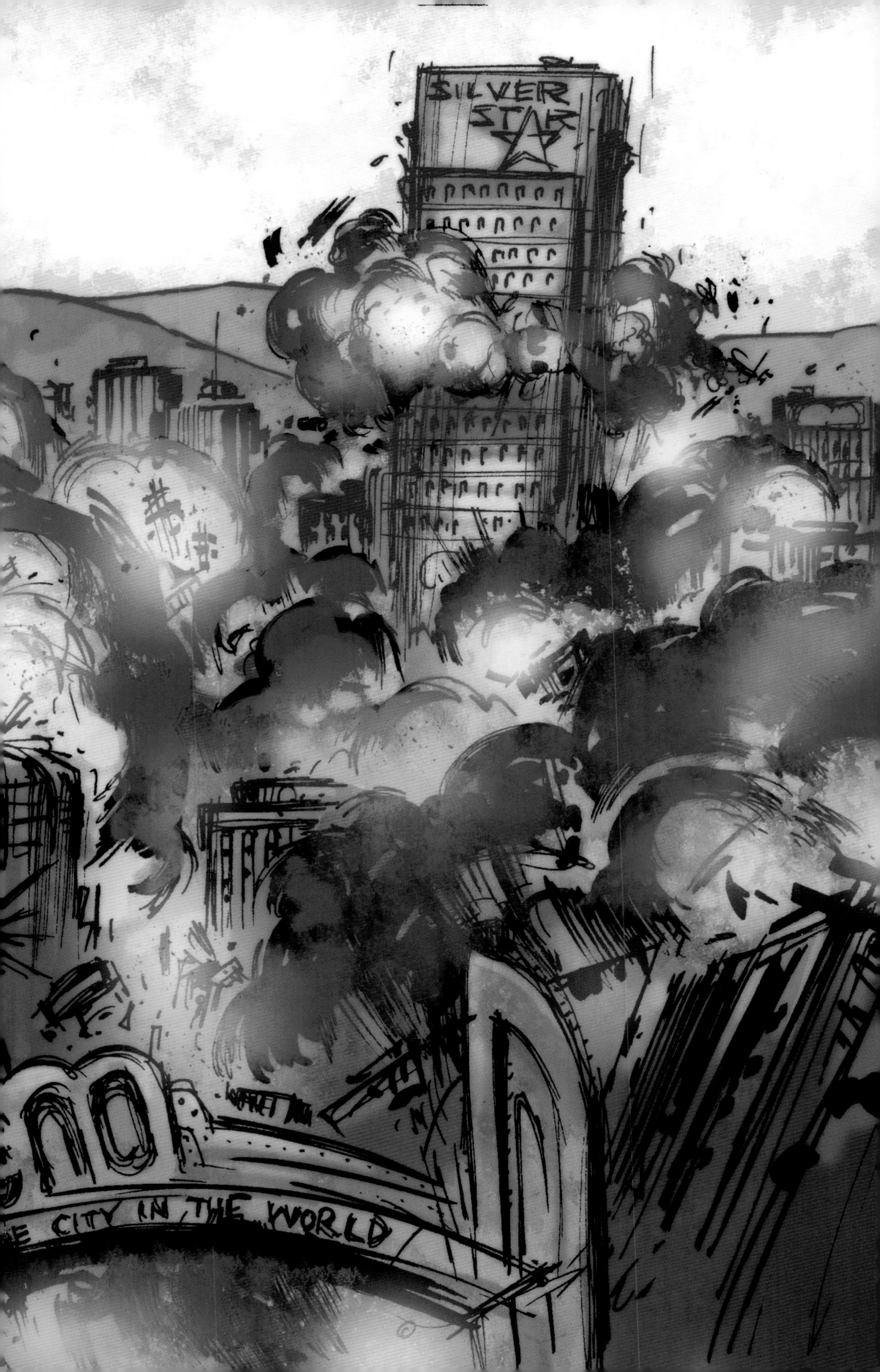
SILVER STAR
CITY IN THE WORLD

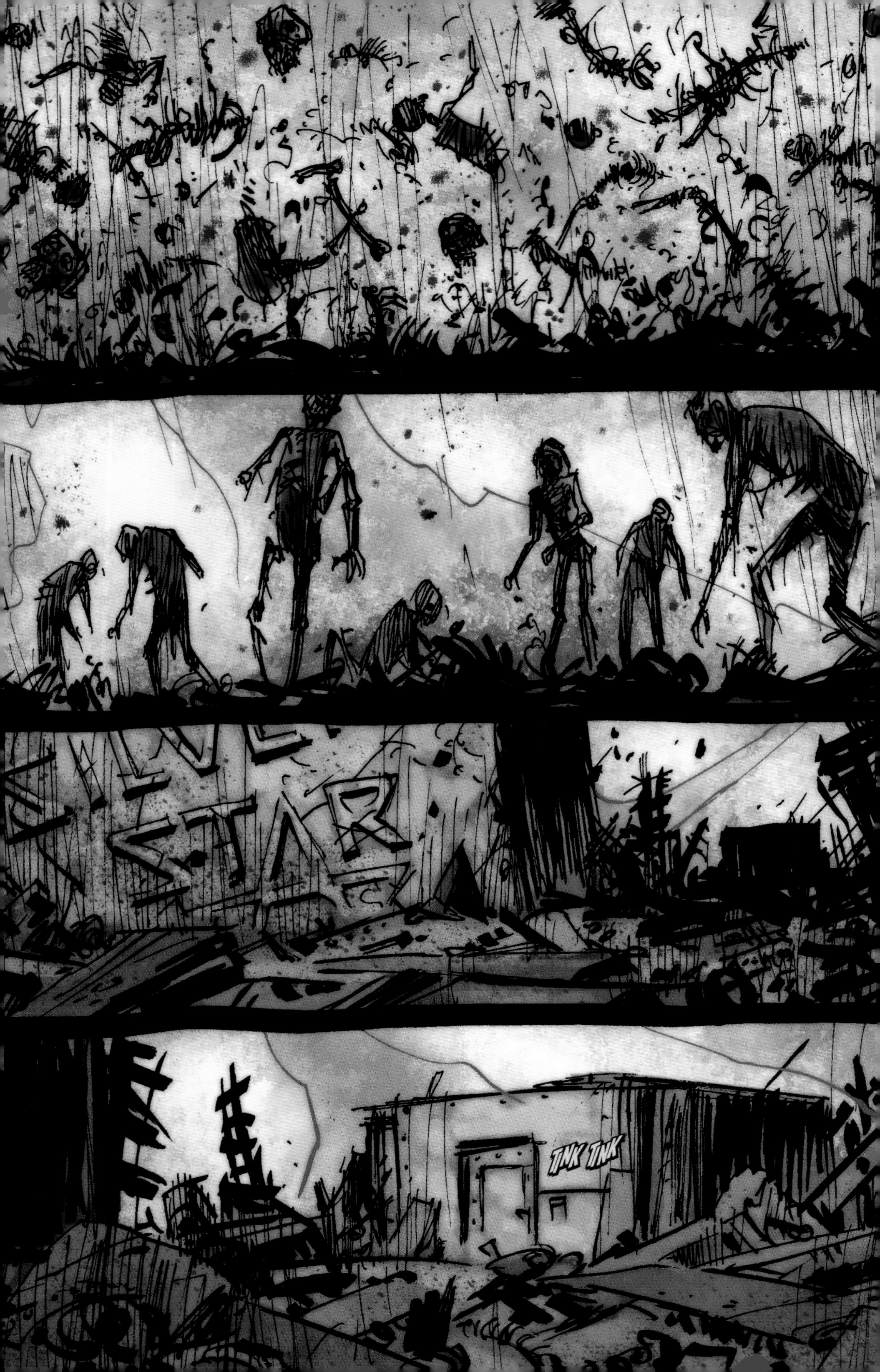
TINK TINK

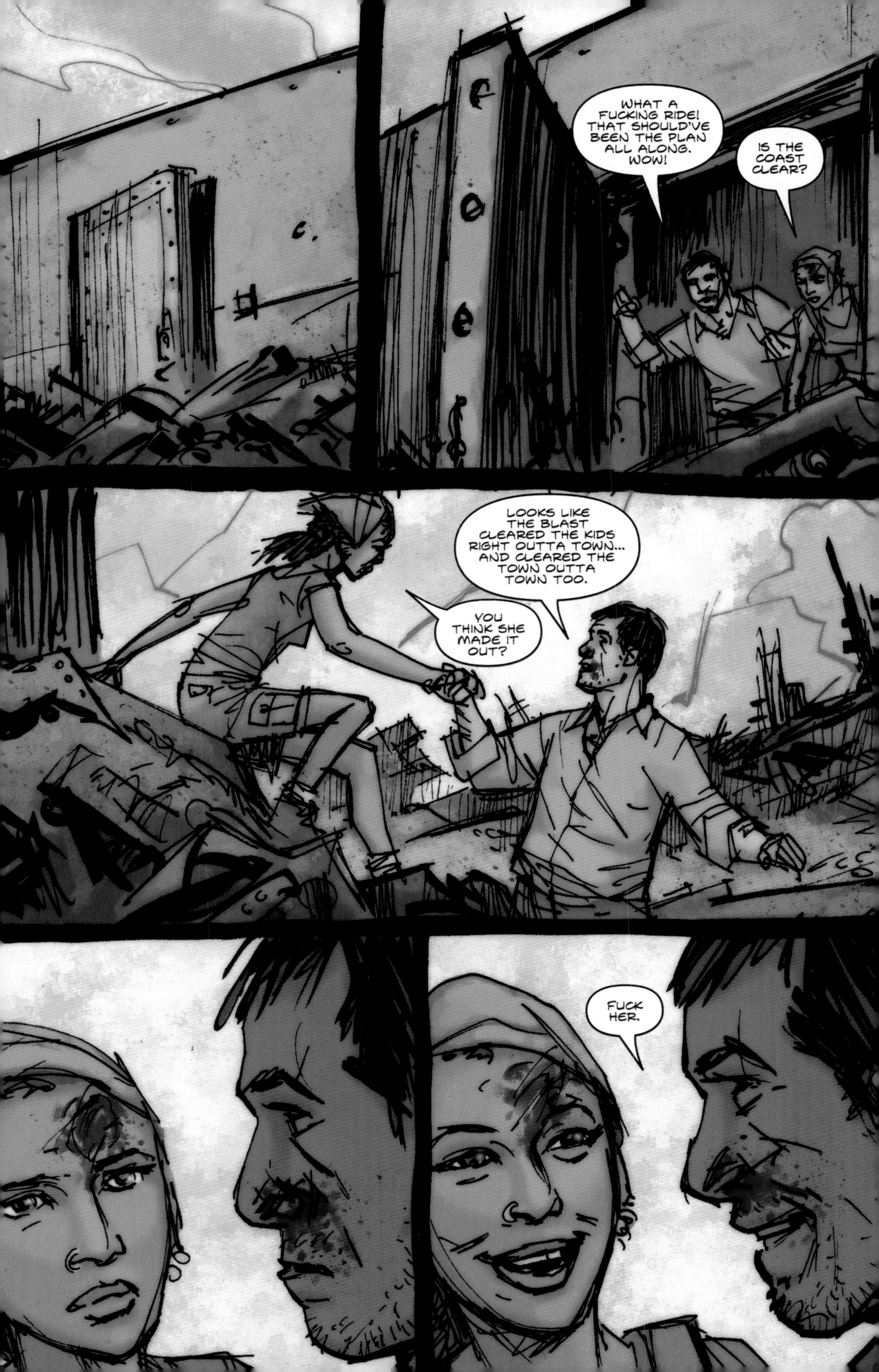
WHAT A FUCKING RIDE! THAT SHOULD'VE BEEN THE PLAN ALL ALONG. WOW!
IS THE COAST CLEAR?
LOOKS LIKE THE BLAST CLEARED THE KIDS RIGHT OUTTA TOWN... AND CLEARED THE TOWN OUTTA TOWN TOO.
YOU THINK SHE MADE IT OUT?
FUCK HER.

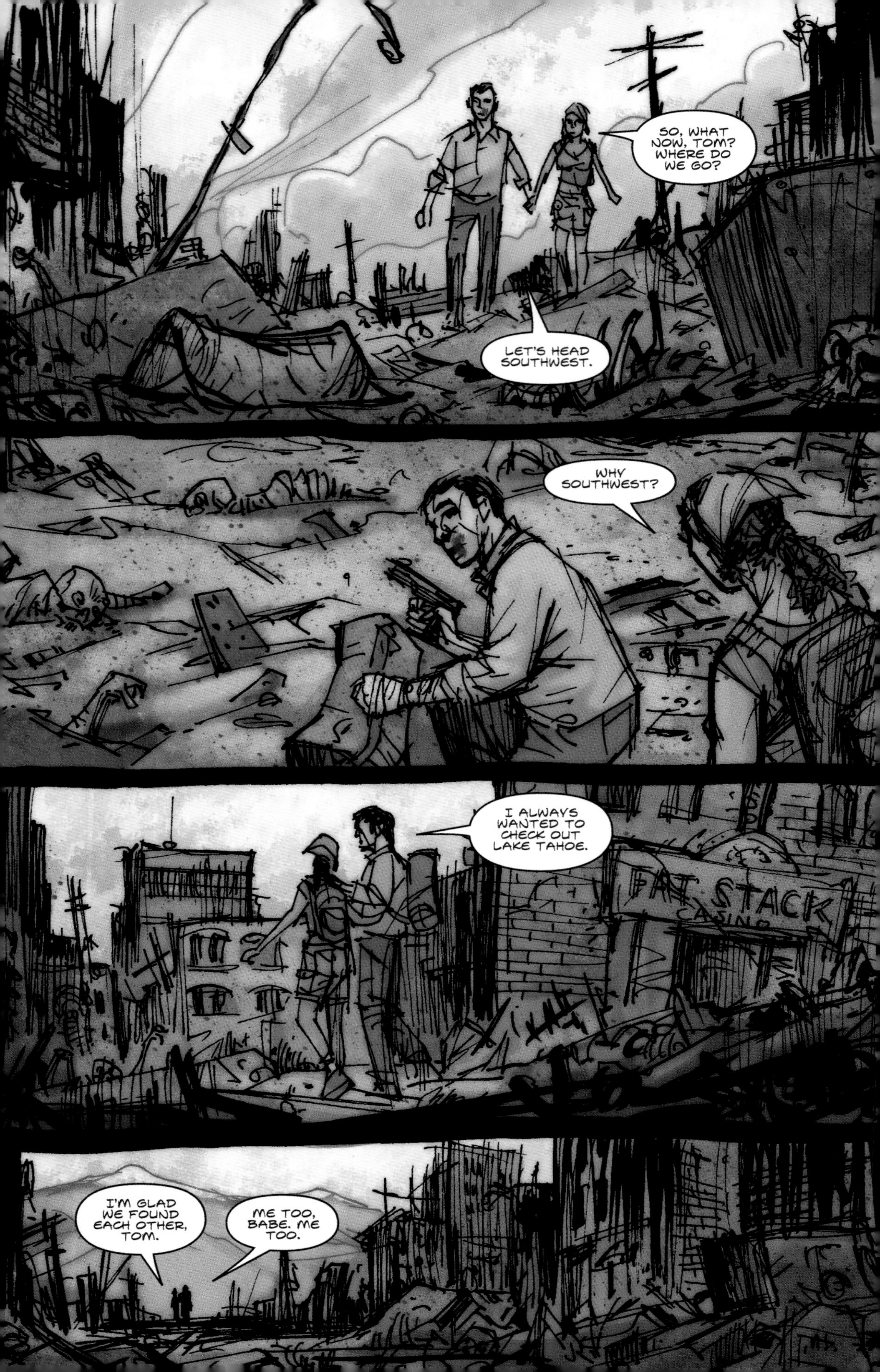
SO, WHAT NOW, TOM? WHERE DO WE GO?
LET'S HEAD SOUTHWEST.
WHY SOUTHWEST?
I ALWAYS WANTED TO CHECK OUT LAKE TAHOE.
FAT STACK CASINO
I'M GLAD WE FOUND EACH OTHER, TOM.
ME TOO, BABE. ME TOO.

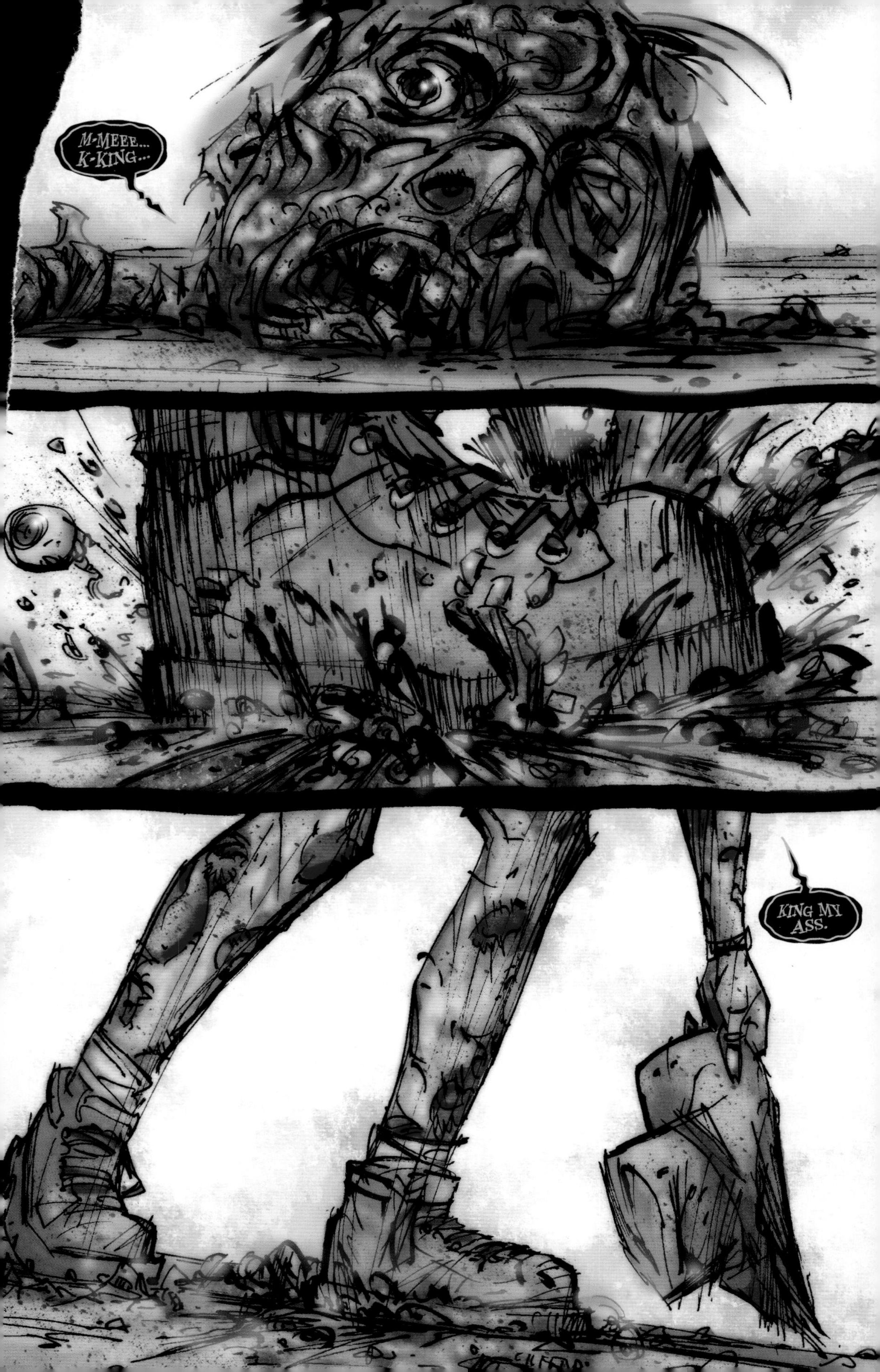
M-MEEE... K-KING...
KING MY ASS.

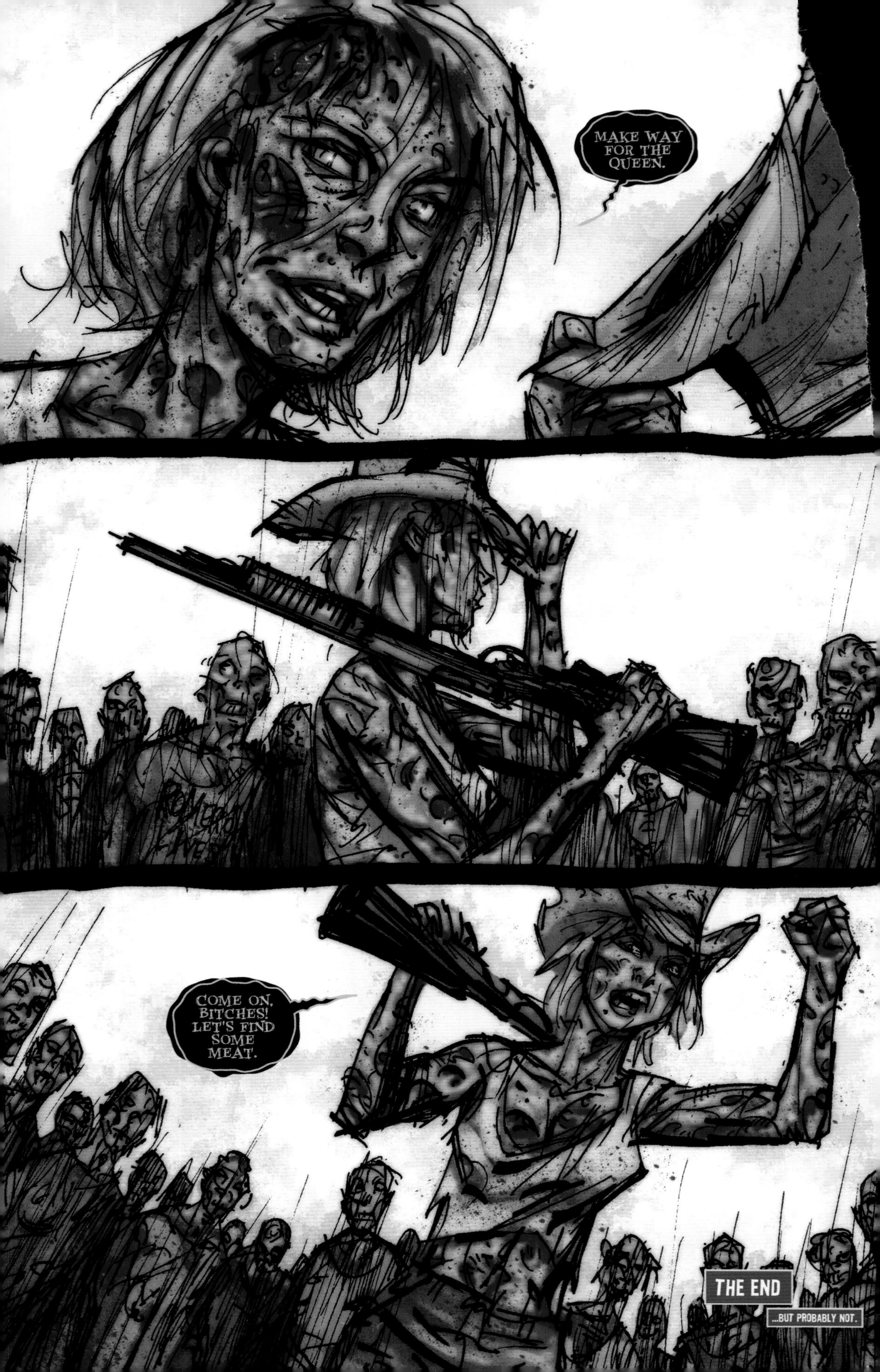
MAKE WAY FOR THE QUEEN.
COME ON, BITCHES! LET'S FIND SOME MEAT.
THE END
...BUT PROBABLY NOT.